Holy Hostage
My Journey from Saddam's Prison to Healer

by
David L. Cunningham,
with Linda Lee Ratto, Ed.M.

First Printing October 2008
Second Edition, March 2009
Third Edition, Fall 2010

Power! **Press**
Post Office Box 622
Tyrone, Georgia 30290 USA

Holy Hostage
by David L. Cunningham,
with Linda Lee Ratto, Ed.M.

ISBN 978-0-974850-89-4

1. Healer's Biography; 2, Health—Physical and Psychological; 3. Wellness—Mind, Body, Soul; 4. Counseling—How to repattern self; 5. Healing Energy and Disease Relief; I. Cunningham/Ratto; II. Title: *Holy Hostage*

"FOR THOSE WHO BELIEVE,

NO EXPLANATION IS NEEDED.

FOR THOSE WHO DO NOT,

THERE IS NEVER ENOUGH."

www.SpiritualHealingCentre.com

English Contact: 44 (0)191 417 8231
Mobile: 07903 6274333
Skype: Davidlc21

cunninghamd1@sky.com

www.LindaLeeRatto.com

USA Contact: 404.406.7432

Ratto@mindspring.com

Table of Contents

ACKNOWLEDGEMENTS

DLC:

I thank God for this incredible, wondrous gift of healing, counselling and teaching. In addition, I thank the thousands of people I have worked with for their faith and trust in me. In particular, I send special acknowledgement and honour to my lifelong mentor Don Galloway of the College of Psychic Studies, for leading me on my spiritual journey. Thank you, Sir, for guiding me in 1966 by saying, "Healing is going to be your destiny." I took this to heart, as you can well see.

I would like to thank, most sincerely, Linda Ratto, my dear friend who encouraged me to delve into my life to write this book with her, and for the thousands of hours of love, dedication and hard work in bringing this story and helpful book to you. Thank you Linda—what would I have done without your loyal friendship and love. Many, many blessings upon you.

LLR:

I humbly thank David Cunningham for allowing me the privilege of walking into his life and telling his story. My spiritual journey has been enriched and evolved with his loving presence in my life. In addition, I share heartfelt appreciation to David's sister, Margaret, her husband Jim and their children, Lynsey and young David, who have welcomed me into their family as a sister. I thank my family: David, Courtney, Eric, and Ryan for their years of love and unwavering patience during this book project, even with material that they found surprising and at times unbelievable. Thank you for accepting my work.

We encourage you to contact us with your comments and your own healing stories, if you so desire.

PREFACE

the years leading to my capture...

***1982-1990. Eight years of military struggle between Iraq and Iran created massive regional tension.

***July 1990. Well positioned Kuwaiti bankers and money lenders unexpectedly go on trips abroad, secret travels no one knew about, not even their closest advisors.

***July 28, 1990. The Kuwaiti royal family disappears. A family friend receives a call from a distant land saying the royal family is traveling for a time. Another royal friend receives a long distance invitation for him to join a royal family reunion. The friend flies to this unplanned event.

Back in Kuwait, local business people begin to notice that key officials have disappeared from daily life; the entire royal family and those holding the majority of the financial power in the Kuwaiti banking industry are gone...

INTRODUCTION

A Healer's Life

*** A distraught mother comes to me through a series of acquaintances and numerous doctors. Her baby has leukemia. I quietly begin counseling, learning all about Mum and infant Jennifer Marie. We spend a full hour together in a healing session. I hold the baby, find and release her eight energy centers. I meditate, touching her little head, asking for healing energy to flow again clockwise through her body giving the infant back her health.

Days later Jennifer's mum telephoned. "Our doctors said Jennifer Marie is in remission. Jennifer Marie's blood tests are normal !"

*** London born Jack, age three, was brought to me by his parents. Jack was autistic and had not slept save dribs and drabs since birth. As with most autistic children Jack did not speak. To cope, Jack's folks took shifts and I saw why. Jack virtually climbed the walls of my Hale Clinic office scurrying about like a bumblebee seeking nectar. We seat belted Jack in his push chair, while I explained the eight energy centers healing process. I moved my hands over all of Jack's chakras, opening his energies full steam. The family returned for another session three days later explaining, "Jack slept soundly ever since your first session and spoke several words !" We hugged one another. On the second visit, Jack was calm—not the same toddler first presented to me. We did another healing and I sent them home. On Friday, October 22, 1999, I received word that Jack now attends normal public school.

*** I awakened in the middle of the night to a message: a close friend's face appears telling me, "Don't worry,

David, I just passed into the Spirit world. It is fantastic !"
The next day I telephone my friend's family and they tell of
his funeral arrangements.

Angel

*** A woman named Hayley requested my services
through a friend whose horse was gravely injured. Animals
have similar energy centers as humans and we were
successful in helping the horse become well. The Hayley
turned out to be Ms. Hayley Mills, a beloved movie heroine
of my childhood. It is of interest to note how one's health
can be blocked and Hayley is a perfect example. With her
gracious best wishes, I share our experiences.

I often counsel in the comfort of a person's home. Hayley
invited me to her Hampton house on the Thames just outside
London. I was excited, having watched her grow-up in films
such as *Pollyanna*. One of my first jobs as a young teen
was in a local theatre. I knew every movie by heart, especially
Hayley Mills'. She portrayed girls I would have loved meeting.
It so happens that Hayley is exactly my age; we found much
in common and made fast friends.

In 1995-96, *Dead Guilty* was the play in which Hayley
portrayed a murderer. She chose the character because
it was quite different. Hayley revels in acting challenges
and did enjoy this play on some levels. However, the
dramatic implications of murder and the live performance
schedule upset her entire being. Hayley's deteriorated
condition brought her to seek my aid.

We worked together for several healing sessions,
helping her through the final month of the play. She saw
great results, feeling lighter, brighter and began enjoying
life and performing again. The Almighty's healing energy
through my hands eased her back into the best of health.
She expressed delight in her renewed strength and overall
wellness in body and spirit.

After our healings, Hayley wrote an article highlighting her healing work with me, which was published in London's *The Daily Mail*, December 1996. She said, "My article is a gift of gratitude for what we have accomplished together." She is today refreshed and happy, in a lovely, healthy state of being. I appreciate deeply that Hayley chose to go public concerning her healing with me. It was the first publicity of a larger scale that I experienced and she literally opened floodgates in my life as a full-time healer.

Hayley grew to trust my professionalism and asked me to house sit for her after the London play; she was going on tour for *The King and I*. What an honour this was to have placed her home and trust in my hands. I lived there sixteen months with Hayley's permission to see people for healings. Hayley's gracious friendship fostered the health of close to one hundred people whom I counseled in her home. Hayley's house in fact took on the positive energies emitted in sessions. It was Hayley who mentioned the energy changes. She noticed how exquisite she felt whenever she walked through the door. Her home to this day is filled with positive vibrations which enhance health.

Over time I met and worked with Hayley's parents, Sir John & Lady Mills. Hayley and I remain very good friends, keeping in touch by phone and meeting for healings when she is in need. I was welcomed into the family with many kindnesses, including an invitation to Sir John's ninetieth birthday celebration. It was a marvelous night of stars in London's Dorcester Hotel. I am blessed by this family. To those clients and myself Hayley Mills is an angel.

Sadly, Sir John and Lady Mary have now passed in Spirit. Yet, I had the honour of being invited to Sir John's memorial ceremony in London's Trafalgar Square St. Martin in the Fields Church, with all the family celebrities and dignitaries. Their family is such a blessing.

OVERVIEW

The Almighty has created a miraculous human body. It is a humming, vibrating, pulsating system that maintains itself with an ease that is often surprising. All we need do is properly feed it, exercise it, fuel the mind and soul, and we are able to withstand much of what life throws our way. We can survive.

Existing with good health and for a very, very long time is another matter.

We cannot optimally function if the inner energy, our life force, is not running. No pills, potions or lotions can free the ills from blocked energy. We must keep our healthy, flowing systems going. We accomplish this by freeing ourselves. Those who have learned the art of quiet stillness, meditation or prayer can significantly influence their daily energy stream. Releasing troubles to the Divine helps people cope with emotional pain and maintain wellness.

Every living soul's energy flows naturally in a clockwise direction. Healthy energy surges from the Almighty above the body, down through the eight energy centers to earth, where we are grounded. The mind, body and soul remain balanced if we seek the positive side of life and the good lesson in each situation. Alas, most of us need reminding. Even the highest living soul has to work on staying healthy. The best way to keep the energy centers surging is to become silent and peaceful. In so doing we hand over to the Divine our worries and negatives of the day.

God's energy is blocked when we are not in harmony and unable to deal with today's or yesterday's events. We place barriers and build walls to protect ourselves. By building protection against pains, we cause imbalance (dis-ease) in mind, body and soul. Rather than being safe from the emotional upheaval, we block the very energy that releases pain.

Within these pages is the story of my life, work and continual quest to begin the healing process in those who seek assistance. Spiritual energy healing involves unblocking the energy centers called chakras. My work changes people. Releasing energy flow causes a person to relieve buried hurts. It is surprising what can be let go and forgiven when the healing process is begun.

HOLY HOSTAGE is the story of my personal healing journey, but also yours. Spiritual healing has been frequently misunderstood. Healing is not just for a few but for all souls. It is my humble desire that you come away from this biography filled with greater compassion and useful tools for healing yourself and those around you.

* * *

The word 'God' used in this book is my definition of The Universal, Loving, Creative Energy Force. With respect to the reader, the use of God does not conflict with any man or woman's religious and spiritual beliefs, it encompasses ALL.

David L. Cunningham, 2008
Tyne & Wear, Northeast England

Chapter One
Captured into Freedom

Scott Peck, MD, tells us in *The Road Less Traveled* that the purpose of his chapter on grace is to help readers understand not only the perfect fit of grace's serendipity, but to realize that opening our awareness to it makes a grace-filled opportunity a miracle of perfect timing. Grace and serendipity, what I call synchronicity, abound in this life, if we only open our eyes and hearts and listen.

August 2, Durham, England

Today is the anniversary of the early skirmishes of the Gulf War. By August 9, 1990, I was an Iraqi prisoner. Along with scores of others Saddam Hussein wanted captured and used as human shields, I was held at gunpoint. Most were imprisoned until December or well past the end of 1990; I was held captive until October 1990, for almost one hundred days. Dozens of us were fenced in a makeshift Baghdad prison called a tractor factory. In reality, it was a T-72 tank mill next to a gas bomb plant.

4 a.m., August 2, 1990. Peaceful sleep shatters as gunshots blast from the Kuwaiti street below. I was housed in the Kuwait Plaza Hotel as their new deputy manager and the only overseer on site. Jumping out of bed, I peered out my window to view the commotion. Soldiers and tanks caused mayhem everywhere, firing indiscriminately popped in my ears. My first reaction was

the realization that recent rumours were true: Iraqi soldiers had crossed the border. They were invading Kuwait !

During the days leading to my arrival in Kuwait on July 26th, British newspapers and television reported that a 'military machine' was building on the Iraqi/Kuwaiti Border. Back home in England I telephoned my future boss with concern. Our Kuwait Plaza Hotel contract was still in negotiation and I could have backed out. He assured me that Kuwait was conducting business as usual. Still worried, I telephoned the British Embassy. They were emphatic. "Iraq does not invade Kuwait. These are the games in which soldiers commonly engage," said an embassy official. I appeased family and friends with those updates and decided to keep the job. I flew to my new adventure in Kuwait City. *It is perfectly safe to travel in Kuwait.* Those words rang in my ears as I was familiarized with management responsibilities, met the boss and his wife and unpacked my life.

4 a.m., August 2, 1990. Just seven days after landing in Kuwait City, there I stood as the only manager of a hundred hotel guests in the midst of military attack. I had to remain focused on my duties in spite of my fears or we'd have pandemonium. Intuition told me that communication avenues would soon be severed, especially those connecting out of the country. I rang my sister, Margaret, and told her of the local war. "Please call Mum. The lines will probably be cut soon and you may not hear from me for a time. I will all right."

*We **will** survive.* My mind screamed, while I fumbled in the dark as I dressed. Lights would have attracted attention, perhaps bullets. The receptionist rang. Guests were swarming the lobby. Unsure but clear-headed I rushed to the elevator lift. *How does one deal with this?* I tried to get my arms around the situation. I had always had faith, but this… The elevator numbers ticked 7, 6, 5. The lobby floor was only four floors away.

Solutions?
There were none.
Couldn't get rid of an army could we?
I resolved to be professional and fall back on organized action, an old hotel business motto. There were only two primary issues: the safety and basic needs of the guests. In whatever routine I could muster, we would satisfy these needs together. Such was my quest. The lift bell rang and the doors opened to the throng.

The scene was colourful, luxurious chaos. I swallowed more pangs of fear. In the surrealness of the moment there was no time for negativity. Women and children, their eyes in tear-filled terror, gaped toward me. I took a deep breath, "Attention!" I called above the crowd.

Glancing about I was grateful that it was high summer. Thank God it was not the height of the tourist season with a capacity crowd. "We are going to the breakfast room on the lower level where there are no windows. We will be safer there," I announced. The group followed in surprisingly attentive order, in spite of dozens of small, sleepy children.

Once in the linen caressed breakfast room mumblings grew loader. I surveyed my staff, only half a dozen. Guests' shouting snapped me into their focus. A British engineer panicked shouting, "What are **you** going to do about all of this, David?" The question cut the crowd into silence. His glare pierced my brittle calm. There were numerous oil rigger engineers, the hotel's business staple, expecting excellence in service—even during a siege.

As a British national, I replied quite in character, "Well, the first thing we should do is sit down and have a nice cup of tea." We staffers set breakfast in motion, serving tea as rapidly as the water steeped the leaves.

The guests quieted. It was then that I realized how difficult it was to assess the invasion's progress. We could not see nor hear the soldiers and tanks as earlier. I escaped up the back stairwell to peek out the windows. All had miraculously quelled. Now the next best place for everyone was in their hotel rooms where they had personal affects and lavatories; they would be less at risk than in one central locale. I flew back downstairs and told them the strategy. Even the grumpiest agreed.

9 a.m., same day, August 2, 1990. No other hotel employees reported for duty. The roads were surely blocked. We were on our own: the chef, six waiters, one receptionist, two extra staffers, and a brand-new manager, me. So far we'd provided good service with guests tidying their own rooms, towels in the dryers. A telephone call to the British Embassy was in order. "This is David Cunningham of the Kuwait Plaza Hotel. May I speak to the ambassador in charge?"

"There is no one available," the telephone operator replied.

"Could you tell me what the contingency plans are, please, for emergencies?"

She asked, "What do you mean?"

"Well, Iraq has invaded. What must I do with the hotel guests at the Plaza?"

"We do not have a plan."

"What am I supposed to do?"

"Keep your head down and listen to the radio." So much for obtaining help from my embassy.

What about seeking other Kuwaiti-stationed help? I paced about my office, mulling over that I had only just arrived seven days ago. Normally, I would have developed relationships with local security and business people, neighbouring hotel staffs, community leaders, and the like. On whom could we rely? The best we could do was stick together; the staff and guests must be united and befriend the soldiers.

And the army flooded us.

The hotel was intermittently invaded with troops storming and ransacking, demanding food and drink. This happened in every hotel on the street as I watched from the Plaza windows. The staff became an oiled machine: serving meals, cleaning, keeping needs met. Fortunately, we had two weddings booked for the weekend of the invasion, so there were ample supplies stocked in the pantries. We fed some two hundred military personnel wedding quality prime filets along with staples of rice and water, besides the now hostaged one hundred guests served. Professional training kicked in as I taught the staff how to stretch the luxuriant bridal delicacies, including shrimp and pastry flour, to ensure the resources lasted. How long we would wait for food shipments was anyone's guess.

The guests kept occupied with their families, even helping with the laundry and followed my directive to generate a list of immediate relations' telephone numbers. I again called the British Embassy and informed the telephonist that I had a list of all the British people and could she please pass on the names to the Foreign Office in London. She replied that the phone lines were down. I said I know, but you have a satellite link up with London. Haughtily she answered, WELL, THAT IS PURELY FOR EMERGENCIES. *What was a war if not the ultimate emergency?* I dropped the receiver. *My God, I truly am alone*, my mind cried.

I shook my head, clearing it.

Maintain routine. Comfort the guests. Feed the soldiers.

All the while I had to keep my British heritage a secret from the military. Early on, I learned that Saddam Hussein commanded that all British nationals and other westerners must be rounded up and shipped to him in Baghdad. He disliked westerners with a passion, especially Americans and their allies. I had been 'acting' Swedish, as I believed Sweden was neutral in this conflict.

When a soldier appeared, I nodded or flavored my accent; along with my white-blond hair, it all fit to them. It was a way to keep sanity. Someone had to stay organized. What would have happened had we not been able to feed everyone?

Safety was critical and very risky. A security strategy emerged as the families with young children were moved to the top floor. With the help of the engineers, the lifts were reprogrammed to stop at the eighteenth floor. The guests hidden two flights above would use the back fire stairs. This way, random military searches would not affect the children's repose nor would soldiers hear noise with the nineteenth floor as buffer. The families with children under ten were amiable for it created a bit of peace for them.

August 5th, Day 3. The Kuwait Plaza general manager found his way to us. He was Palestinian and allowed to walk the streets, a NON-westerner still on Saddam's acceptable list. We discussed the invasion from his recent viewpoint. After I explained the soldier rampages, a refined strategy developed. We set out to foster beneficial relationships with the soldiers by coddling military officers. We still had good food and a fine environment. Iraqi military leaders had been struggling in their country for years. These accommodations were gold. Coupled with a friendly attitude, we hoped to bring law and order to the renegades storming the hotel with untamed hunger and demands.

An Iraqi named Major Abu - Rhyd came in with his battalion. We gave him, as well as his Aide De'Camps, the second in command, our finest suites. We royally fed and looked after them with fresh laundered towels round the clock, room service, the works. In return, although not spoken nor agreed upon directly, a calm reigned at the Plaza. Far fewer soldiers invaded with the major in residence and satisfied.

It was hilarious irony. When the major, his aide, our general manager, and I sat down for a meal, the waiters literally tip-toed behind the major's back and up the lifts to feed those hidden hotel citizens. It was difficult to eat given the scene. It reminded me of Anne Frank hiding Jews during World War II.

August 6th. I continued concealing my nationality to the major and military personnel as a couple of relatively routine days passed. Then I overheard soldiers who stated that, by Saddam's orders, allies of America and England—all westerners—were to be shipped immediately to Baghdad. I waited in nervous, silent anticipation, while the major and his aides rounded-up every passport in the hotel, save the top floor's hidden families'. My passport was seized and they discovered my British secret. "You have half an hour to get your bags together," the major commanded. I snuck to the twentieth floor and told our families that I no longer could help them. To my astonishment, the group insisted on joining me. I dropped into a chair, overwhelmed, as pride and fear seeped into my very soul. They were standing by me.

What now?

I was even more worried and responsible for them if they joined me. Who knew what foreign ground, what situations were to come? We had gotten close, the staff and guest families, through this war. How would I protect them?

I told everyone that we were expected to leave in half an hour; they agreed and set to task. I rushed to my room where life had so recently been unpacked. Soldiers pounded my door. We banged my luggage down the elevator, shocked at what met us in the lobby. The major peered my way, aghast at the numbers to be transported. While he grumbled, I said my good-byes to the General Manager and personnel. Their eyes brimmed with tears. We loaded into a coach under the hotel portico. The driver then drove to the stop light at the end of the Plaza Hotel street, U-turned back and parked in front of the Marriott opposite the Plaza. We were commanded to get off, haul our bags and enter the hotel across our very street.

We protested loudly. The major said something about waiting for more people, transport and security. We were assigned palatial, five-star accommodations by the soldiers. My inner calm was shaken with uncertainty and nothing to do. Time ticked on toward noon when I heard the soldiers talking: the Marriott had no food.

"I am David Cunningham, manager of the Kuwait Plaza. We have supplies there, why don't I ring them and have the staff deliver?" The soldiers telephoned themselves to guarantee I was not tricking them. Our waiters arrived and served us in the Marriott ! I was proud of them, knowing they had only a week of on-demand training with me. The guards instantly demonstrated respect following a good meal. Someone found the alcohol stash, so we had a little party that evening. It was quite a comedy of paradox.

Dawn, August 7th. I knew of the swimming pool on the Marriott's roof. I asked the major if we could swim and, while I had his attention, would they restart the air conditioning. "Well, you are here and have nothing to do. By all means, please use the facilities. I will see about the air conditioning." It was almost amusing, how matter-of-fact he replied, saying we should make ourselves feel at home during a war.

The Iraqi soldiers marched us to the top floor where we splashed in the pool, gleefully throwing balls with the children. All the while armed guards, with submachine guns slick in the bright sun, stood on defense. *In defense of what, of whom?* I shook my head. Paradox upon paradox, there was no time for worrying about something I did not understand for there were too many lives at hand.

Must press on, think and act in the best interest of survival. This was my anchoring thought, a Divine strength inside. It came to mind that I should do what I always sought to do: build relationships. I swam over to the guards. "Officers, this is silly. We can't go anywhere, nor escape. We're on the top floor of a high rise hotel with no clothes. Why not put your weapons down and join us? It must be 115 degrees up here."

They looked at each other, shrugged their shoulders and stripped down to their underwear. Those Iraqi soldiers, in their skivvies swimming and cavorting with the families in their charge, were quite a sight. *What was this about God?* I kept wanting to shake myself to make sure I was awake and not swimming in a nightmare.

That evening, after more food from my Plaza Hotel staff, the major commanded us to depart for Baghdad promptly at 6 a.m. the next morning. "If you are not ready, your belongings will be left behind." We obeyed, spending the night assembling our things and worrying. *Would this journey bring us closer to home or even farther away?*

August 8, 1990, 6 a.m. We convened efficiently in the Marriott lobby. There we were kept in suspense sitting atop suitcases and fine furniture waiting for the seized Kuwaiti buses. It was hardly quiet, nor dispassionate. *What next?* We felt somewhat safe in that hotel building. It was the immediate future that had the group murmuring, fear-stricken. To forego serving us again at the Marriott, I had asked the Plaza staff to pack survival rations for the hundred being transported to Baghdad City. The children were getting hungry. Tensions mounted.

9 a.m., two buses arrived. We sardined-in with captives from other locations and chugged off. At the Kuwait/Iraqi border we witnessed scores of Asians clamoring to get out of the country. Our coaches finally crossed and took a little-traveled road across the desert to Baghdad City. It was the dry, hot, desolate route through

deep desert country. For twelve hours we rode straight away, enduring the baking desert heat and withstanding temperatures surpassing 120 degrees. We had a couple of bathroom stops, both appalling. There were no facilities for so many. Whispers of "Where are they taking us?" filled the thick air in the bus. Disgruntled children cried. One woman sitting in front of me leaned over and proclaimed, "We're never getting out alive." Others overheard and fear rose with the noise level.

At last, we reached Baghdad City in the dark of night, exhausted. Again we were presented with five-star accommodations at the MansAmelia Hotel equipped with armed guards at the end of each corridor. They led us to the glorious dining area lush with fine fabrics richly coordinated and textured, where we joined some 400-500 other detainees. The mass of hostages lined-up to eat rice. Later we were told that we could come out of our rooms but must not leave the floors, nor take the lifts. Few slept and children moaned helplessly.

August 9, 1990, dawn. After watery porridge the women and children were grouped together and readied for departure. A guard told us a mercy plane was being sent from England only for women and children; males, fifteen and older, were to remain imprisoned. Hushed cries flew as women grabbed their husbands and adolescent boys. Flashes of Hitler's tactics entered my mind. Families torn apart—it was sacrilegious, intentionally cruel. *Would Hussein do as stated and safely return the babes and mums? Was there honestly a mercy airplane? What would become of the men?* Of course this was not discussed openly. We did not antagonize the soldiers with questions. It was as if we read each others' hearts as we sobbed our gut-wrenching good-byes. The children's screams ripped our hearts.

Then silence blanketed the hotel.

The number held captive was greatly reduced to some two hundred males. It was a bitter, uncertain quiet.

Maybe we would be safe. After those lovely, colourful, laughing women and children exited, the hotel felt like a tomb. Any means of security was no more.

The day droned forward. The soldiers kept tight-lipped so little information came from the outside. Out of human habit another routine developed for yet an additional week. We awoke, showered, ate, and swam, then back to our rooms. We congregated in the hallway corridors, talking between rice rations. We heard from new prisoners that the Americans had sent ships to the Gulf. President Bush was acting but would we be freed? I felt like a counselor keeping tempers at bay. Masses of other male hostages came through the hotel, ate, lived amongst us for a day or two, then vanished in the middle of the night. This kept us on edge, the dark exiting; we heard men were taken to various military installations to locations unknown.

Locations unknown.

August 16th, nightfall. After a week in the MansAmelia Hotel, the soldiers instructed me to prepare to leave—just me.

My heart sank.

I obeyed, stocked my belongings and stood before the guards with not an ounce of information. *Where or what was next?* Out of the hotel reception area I was led by four armed soldiers to a jeep. I sat in the back seat with a guard on either side and two in front. With not a familiar hostage face to be seen, I was driven into the black unknown terror of night.

The minutes felt endless, although it was only about an hour's journey when we stopped in the pitch darkness. I was shuffled into a small house and discovered inside other Westerners: British, American and Irish, five in all. This was my new prison.

Another routine evolved as days passed. We awoke, shared the loo, were fed rice and water, then allowed to talk and pray near the house. Guards were everywhere.

2 a.m., August 19th. Spotlights and banging woke us. I was indignant at having been blasted out of my sleep and shouted, "What is bloody going on?"

"Get your things."

We obliged, stashing our bags as we witnessed the looting. Everything in the house except the toilet was dumped on military lorries, along with us. We drove barely a few hundred meters through huge guarded, black iron gates. It looked like a factory with scores of bayoneted guards and countless machine gun towers. We marched past plain industrial buildings and into an office block. The smell of paint permeated the night air. Military personnel whitewashed windows and riveted them shut converting the factory and office block into a prison. It was incredibly well secured with displays of weaponry every few meters.

"What is this place?" I asked.

One of the well-educated, English-speaking Iraqi soldiers replied, "It is a spare parts factory for tractors and such." (In reality it was a T-72 tank factory next door to a bomb plant. We were pawns in the game of human shields against any forthcoming United Nations defense maneuvers.)

In the bustle of the move, I had forgotten to use the toilet. "Toilet facilities, please?" I was taken to a room with a hole in the ground and a sink. "What is this?" I asked in disbelief.

The soldier said, "It's the toilet."

"What do you mean, this is not a toilet?"

"It is an Arabic toilet."

"I can't use that, I've not been trained, nor am I used to implementing that sort of thing." My dignity got the better of me and I forged on with my demands. "Look, I want to know if what we've been told is true or propaganda. We are supposedly guests of Saddam Hussein's or are we prisoners?"

The soldier squeezed his machine gun. "You are guests."

"Then as a guest of Saddam Hussein I want to be treated as such and given acceptable accommodations, at the very least a proper toilet." I glared at him for a long moment. *Dear God, is my blatant honesty going to work or get me killed?*

He grabbed me out of the cell block, shoving me back into the jeep. *What next? I still had to relieve myself.* My heart raced and bowels moaned, as the jeep jostled us out of the compound through those imposing, black gates.

He simply parked in front of the looted house.

I was led to a 'real' Western toilet, which I was permitted use with an armed guard standing by the door. It was hilarious using a loo in front of a man with a rifle. Using a loo in front of guarding soldiers with guns reminded me of the famous Italian Job movie with the incredibly gifted actor Noel Coward in the scene where the prison guards carried his loo paper for him and stood guard outside the loo door.

We returned to the factory-turned-prison. I was released to my room, when shortly thereafter I was forced to ask the guard for the facilities again. "NO !" The soldier took his stance erect with gun angled and proper ready. "No, that is it." He nodded his head toward the loo. "That is it, the Arabic one."

"Come on, this is silly. That is your life. You are used to a hole in the ground but I am not." Stomach cramps waved, as I felt increasingly ill. Feeling so awful, it seemed I had nothing to lose and I said, "I have my rights as a guest of Saddam. Isn't there anything you can do for me?"

He nodded in military fashion, turned on his boot heel and left.

I watched the soldiers exit, not knowing what was next. I had seen 'complainers' from other prison blocks permanently removed out of the factory compound after disagreements with the guards. The jeep took off and I went back to my bed, very sick, and I prayed. The Arabic hole seemed my only solution. Then I heard the jeep return, followed by the clamor of soldiers, equipment and loud pounding. I rushed to my door as I could not hold-out any longer for some form of bathroom.

"Go here," he ordered me back into the Arabic bathroom. I was astounded. They had uprooted the looted house toilet and placed it on top of the hole and rigged sink water as a flush system. I was massively relieved.

What a comedy-of-the-absurd.

Inside the military installation another semblance of daily routine emerged. Seven of us shared a bedroom in the office block; each prisoner had a single metal framed bed, table, and small lamp. We even had air-conditioning. There we were complete strangers sharing life and another new adventure.

Minute upon minute, day to day forced us into talking to one another and getting to know the lives we led apart from the prison. It was the best solution to our predicament. I had always been a communicator and bridge builder. We found talking a comfort in the middle of a desert war.

Ultimately, we became nine in our office block: Irish, British, American, German, and Japanese. We were almost one-on-one with six soldiers forever present. Strangely, they discarded their uniforms and did not hoist weapons unless a big Hussein official was expected. The young guards were quite educated and articulated English well. We were able to converse with ease and slowly developed a rapport with each soldier.

All together we fifteen—prisoners and military alike—shared a shower. A room converted into a kitchen and a lounge/dining room equipped with a television exclusively broadcasting propaganda. Saddam was the leading man on every channel with children playfully laughing about.

Military stars and hero-like cinematography topped off the Iraqi trash. As the days turned into weeks and August drew to a close, we made a semblance of comfort in the oppressive uncertainty. We always had the telly to grumble about.

The guards gave me kitchen duty with two young soldier boys barely 16 years of age placed in my charge. We managed all food preparations and cleaning. Ironically, I had the privilege of telling two of my own captors what to do ! We kept busy, which filled a few hours of each day. My career trade brought me day after day blessings. Morning bread and coffee with two meals of rice, cucumber and tomato were our daily rations. All roads were closed and food shortages rampant. Some of us were grateful for anything edible, others complained heartily. Laughably and fortunately I became known as 'the manager'.

To help with bland food complaints I persuaded the soldiers to obtain any spices, salt, pepper, whatever flavoring they could. Insignificant? Quite the contrary. The complainers were mostly large men who were unhappy with so little food, let alone the tastelessness; hunger contributed to angry moods. I believed I was saving lives in requesting spices.

To my relief several guards produced half a dozen varieties of herbs. I played with these ingredients in our twice daily rice pilaf. This appeased the group a bit until the days when we ran out of rice. My fellow inmates cried, "Where is our rice, cucumber and tomato?"

"I thought you were tired of it?" I teased to lighten the crisis.

"But if that's all we have, we want at least our rice. We're starving."

"Sorry fellows, if we haven't got it, we haven't got it. We have to make do with bread, cucumbers and tomatoes." I was compelled to avoid an angry outbreak

by easing their moods. Rest assured the days after we
received the next rice shipment, the standard fare of rice,
cucumber and tomato satisfied every man, whatever the
spice.

I lost seven inches of my waistline. When back in
Britain, I was going to market this rice, cucumber and
tomato diet and call it the *Baghdad Diet*, guaranteed to
work. I call it my boyhood diet, for after all, this all matured
me beyond my wildest imaginings.

We gradually found out much in talking with our
captors. If others in the compound outside our office block
had abused the guards or complained bitterly, they were
removed in the middle of the night to an underground
tomb inside the wall of a dam on the outskirts of the factory
property. This was the resister's and trouble-maker's
isolation cell. With this information our small group kept
a lid on our tempers and mouths. It was far easier to
keep a stable, daily routine when the drastic alternative
was known. Bits of stories were overheard or shared.
Talk of chemical warfare abounded and gas masks
surfaced for the guards' equipment stashes. Missile fire
was heard often, sometimes every few minutes. One
night while deep in sleep, we awoke to the loudest banging
with bright lights flashing through the white-painted
windows. We jumped out of bed and congregated by the
office door and witnessed workmen erecting an eight-
foot corrugated iron fence surrounding our block. I yelled,
"What on earth are you doing at two a.m.? Why can't you
do this during the day?"

Some of the guard constructors approached and
gruffed for us to go back inside. We kept negotiating until
they threw down their tools. They returned the next day
and completed their task, including removal of the white
paint from our windows and the riveting. They built a secure
exercise yard which we saw from the windows. If not too
hot, we were even allowed to open them for fresh air. It
was minutely liberating as we clung to any shred of light.

The new day following the construction brought a revised routine, which included permission to roam within the new fenced arena, exercising and basking in the morning sun, which was much more tolerated than the mid-afternoon blaze that forced us indoors. I found myself praying and meditating every day after calisthenics.

A strange thing happened. My closed-eyes meditation intrigued the others, both the captives and the captors circled around. After quiet time, we reminisced about family, occupations and shared feelings, questioning life. It was a natural occurrence, these energizing sessions. An even closer personal atmosphere evolved, conducive to the guards talking to me, even one-to-one whenever they could. I became the prison's cell block counselor.

We desperately needed one another to keep sane and our friendships had a calming effect on us all. To my surprise the young soldiers said they were prisoners, too. Each guard confided privately that they were miserable, tired and entirely frustrated. They had fought an eight-year war with Iran and hated everything, including Saddam Hussein. They missed their families and wanted to go home and eat well. We all had such commonality. I thanked the Almighty often, grateful for the guards' openness and confidences. They simply obeyed their Commander Saddam's edicts and truly, deep down, intended no harm.

One morning during quiet discussions together outside, the tone and focus centered around, "Why are we here, David? What is God punishing us for? We've done nothing wrong." Certainly this reflected our mutual desperation as I struggled with this issue in my heart every night.

Over the years I had dabbled with God. He had given my sister Margaret and me a sixth sense and a special talent for intuition. I also had a massive energy force given to me. Through my body there was a warm, constant vibration in both hands, which I had used spontaneously over my lifetime. I even managed to heal some of my friends by simply placing my hands on them. I had struggled for most of my 44 years trying to understand what made me tick. Night after night during the capture the reason I was on earth gradually became clear. In realizing my gift for counseling, I put many of my life's events into a sort of mental order. Through the years, job after job, I had been much too busy to think or be still. The hostage time fostered hour upon hour, night after night of inner contemplation. The question, "Why are we here?" had far more personal meaning to me than the guards and prisoners knew. The Divine, in Her perfect timing, was leading me to healing my fellow man. I knew this, as naturally as intuition, but during the imprisonment I was reawakened to my purpose. Life was heading in a fresh, energizing direction; I simply had to live through the hostage crisis first.

My answer to "Why did this happen to us?" was kept simple: "I'm sure that God is not punishing us. We are victims of circumstances." However, in replying I dug way down deep for self-control. "We will all be allowed to go home, but what can we learn in the meantime?"

Later that day I queried God. *If I am meant to counsel and heal others when can I go home and get on with it?* I broke down into tears praying that night, something I tried hard not to do. *When can I go home? My mother has cancer and was not well when this incident began. She must be sick with worry. My whole family is being tortured along with me. When may I go home?* In the stillness, the voice in my head said, *"After the eighteenth of October."* It was early September.

I then realized I was already healing people by counseling in prison.

If the voice was right, I had weeks to go and must make the most of it. I continued reflecting and began looking on my hostage situation as I would an actor on stage; I walked in and out of the routine. Perhaps it was a defense mechanism. Each day I kept conversations with the Almighty going inside while performing my prison duties and consoling the others. Baghdad offered me time to look deep within. When freed, I pledged to use my talents. Counseling and healing was what I wanted, what was so comforting, so natural to me. I handed over my promise to God and slowly, gradually developed a peace inside me that felt stronger and stronger. Praises for this and the blessings of daily routines.

Remarkably, after morning prayers, letter-writing and counseling discussions, we were given items to read. From week-old newspapers to month old magazines, we devoured anything the soldiers gave us. These tidbits were lifelines: "Ship build-up in the Gulf" and "Increased European Troops Engaged in the Gulf". We discussed possibilities such as would the Iraqi/Kuwait war last as long as the Iraqi/Iran conflict or even Vietnam? It was frightening, yet we kept reading every scrap, stimulating our minds.

At 1 p.m. the young soldiers and I prepared lunch, comprised of the old stand-by of rice, cucumber and tomatoes, which did not take very long to eat. Once tidying-up was complete we had an afternoon siesta. We were forced to avoid the sun, which hovered between 100-150 degrees daily, so no one went outside unless they had guard tower duty. Often I read and fell asleep, arising to refresh myself with a wash at 4-4:30 p.m. In preparation for the evening we talked and prepared food until the 7 p.m. dinner time of—yes, rice, cucumber and tomatoes. We settled down to card-playing or if luck would have it, watched a video the guards brought to pass the time. At 11 p.m., I would turn in to lie privately in my bed for night prayers and sleep. God had always given me the sanctuary of sleep—through thick and thin, I had few sleepless nights.

Sleeping was an escape mechanism and survival instinct. My diabetes was not well maintained with haphazard medications and thus I was exhausted most of the time. Sleep came easily. In contrast, one of the Irishmen never slept. He slowly transformed into a walking nerve increasingly agitated and volatile. I counseled him frequently, teaching prayer and breathing for some semblance of relaxation for the poor chap.

It is difficult to communicate how it felt being held against one's will 24 hours a day for months. Although the guards had not shown any abuse, we still hung on the hostage/prisoner fence. Always in the back of our minds was the question: *Why is this happening? Will we be taken into the night to vanish without a trace?*

Rumours flew about confounding us. *What was true, what was exaggeration or complete fabrication?* On a small radio we obtained from a gracious guard we sometimes got word from the BBC. Prime Minister Margaret Thatcher proclaimed her sympathies regarding the hostages and their families. Blah, blah, she seemed to go on and on with a tough luck attitude. The message felt loud and clear to us: neither Prime Minister Thatcher nor President Bush were going to give in to terrorist threats from Saddam Hussein. We felt oppressively lost and isolated.

No one was negotiating for our lives we surmised.

All the evidence we had said this to us.

The Iraqi secret police visited our compound to orchestrate fresh prisoner news footage. We were ordered against a wall with cameras shooting up out noses and large spotlights piercing straight into our eyes. Answer this. Answer that. Questions concerning politics, our leaders and presidents, Thatcher and Bush, were shot at us from uniformed cameramen. This was a joke as we soon discovered. The police edits ran on the television; we watched our sentences bleeped and cut to nonsensical lies. We learned to seldom answer their questions seriously. We knew our faces and responses would repeatedly glare on Iraqi television in supremely fictitious context. Where else we were broadcasted? Had Mum and my sister seen the edited garbage?

Prisoners and soldiers alike developed critical exhaustion symptoms such as agitation and angry disagreements and either severe sleep deprivation or continual sleepiness. We comforted one other as close friends. The guards tried hard to please us, believe it or not. One day it was an Irishman's birthday and the soldiers brought us a cake and flowers and held a birthday party. I was actually allowed to take a photograph of the birthday man and our guards with my camera. It was amazingly not all bad when I think of these little pleasantries.

Thanks to my professional hotel experience, the factory-prison warden appointed me the group's negotiator. I sat down weekly face to face with him, presenting a list of hostage requests. The warden would either say yes or no to each line item. His one stipulation was that no one ask him directly for anything, but rather everyone had to go through me. I was honoured but at the same time placed in an ironic light. I was the smallest and weakest amid all the burly, oil-rig engineers.

It was an important peacemaking solution and melded beautifully into my nature and current mode of nurturing relationships. With the major general's directive, I intentionally asked each man what he would like. It was therapeutic for us to consider a wish list of sorts. Granted, not everything we desired was given over, but it was good for us to commiserate and dream together. It turned out that the major general was one of Hussein's 'inner sanctum' members, of which there were only twelve direct advisors. I believe my relationship building with Saddam's inner man fostered my freedom.

One of the underlying reasons for my release was the diabetes diagnosis I had received prior to the move to Kuwait. As the captivity time lengthened, my health deteriorated with neuropathy of the ankles and feet. I barely felt them some days nor could I walk well. On occasion the guards brought a doctor to check my feet by sticking pins in me. Other times I was taken to a Baghdad hospital for blood work and sugar level tests. They ultimately gave me the same medication I had obtained from my own physician, blue tablets for sugar control.

At 3 a.m. one night, we were abruptly awakened with lights blaring. New guards dressed in green with red berets marched to my bedside. In perfect English one demanded, "Are you David Cunningham?" I blinked. "Get up. Get dressed. You are coming with us."

"Why?"

"You do not have a choice. Get on with it."

By this time our cell block's hostages were wide awake and panicked, including our usual guards who knew nothing of the current invasion and plan. The men in berets waved military orders in our faces. All pandemonium broke loose as men shouted and shoved one other. I obeyed the guards and got dressed but also grabbed my address book. I showed the fellows my family's telephone numbers and addresses. "Please, when you get out of here contact them for me." *I had to get word to my family somehow, in case I did not return. I wanted them to know I loved them.*

Once outside I strained to see through the pitch black darkness. Two brand-new Range Rovers, confiscated from the Kuwaiti oil fields with oil company logos on them, overflowed with green clad Iraqi guards. The placed me in the back seat, sandwiched in between soldiers. My heart thundered. Each of the men gripped a submachine gun with countless rounds of ammunition clanking from their belts. As I glanced back to the second Rover following, counting half a dozen more guns and guards pointed toward me, I thought: *firing squad*. Cordial manners flew out of my head as I screamed, "Where are you taking me?"

Stone cold desert night silence was their reply.

As we drove, resignation washed over me. My mind raced. *Well, I've had an interesting life, God. If this is my end then let it be done.*

The ride was interminable, black and mute, yet another hour of sheer terror.

The lights of Baghdad suddenly appeared. We rolled right in front of a hospital. I was marched into a consultation room with a physician asking questions concerning my diabetes. I was examined for over half an hour. I don't think I ever had such detailed medical attention. Eventually I was loaded-up and taken back to the compound.

"Why? Why could you not tell me? Why all of this in the middle of the night?"

"For your own safety. During the day there are deadly attacks, especially on English and Americans. We did not want your security in jeopardy." My eyes burned closed. I said a prayer in thanks for the care I'd just received. I even had proper medication in hand. *This was my own personal miracle.*

An inner calm melted through me. However, my outer world was pandemonium. As we approached the prison I saw men running, shouting, smoking, lights blazing, and guns firing. We parked in front of our block where my own guards and fellow hostages spotted me. They came running, genuinely elated to see me. "What happened to you? Where were you taken?" Hugs and kisses-on-cheeks flew about.

"You'll never believe this but they took me to a hospital." More hugs and pats-on-the-back were exchanged. What energy ! It was overwhelming, their blanket of affection. I could not wipe the smile off my face.

Gratefully and almost happily we went back to bed hoping to grab some moments of rest and sleep before dawn.

A formula of peace, fear, peace, fear during the days and nights played havoc with my health. I could barely walk the next day. I suppose the stress affected my circulation and sugar levels. *God, will your predicted date of October 18th ever get here?*

I lived for evenings and nights filled with sleep-escape. About 9 p.m., we listened ever more intently to the BBC World Radio Station. To our delight a certain frequency began carrying messages from hostages' loved ones. We glued ourselves to the radio listening to the broadcasts of love. Shockingly, one night my sister's voice filled the prison walls.

"I am Margaret, David Cunningham's sister. We love you." Then, "I am Jim, David Cunningham's brother-in-law. I am well, your nephew David and niece Lynsey are both fine. We miss you but know you are strong. You can make it through, David. We are counting on you." Margaret came back on, "David, Mum is not well but she is hanging on, wanting to be here to welcome you home. Your family and friends send you great love."

I broke down in tears for the first time in front of my inmates. Listening to that beautiful message, my sister's voice ringing in my ears, was too much to bear. I had been steadfast far too long. My emotions took hold as I cried for hours. The hostages and guards even enjoyed my family's message and complimented me; it was as if the message was from their sisters. We hugged, smiled and sobbed until bedtime. In my nighttime cocoon I felt completely blanketed with love. Filled to my very core, I had myself another good, long weep in thanksgiving.

Sadly, out of all the people who came and went in the prison, I was the only one who received his own family message. To this day that knowledge overwhelms and confounds me.

October 1st. The heat of the summer lessened but we were all very much on edge. Listening ever diligently to the BBC broadcasts we learned that Sir Edward Heath was coming to Baghdad. A member of the British aristocracy, Sir Heath's mission was humanitarian: to negotiate release of the sick and infirmed hostages, British and all other nationalities. Within a couple of days of this news, a guard cautiously confided, "David, your name may have been placed on the sick list due to your walking problems."

Well, God said after the 18th of October!

I dared not share this news with the others; I dared not even think of it or ponder the sick list idea. What if I died before they freed me, before Sir Edmund could get here?

On the 20th of October, two days after the voice in my head told me I would be released, I stood in the kitchen preparing dinner with the two boy soldiers. It was a special day because for the first time we received a shipment of potatoes. I was instructing the boys on how to prepare a new dish when the telephone in the guard's room rang. My body immediately shivered uncontrollably. I knew the call pertained to me. Within seconds after the receiver clicked down a guard stood before me, "David, get your things. You are going home!"

I dropped the potatoes and ran to my room yelling, "They're sending me home! I am being released!"

I looked straight into the eyes of my befriended comrades. To my horror and through my own self-centered excitement I realized I was the only one going home. I lost my composure completely and became dreadfully tearful and apologetic. "Look guys I am so sorry. I wish you could come as well."

They stood staring at me mumbling my lame apologies for being freed.

"I will take letters for you," I suggested. "Please go write them and give me their addresses, phone numbers. I will assuredly connect with them all."

I had the customary stressful thirty minutes to pack and say good-byes to my cellmates. Upon leaving the other remaining hostages in my prison block lined-up, kissed my cheeks and shook my hands, giving me their family letters for personal delivery. I wished them well, right down to the end of the line where all six of the guards hugged, kissed me, and wished me well on my journeys. I stumbled to the door in shambles, an emotional wreck. I stood gazing at that line of men—captors and captive alike, every face grinned, every hand waving in good will. With their warm love inside me I stepped into the cold, desert night toward freedom.

Freedom did not come straight away, however. Luggage was stowed and the black of night enveloped me once more. It was a silent, jarring ride made longer by a sudden surprise. Nearing Baghdad we approached the sign for the airport…and drove right past it.

"Where are we going?" I shouted with no control left in my bones.

"We have to go back to Baghdad for a while."

"We have to go back to Baghdad for a while?" I echoed.

To my astonishment, we were heading back to the previously occupied MansAmelia Hotel. Once off-loaded, the military authority told me, "We must wait for the rest of the sick hostages being released from all the various installations."

I lived in yet another luxurious hotel room with armed guards stationed at my door. For two and a half days I ate, swam and conversed with more hostages who were being freed, some quite ill. I tried comforting them by passing on the loving care I had received from my previous prison block residents. I uplifted one gentleman in particular, a distant member of the Kuwaiti royal family who had not escaped before the siege. He was to remain at the hotel because he was deemed not ill enough. Distraught, he gave me a letter and telephone number to contact his relatives staying in Switzerland. His smile of hope was worth a million.

On October 22nd the sick hostages gathered in the foyer. Some sat in makeshift carriers with wheels crudely screwed into wooden armchairs. Nothing on that day seemed too awful or too difficult to do, we simply helped each other into the freedom buses. The bumpy ride to our final destination was a blur.

At last, released inside the Baghdad airport terminal, we were escorted to the famous British diplomat Sir Edward Heath. I bowed.

Eventually we moved through normal customs procedures in a cordoned area of the terminal. I was first in line. As I gave over my passport, which had just been returned to me by the guards, the customs agent said, "Oh, you're David Cunningham. We've a lot of mail for you."

Amazed I said, "May I have it?"

"No matter now, you are going home." *Oh, I wish I had those well wishes months ago.* The immigrations officer then asked, "Where is your entry visa into Baghdad?"

Until that moment, I had remained for the most part in control and professional. After all, I was finally going home. However, his question was the straw that broke the camel's back. I shouted, "How the hell could I obtain papers into Baghdad when I entered as a hostage?" The entire airport hushed.

"Oh." The officer closed my passport and placed it gently in hand, his face as red as a beet. I swallowed, keeping quiet until the plane.

As I boarded the posh 747 jet, there stood Sir Richard Branson, President of Virgin Airways, with a full volunteer staff. They had joined Sir Edward Heath on the mercy mission. He shook hands and led us to his medical personnel. It reminded me of "A Close Encounter of the Third Kind" when the people were released off the spaceship and handed directly to medical examiners. After a thorough examination in the makeshift airplane clinic each of us was slapped with a sticker on our chests stating we were fine to fly. Then glasses of champagne flowed !

Fabulous, exquisite food and drink surrounded us. Imagine a 747 first class aircraft staffed with wonderful medical people and young, enthusiastic airline volunteers who had donated their time for us. It was a royal dream. Adding to the excitement were the attentions of a large media and journalist crew photographing and interviewing us with Sir Edward Heath and Mr. Branson. It was as if I were watching a play, some divine tragic comedy. I could not drink for all was far too heady. The six-hour flight from Baghdad to London was a lovely fantasy.

At 2 a.m., October 23rd, London's Gatwick airport appeared through the portals. We were escorted to a special room where finally, after off-loading and secure, alternate doors opened and family appeared. Margaret, her husband Jim and my nephew David ran to me. The room was a sea of delightful emotional hugs, tears and cheers of sheer love.

My nephew said, "Uncle David, I never thought we'd see you again." I picked him up and hugged him for dear life.

Chapter Two
Home

Press cameras flashed, fireworks surrounding us in a miraculous light. As we exited the airport reception room reporters shouted, "Over here !"

"No, here ! Come to our microphone straight away !"

A rainbow of international television logos danced before us. My body and mind dizzied with gratitude. This, coupled with my characteristic manner of just speaking out, pushed me to the reporters where I humbly answered their questions. It felt exquisite talking and basking in the novelty of freedom. From where we were imprisoned to how we were treated, when the soldiers swam with us, to the healing I intended to do, a former hostage's life details fulfilled the press requests.

'Former hostage' sounded incredibly delicious.

Margaret, Jim, David, and I then drove up the motorway for Northeast England and their home, which was mine for the time. A joyous four-hour journey from Gatwick Airport was highlighted with a stop halfway for breakfast. Imagine the mouthwatering joy of a hearty English breakfast: bacon, eggs, sausages, baked beans, black pudding, toast, and tea after endless meals of rice, cucumber and tomato? It was sheer luxury. My body and mood soared as I devoured some of each. Not a very healthy food mind you but pure Nirvana from my perspective.

When we arrived in Margaret's hometown of Tyne & Wear, the first thing I did was visit my mother. Cancer had been part of Mum's life for years, culminating in her now bed-bound condition. I knew she'd hung on to see her only son home safely. I desperately wanted to see, yet when I stood seeing her suffer, sensing she was not long for this earth, the pain made me want to run away. *Love and fear, joy and sadness, was life ever going to let me off its roller coaster?* Since the hostage experience I wanted to make things right between everyone, especially to heal relationships in my family.

Mum was a monumental paradox in my life. She had always tried to be a good mother and had been, but in 1964 she left my father and me, taking my beloved sister with her. In the years following this separation I managed to see my sister occasionally and remain close with her. However, the rift between Mum and me grew as I witnessed my father in profound depression. I took care of Dad in his darkest period. Finally, at age eighteen I left everyone, bound for work around the globe, only seeing my mother perhaps once annually.

My heart broke as I saw her trying to smile at me and making small talk. I managed only one hour with her, just one hour. My stomach turned to knots and nausea forced me to leave. I deplored her dying like this.

Safely back at my sister's I tried to relax after visiting Mum. Such agony. *What more could be asked of me?* I flipped through TV channels finally free to watch non-propagandized broadcasts. Comically, my face turned up in countless news programs. Shots from the lengthy airplane journey and Gatwick arrival interviews filled Margaret's television screen. Any time we turned on the set my mug appeared. Freedom had strange dimensions.

October 23th,1990, was my first full day of freedom in Tyne & Wear in Northeast England. As I headed out for a second visit with Mum I opened Margaret's front door to throngs of journalists and reporters. Cameras snapped and flashed with interviewers shouting questions. I was aghast.

Perhaps I was in shock. I don't quite know to this day. All was so stage-like and surreal. I had lost months of life as a prisoner and felt unworthy of anything, let alone media attentions, and yet I was oddly drawn to their questions as a moth is to light. I interviewed from 10 a.m. through 6 p.m. that first full day, including a live report with Mike Nevile, BBCTV news anchor. Mike soon became a family friend because of his profoundly professional and respectful care of us.

It had not been a full twenty-fours since I was a human warshield and I was on world television live. My emotions scrambled: on the one hand I reveled in the warm welcoming good-wishes, on the other hand I was continually put off and in awe by it. Perhaps I was even in denial at the nature of my life's events. Waves of feelings flooded over me: joy and grief, love and loneliness, alienation and now family and a community surrounded me constantly.

"Would you please do a quick interview?"

"Oh, I recognize you—you're David Cunningham, the hostage."

Smiles, hugs, strong, and loving handshakes greeted me every which way. I had no time to grieve or mourn lost lifetime. The Almighty through strangers energized me to carry forward. Embraced by my sister, her loving family and the scores of unnamed citizens who wished me good future, I was propelled through the first week.

Then all ceased.

Hollywood moments are short-lived and soon I was stale news. By the second week of David Cunningham's 'freedom journey' I was moved out of the spotlight. I freely traveled the streets of England un-interviewed and left with my life to live.

It was a grim time; some of it is a blank as I look back. Amid the warmth and love that surrounded me more than I could have ever dreamed, I did not feel connected to a soul. Not one person had been to Baghdad let alone imprisoned there.

What was I to do with this experience now? Where do I place its learnings?

Fortunately, I could talk with my sister. Margaret anchored me. In spite of the personal upheaval she helped me rediscover myself. I needed love and a paying job. From my Baghdad days and hour upon hour of self-reflection, I knew I had a true and loving, healing purpose. *Where was it?* I prayed and waited anxiously for my new life to begin so I could rent a place and become my own man again.

To add to the emotional turmoil that had become my daily companion, any inner peace I found seemed to have no effect on Mum. For all the counseling I had done with prisoners and guards I could neither counsel nor heal my own mother. I held her hand, told her of Baghdad and the goodness of the young soldiers. One day she asked me not to take any more job assignments out of the country. I promised to stay close to Britain. She knew her time was near and wanted both of her children by her bedside.

I had done some hands-on healing with friends before the captivity. My hands held an energy, not mine alone, but a sort of Divine Light surged through my palms and fingers. I did not know why or how my healing worked, but it helped people. I hadn't dared show this gift in Baghdad, not knowing what they would have done if they saw a healing. Now back in England, I had profound personal healing difficulties such as unstable blood sugar levels, stomach problems and self-imposed hospital visiting time constraints; all this kept my relationship with Mum horribly strained. The unhealed cannot heal others.

Guilt set-in. I was overwhelmed realizing the cancer had been allowed to fester too long. *If I had only been here instead of prison could I have healed my mother?* My own physical and mental dis - ease compelled me to watch the hospital clock, night or day, praying for forgiveness between us. The minute hands ticked away the one hour I allowed myself to stay. Looking back, the protection of my 'self' must have been a misguided survival instinct. I had unintentionally blocked my energy and ability to forgive in an effort to protect myself from any more pain. I did not realize at the time, but I was a walking shell; every day it was an effort just to get out of bed.

Mum's condition deteriorated slowly and painfully.

I had promised God I would be a healer and I could not seem to do much of anything. Given days and weeks of visiting the hospital and ultimately a hospice, I could not improve Mum nor sort my life out. All I could do was establish a safe routine: cling to my sister and family, visit Mum and get through each day.

I sometimes seemed to crawl through each day. I dejectedly decide the future would have to unfold at God's will. I was not able to clear the way with my mother's death looming.

Let the Creator help me, I think this was a turning point prayer and I moved forward, albeit slowly.

I actually healed strangers. Every day I could, I called the family members of my fellow hostages. This was a gift I gave them, but how I received love in return ! The Kuwaiti royal family fairly jumped through the phone with joy hearing that their loved one was still alive. Of course every family feared the worst so it was uplifting talking to them with good news of moderate good health and fair treatment going on in the compound I had left behind. Sometimes we met for tea and they read their letters. Other times just the phone call mutually warmed us all to the bone. What had begun as a matter of honour and fulfillment of a promise became a profound act of giving to others and to myself. The meeting of our hearts and souls generated new life in me. It closed wounds, dissipated guilt that I was free and not their loved ones.

The final news ended that horrific chapter. To my elation the remaining hostages were freed before the end of 1990.

Then another personal crisis emerged: my first wife Suzie divorced me. We'd been apart for the better part of a year when she announced the proceedings, in June of 1990, just before my move to Kuwait. She carried through during my hostage time. Her actions culminated in the divorce papers I found in Margaret's post box. She had been unfaithful. I in turn had blocked her out of my mind and very existence during Baghdad. (See My History, chapter five.) Being divorced compounded my sense of abandonment. Time ticked away. I still had no home of my own, no spouse, no money, and could afford no psychological counseling. The British government, even after two interviews with England's Minister of Defense, was not forthcoming with prisoners' readjustment compensations, nor mental aid counseling to at least the British hostages. (This proved to be the case for all thirty-three returned U.K. citizens. After being held as human shields no financial support appeared. I filed a United Nations Foreign Office insurance claim for 'prisoner damages'. Payment was eventually received.

The word 'alone' took on new dimension. I remember that year as a dark, dark time highlighted by sparks of love that kept me alive. If it had not been for Margaret, Jim, little David and Lynsey, their young daughter, I would have been homeless and destitute out on the streets.

Christmas loomed when an old friend, David Northey, called. "Welcome home, David ! Do you want to be kept busy?" David had been a boss at the Londonderry Hotel and had moved to Yorkshire in a small village called Luddendenfoot. "Look, if you need work I've this hotel of my own now. I cannot afford a full time manager other than myself but I could use extra help over Christmas."

I was torn but excited. "Part time work is good, Northey. Maybe we can work hard enough to make it a full time job." *It was not a job doing healing work but it paid.* Northey laughed and agreed to hire me on for December and we'd go from there.

Mum was dying. It was Christmas. All I had done was stay at Margaret's searching for work or traveling to the hospital. I needed to move forward. Reluctantly I packed, knowing that I had to leave my family at Christmas time to gain my life back. If I could work I would be on the other side of being a hostage—a free, productive man. My mother was surprisingly supportive, especially knowing the job was just a couple of hours away.

I cannot tell you how good it was in those first months back from Baghdad—the intensity of love that washed over me whenever I met with old friends. There had been desperate times when I thought I would never see anyone again. Seeing Northey was great as he was such a trusted friend and colleague. The last week of November in England was far warmer when I shook Northey's hand and went to work for him.

The country hotel was booked with all rooms and dining areas scheduled for parties and family gatherings throughout December. We worked hard and became an oiled machine serving the holiday clientele. On Christmas Eve we offered lunch and then boom: all was silent for Christmas week closing. We labored on cleaning for the new year re-opening, but there were no party guests or celebrations. I headed back to Margaret's anxious to see Mum.

Early February, just as the 'official' Gulf War broke in Iraq, my mother entered hospice care. I fulfilled my obligations as a dutiful son and continued visiting as Mum slipped into a coma and was placed in a special care private room. In her final days I stayed longer no matter how uncomfortable I felt. On February 15, twice during the day, Mum came out of the coma and said, "I am dying, son."

I comforted by holding her hand and repeating, "Be at peace. Be at peace."

Looking again straight into my eyes she said twice, "Son, have I done enough for you?"

"Son, have I done enough for you?"

With tears streaming I whispered, "Please don't bother with these things. Relax and be at peace. We're fine." At last, in my heart, I knew she meant to do her best and she had realized how she'd affected my life. I'm afraid it had taken over twenty years to accept my parent's divorce and my mother leaving us. It was done just in time.

February 17th at 6:58 a.m., two minutes to seven, Margaret and I bolted upright and witnessed our mother's last gasp of air. (We found out later that at her moment of passing, she woke several family members at precisely two minutes to seven. My mother wanted to make a dramatic exit. That thought made me chuckle. She'd always had a dramatic flare.) Mum was such a strong spirit. I was grateful that Margaret and I were together upon her passing. Margaret kissed Mum good-bye and left with her husband while I remained keeping vigil as the nurse laid her to rest. I sat for a while experiencing a torrent of emotions. Fragments flew through me: Mum leaving Dad and me back in 1964, unspoken grief over Baghdad, not being a better son, not wanting to be with my mother and her final passing into spirit. I apologized and kissed her brow.

Back at Margaret's we planned the wake and burial. I walked outside for a breath of fresh air and checked the mailbox. Next day, the postman had left a cassette tape from my old college teacher, Don Galloway, of the College of Psychic Studies in London. Don taught meditation and shared information he received through his guides, commonly known as a channeler. The recording was of a spirit message Don had received during meditation the week before Mum's passing. The spirit-soul spoke

through Don and the communication was from my father
! I was amazed as I listened intently while his inflections
reminded me so much of Dad, "Tell David and Margaret
that I am waiting on the other side for their mother with a
big bouquet of flowers."

Inspiring.

It was twenty-seven years since their divorce and
my father still loved Mum into the Spiritual Realm after
physical death. Suddenly an unusual and profound
comfort melted over me as I listened repeatedly. I
envisioned my parents in heaven together. It was a little
boy's dream.

I decided to give Mum a very special farewell gift
before the burial, especially after Dad's message. In the
funeral parlour's Chapel of Rest I took a red rose and
visited with Mum entirely alone and peaceful. I ended my
prayers by placing the rose on my mother's chest. The
coffin was then sealed.

Later that day I shared time with an old friend. George,
in his eighties, was the president of the local Spiritualist's
Church and had been a practicing clairvoyant since the
age of fifteen. I told George that Mum passed into Spirit.
As we drove down the lane George shouted, "David, I
have your mother here with me ! She says, "Thank you
so, dear, for the red rose you gave me in my coffin this
morning !"

I was dumfounded.

God has a way of grabbing my attention. It was
absolutely shocking to think my mother yearned to make
her presence known to me, as well as comfort me even
beyond the veil. I was terribly touched and smiled
thankfully at George.

I took one day at a time and tried keeping my two
promises: one to God that I would practice and dedicate
my life to healing; the second to my mother that I would
not leave the country for a job. I struggled unfruitfully, and

since Northey could not hire me on full time, I was jobless once more. Ah, but the Divine gives messages and comfort if we only look, if we only stay awake and aware. One spring day in 1991, I wandered into a book store where a volume literally popped off the shelf and onto the floor, opening my eyes to the following prose:

"WHY" ~ An Allegory

I leaned from the low-hung crescent moon and grasping the west-pointing horn of it, looked down. Against the other horn reclined, motionless, a Shining One looked at me. But I was unafraid. Below me the hills and valleys were thick with humans. The moon swung low that I might see what they did.

"Who are they?" I asked the Shining One for I was unafraid. The Shining One made answer: "THEY ARE THE SONS AND DAUGHTERS OF GOD."

I looked again and saw that they beat and trampled each other. Sometimes they seemed not to know that the fellow creatures they pushed from their path fell under their feet. But sometimes they looked as he fell and kicked him brutally.

And I said to the Shining One: "Are they all sons and daughters of God?"

And the Shining One said: "ALL."

As I leaned and watched them it grew clear to me that each was frantically seeking something and that it was because they sought what they sought with such singleness of purpose that they were so inhuman to all who hindered them.

And I said to the Shining One: "What do they seek?"

And the Shining One made answer: "HAPPINESS."

"Are they all seeking happiness?"

"ALL."

"Have any of them found it?"

"NONE OF THOSE HAVE FOUND IT."

"Do they ever think that they have found it?"

"SOMETIMES THEY THINK THEY HAVE FOUND IT."

My eyes filled, for at that moment I caught a glimpse of a woman with a babe at her breast. I saw the babe torn from her and the woman cast into a deep pit by a man with his eyes fixed on a shining lump that he believed to be (or perchance to contain, I know not) *happiness.*

And I turned to the Shining One, my eyes blinded.

"Will he ever find it?"

And He said: "THEY WILL FIND IT."

"All of them?"

"ALL OF THEM."

"Those who are trampled?"

"THOSE WHO ARE TRAMPLED."

"And those who trample?"

"AND THOSE WHO TRAMPLE."

I looked again, a long time, at what they were doing on the hills and in the valleys; again my eyes went blind with tears, and I sobbed out to the Shining One:

"Is it God's will, or the work of the devil?"

"IT IS GOD'S WILL."

"And it looks so like the work of the devil !"

The Shining One smiled inscrutably. "IT DOES LOOK LIKE THE WORK OF THE DEVIL."

When I looked a little longer, I cried out protesting: "Why has He put them down there to seek happiness and to cause each other such immeasurable misery?"

Again the Shining One smiled inscrutably: "THEY ARE LEARNING."

"What are they learning?"

"THEY ARE LEARNING LIFE AND THEY ARE LEARNING LOVE."

I said nothing. One man in the herd below held me breathless, fascinated. He walked proudly and others ran and laid the bound, struggling bodies of living men before him so that he might tread upon them and never touch foot to earth. But suddenly a whirlwind seized him and tore his purple robe from him and set him down naked amongst strangers. And they fell upon him and maltreated him sorely.

I clapped my hands.

"Good ! Good !" I cried, exultantly. "He got what he deserved." Then I looked up suddenly, and saw again the inscrutable smile of the Shining One.

And the Shining One spoke quietly: "THEY ALL GET WHAT THEY DESERVE."

"And no worse?"

"AND NO WORSE."

And no better?"

"HOW CAN THERE BE ANY BETTER? THEY EACH DESERVE WHATEVER SHALL TEACH THEM THE TRUE WAY TO HAPPINESS."

I was silent.

And still the people went on seeking and trampling each other in their eagerness to find. And I perceived what I had not fully grasped before, that the whirlwind caught them up from time to time and set them down elsewhere to continue the search.

And I said to the Shining One, "Does the whirlwind always set them down on these hills and these valleys?"

And the Shining One made answer: "NOT ALWAYS ON THESE HILLS OR THESE VALLEYS."

"Where then?"

"LOOK ABOVE YOU."

And I looked up. Above me stretched the Milky Way and gleamed the stars. And I breathed: "Oh !" And fell silent, awed by what was given to me to comprehend.

Below me they still trampled each other.

And I asked the Shining One, "But no matter where the whirlwind sets them down, they go on seeking happiness?"

"THEY GO ON SEEKING HAPPINESS."

"And the whirlwind makes no mistakes?"

"THE WHIRLWIND MAKES NO MISTAKES. IT PUTS THEM SOONER OR LATER WHERE THEY WILL GET WHAT THEY DESERVE."

Then the load crushing my heart lightened, and I found that I could look at the brutal cruelties that went on below me with pity for the cruel. And the longer I looked, the stronger the compassion grew. And I said to the Shining One, "They act like men goaded, what goads them?"

"THE NAME OF THE GOAD IS DESIRE."

Then, when I had looked a little longer, I cried out passionately, "Desire is an evil thing."

But the face of the Shining One grew stern and the voice rang out, dismaying me:

"DESIRE IS NOT AN EVIL THING."

I trembled and thought withdrew herself into the innermost chamber of my heart. Till at last I said, "It is desire that nerves men to learn the lessons God has set."

"IT IS DESIRE THAT NERVES THEM."

"The lessons of Life and Love?"

"THE LESSONS OF LIFE AND LOVE."

Then I could no longer see that they were cruel. I could only see that they were learning. I watched them with deep love and compassion, as one by one the whirlwind carried them out of sight.

by ANONYMOUS

This passage from the Almighty gave me strength as I struggled for patience and employment. I prayed daily as I had been used to doing in Baghdad. The family followed world events as they developed in the Middle East right before our eyes on the living room television. The press carried daily coverage of the Iraqi invasions as the war took hold. The Kuwait Plaza Hotel became an important military base. I was grateful to have escaped

Baghdad and Kuwait, then suddenly realized I could help. I rang the Minister of Defense.

"I am David Cunningham, a former Hussein hostage."

"Yes, Mr. Cunningham, I remember our debriefing. How are you getting along?"

"Sir, I have some information you may find of use. I know the Kuwaiti Plaza Hotel floor plan has a labyrinth of underground rooms and storage areas by its generators. I wanted you to know this perhaps to pass on the information. In all likelihood some of the Iraqi soldiers who had lived in the hotel with me know of these hideaways and could keep prisoners or themselves in high secrecy."

"Thank you, Sir. I shall contact the ground forces with your valuable information. You are good to call."

As the war escalated the press called upon my historical perspective again as a former imprisoned Kuwait Plaza manager. I was back on the telly ! "How do you feel about the conflict now, Mr. Cunningham? Would you be afraid if you were there when they took over the hotel as a military base?" I explained that our hotel had actually been a military establishment back in August 1990.

Subsequently, in the Spring of 1991, two British airmen were shot down, captured and paraded before Iraqi television cameras looking battered and bruised. There was another flurry of newspaper and TV reporters' calls, "What do you think will happen to those individuals?" My stomach rumbled with each question. "How do you feel about this new war development?" Fortunately, just as that interview ran on the networks the Iraqi/Kuwaiti war ended.

The television interviews were not a paying job, just volunteered conversations that took up loads of my time. The only trade I had ever known was in the hotel and catering industry. If a career in healing and counseling others was not going to present itself soon I would be forced by circumstances to take any job offer. I was in a state of monetary desperation. As the Gulf War concluded so did even that active part of my existence: interviewing with reporters.

In June of 1991, I received an entirely unexpected telephone call. It was my previous Kuwaiti Plaza Hotel manager, "Would you like your old position back? After all the war is ended."

My heart jumped then stopped short.

Kuwait? Not that danger zone again.

I remembered the promise to myself and my mother not to go to that part of the globe again. "Let me think about this and get back to you." I sought my sister's counsel.

Was I cracking?

Was I out of my mind?

How could I consider the Middle East again?

I was desperate with seemingly no other choices. Guilt crushed over me as my promises started breaking. "This is the only job I have been offered. I cannot continue like this forever unemployed. Getting back to a work routine is what I need." Margaret agreed that working should help get me back on my feet. I knew I was always welcome in her home and that she understood. With Margaret's blessing I telephoned and accepted. The Plaza would arrange for a private plane to take me back to Kuwait.

On a whim I phoned the television anchor who had the most interest in my family, Mike Nevile. "You will never believe this but I am forced to go back to Kuwait. The Plaza has offered me the manager's job again ! Since I have not had one full time, local job offer I have to take the position back."

"Will you do a quick interview before you leave?" Mike loved these kinds of turnabouts. I said yes. Enthusiastically Mike had the television studio send a car around for me straight away. A few days before the Plaza plane was due in I went on the British airwaves one last time. I stated, "I have no other options but to take my old wartime job back. It's closing in on one entire year since gaining my freedom with a mere four weeks of employment. I had an awful experience in Kuwait. Not returning to that part of the world was a promise made to my mother. She has since died. Farewell Britain, Mike Nevile. " He shook my hand and nodded with understanding. What a predicament.

Later that very day I received a call from a prestigious hotel just outside London. "Mr. Cunningham, you are a British hero. We are willing to offer you a job here if you can move to London." The energies in my body took off running. I quickly accepted.

Was my luck changing? "Ask and you shall receive," rang in my ears.

Immediately I telephoned the Kuwait Plaza and thanked them royally for the job renewal. Then I declined explaining the new position in my native England. I ended by asking them to forward the back pay for the week I was in management there defending their establishment.

My life's path had turned the corner. In July 1991, I packed my luggage, again.

David L. Cunningham, 2008
Tyne & Wear, Northeast England

Chapter Three
The Healing Process

Barry Neil Kaufman, author of *Happiness Is a Choice,* tells readers in his chapter called "Nothing is Impossible" of the regeneration of tissue in children. Children have the ability and are documented to regrow finger tips, heal from wounds rapidly, etc., whereas teens and adults who become trained to believe people cannot grow limbs, do not. Mr. Kaufman questions, is it as scientists state that older cells cannot perform, or have the reorganization potential of cells that new, baby and child cells do? Or rather, if humans of any age can regrow cells (skin, liver, etc.) then why can't we change our beliefs and the neuropathways that support them? In the millennium we are continually finding evidence that we can indeed change our inner chemistry. A beautiful line Mr. Kaufman posits includes a fresh and exciting word you, dear readers, might consider: *bodymind*. Mr. Kaufman asks: "If happiness were a seed, what *bodymind* would grow from it?"

That old black magic, white magic, light magic—what is this thing called healing? I have pondered this subject, as many of you have, for decades. The life I have led chronicles my journey and is honestly all I have when it comes to explaining healing. I read, study and speak with others of the miracles of healing but am still a healing student. However, since my captivity, I've pledged my days to the art of healing and seek to comfort and heal all. Perhaps you will find personal healing in my life story. I pray that you will.

One caveat: when I refer to the Deity, He or She is yours as well. Whatever or whomever you see as the Creator is also mine. The healings and gifts in my life, I do not claim as my own, but are the Divine's through me His willing vessel. I do not seek to offend or alienate any religion, ethics or spirituality. My existence is truly congruent with yours; we all have unique qualities, encounters and gifts to bring to the world. I strengthen the energies in people's bodies helping them heal themselves. I am a partner in healing—a team partnership originated by the Almighty.

Healing is an ancient art. People have been practicing healings for thousands and thousands of years. A man called Jesus was an incredible healer, teacher, guide, and beam of love and light. **Healing is universal and for everyone.** The task of a healer is to transfer and transmit the Supreme's Energy into the person with whom the healer is working. Realigned and energized, the individual moves into better health, both spiritually and physically. Jesus said other people will do this work and to a higher degree.

For years before the Baghdad imprisonment, I spontaneously practiced this gift without understanding it. One day in a 1995 meditation the angel-guides addressed my lack of understanding: "David, healing is God's demonstration of Love for His children." My soul warms with joy when I recall that exquisite message. It is a beautiful knowing I carry with me as I journey. I grasp healing more fully now and as future healings unfold I continue learning with each soul I counsel.

Healing eases people with all kinds of mind, body and soul maladies, both physical and emotional pains. Every human being has enough vibrational energy to heal his or her own body and soul and even other people. This is done through energy centers called *chakras*. The ancient energy center medicine of Ayurveda was organized centuries prior to Christ's walk on earth. Since Jesus' time, in the past 2,000 years, increasing numbers of people have trained themselves to use the Almighty's energies. In almost every culture there are legends of their own healing miracles.

These miracles and their passed down stories have resulted in healers having come under centuries of suspicion. The main reason for fear and trepidation is the misunderstanding the art of healing. Countless healers, documented and not, have been persecuted because people were afraid of what they did not grasp. This is universal: every person can use his Love Energy to help a neighbour, friend or any person. Love is the vibration of healing, the God Energy in which I work. The easiest way to understand this energy is referring to it as Love Energy.

At first I did not comprehend healing either. Don Galloway, my friend and mentor at London's College of Psychic Studies, told me when I was twenty that my destiny was as a healer. I had not a clue what he meant. It is clearer now: healing is an act of the soul's free will along with the Creator's presence. In all humility, I am destined to heal during this life and have been a healer in numerous other lifetimes. I take His calling very seriously. I vessel God's Energy. It pulses into the energy centers of the mind, body and soul through my hands to help others. This Life Force is the highest, intelligent energy. It goes directly to the problem area, which is a place of slowing energy or a blockage of energy flow, and aligns the person's Life Force back in order and free flowing, healthy living.

It has taken more than fifty years for me to understand the art of healing. I read voraciously and continually discuss healing with others. I am diligent in meditating every morning and night to sustain healthy energy flow in my own body. Serving others is what I want to do for a very long lifetime. The more I learn the better I will teach healing. Besides studying at London's College of Psychic Studies I have worked extensively with the gifted healers of the Association of Stress Management, UK. I am certified by the National Federation of Spiritual Healers of Great Britain and was ordained a Minister of Healing in the United States.

People often ask, "David, why do we get sick? Why must we need healing?" It is my understanding that when a person is not in harmony, illness can begin. To maintain continual health one should go forward in life with unconditional, non-judgemental love for self and fellow man. "Love thy neighbour as thyself," is a verse everyone knows. "Do no harm, only love", is another golden saying. It sounds simplistic yet this is what fuels the healthy world of living beings.

Being out of harmony is often the unhealthy experience of feeling unwanted or unloved. When a person buries a painful unloving event rather than letting it go the body begins to vibrate its balance of energy differently, slowing it down. Sometimes a barrier is formed to protect against more pain and energy slows to a blocked state. This energy flow difference brings disease if not cleared.

It is my perception, along with others working in the medical and spiritual fields, that illnesses come from within. The word *disease* comes from the root words: not at ease or dis + ease. We are not at peace with the Life Energy when we push our problems inward or think negatively. A common illness pattern of thinking is: "Why me? Poor me, I am a victim." That kind of thinking stops positive energy and creates an unhealthy setting for dis - ease in the body's energy stream. Disharmony filters through the body and can strike the physical body and mind. A healthy way of thinking is: "How can I make this situation more loving?" or "What can I learn from this lesson and these people?"

My healing sessions begin with positive, encouraging conversations with patients. This can work wonders and was a saving grace in Baghdad. Clients are asked why they are unwell. It is tough for people to recognize that events stuffed inside from their past, either recent or far back, can cause present ailments.

To compound our health issues, we do not live in an unconditional, loving society. We certainly have pockets and groups of good intentioned, kind and loving people. However, we commonly find ourselves in unloving environments. These situations can build up, manifesting and creating personal negativity, which frequently moves into illness if not resolved. Humankind does not teach love as the primary human responsibility. **Love is the most important function we have on earth.** Schools teach reading, writing, arithmetic, and how to use a computer. Not enough people teach why we are here: to love. Some communities, churches and families try, but as a whole society, we need far more loving than is currently demonstrated. Most people need healing for this reason. My work has only just begun; the more people I meet the more pain I see that needs relieving.

To follow is a sketch of the classic seven energy centers called chakras, plus an awakening center. I have added the Thymus Energy Center as the eighth chakra. In meditation I learned that the ordinarily dormant thymus gland is evolving in the human body. I often see the thymus unblocked in health regained patients. The Thymus Center is linked to deep emotions. The fluid abilities of a person to achieve and be motivated to do so can be blocked in the thymus. Blockages are frequently due to missing experiences of love or past hurts.

The sketch depicts the framework of the highly refined wellness energy system of Ayurveda. The Ayurveda medical philosophy, founded in India, was documented in Sanskrit as scientifically well developed since 1500 BC, far earlier than Ancient Greek or Chinese methods. It is written that Life Force comes from above the body as Light radiating to the earth and flows into each of the interdependent but distinct chakra energy centers. The energy swirls and spirals clockwise through the chakra points finally flowing out through the Base Chakra. The healthy body feels light, bright and has a full, harmonious sense of the partnership between the mind, body and soul/spirit.

What is this thing called *chakra*?

It is a field of light-energy-vibration connecting mind, body and soul. The Energy Force which emanates through the body is always meant to flow in a clockwise fashion. If the Life Energy becomes blocked, moves counter-clockwise or stops flowing through one of the chakra points, it causes imbalance and the person can become ill.

We have twelve chakras in all. Four chakras flow above the Crown (top of the head) chakra attaching the soul with the body. The remaining eight physical body centers run in a straight line streaming through the body, from the soft spot of the baby's head (Crown Chakra) down the center to the base of the spine just below the navel (Base Chakra). The Light keeps us going. It is Divine Energy entering the body spinning in a clockwise direction through each of the eight wheels of light and grounding the body and soul on earth. Thus we are connected from Spirit to ground and anchored in present life.

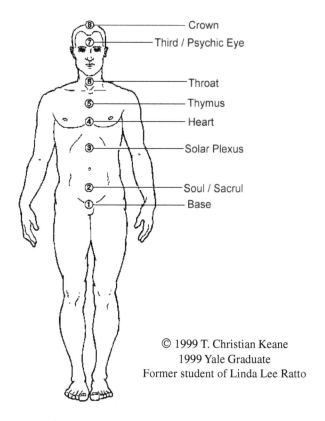

© 1999 T. Christian Keane
1999 Yale Graduate
Former student of Linda Lee Ratto

Crown Chakra: top center of the head; where life force energy enters the body
  • physical connection: full skeleton, all muscles, skin, pituitary
  • mental/emotional: sense of selflessness, spirit, trust, faith

Third Eye Chakra: center of the forehead; connected to our psychic senses
  • physical connection: nervous system, brain, sinus, ear, nose, throat
  • mental/emotional: intelligence, awareness, imagination, intuitiveness

Throat Chakra: base of the neck; thinking and speaking
  • physical connection: mouth(teeth, gums), neck, voice, thyroid
  • mental/emotional: expressing oneself, criticism

Thymus Chakra: situated just below the throat; has been dormant in mankind
  • mental/emotional: deep emotion of all types

Heart Chakra: chest center, below sternum
  • physical connection: heart, circulation, lungs
  • mental/emotional: love, compassion, anger, grief

Solar Plexus Chakra: below breastbone, center 'hole'; linear thinking
  • physical connection: stomach, liver, pancreas, small bowel, adrenal glands
  • mental/emotional: 'who-we-are', charm, charisma, confidence of self

Soul/Sacral Chakra: below the navel; all memories/feelings buried here
  • physical connection: hips, lower back, large intestine, bladder
  • mental/emotional: human relationships, power center

Base Chakra: between anus & reproductive organs; where life force leaves body
  • physical connection: immune system, excretion, sexuality
  • mental/emotional: vitalness, survival instincts, potency

The Life-Energy comes from the Almighty, through our crown, swirling clockwise through the eight chakra wheels of light and leaves through the base chakra to the earth so we are grounded and alive on this plane.

A Typical Healing Session

The initial part of a typical hour-long healing session is a discussion of the nature of illness. I ask why the person has come to see me. Then I further explain the underlying cause of all dis - eases according to my spiritual energy healing beliefs and knowings.** I discern from the patient's comments where the problem lies. I then begin teaching about the Life Force and chakra points.

To diagnose a Life Energy Center blockage, I use a quartz crystal pendulum (any weight on a cord serves the same purpose). I hold the pendulum above each chakra beginning at the base straight to the crown. The pendulum swings the same way that the patient's chakra point energy is moving (or not moving). If the energy is spinning in a healthy, clockwise direction the pendulum will do so. If the chakra's energy is off balance the pendulum will swing counter clockwise. However, if the pendulum does not move then that chakra's energy has ceased flowing at all.

**Point of definition: knowings are things one senses as perfect and right without training and previous knowledge; intuitive understandings

Here are fuller explanations to the diagrams presented. Emotional Body = the first three chakras:

#1 = Base
#2 = Soul + Sacral
#3 = Solar Plexus

If the first three chakras are blocked, the emotional body is being shielded by an invisible barrier to the Life Force. Protection of the emotional body is often traced to personal events as far back as childhood. Anything that has not been dealt with, unlovings or pent-up anger for example, can cause impediments to health filled living and proper energy flow. This can build a defense screen against more pain which only blocks the Life Force further. It is a vicious dis - ease cycle.

If the Heart Chakra is blocked, even if the person is outwardly loving and caring, a 'heart barrier' can prevent the fullness of love from blossoming. Love is always there truly waiting to be shown. God is Love in us.

The Thymus has been blocked and dormant in almost everyone. I have seen signs of it coming unblocked as a new age of increased energy unfolds.

Throat Chakra blockage shields the self from voicing true feelings and thoughts. There is often lack of communication in a person's life due to buried unlovings. A throat block manifests as an inability to tell the whole truth, vocalize who we are, what we are thinking, and/or how we honestly feel. Truth will eventually and always does come out, sometimes in turbulence and often as dis - ease. We must speak truth to self and to one another for our Life Energy to flow freely.

The Third Eye Chakra block prevents the person from using his or her psychic ability and potential. Listening to our gut reactions and intuitive feelings is a first step in using this center. Paying attention to messages in dreams is one use of the third eye.

The Crown Chakra blockage materializes as lack of energy. If the first avenue of free flow Life Force—God's faucet of energy so to speak—is slowed or stopped, the entire body is affected. "I have to get out of bed, I have to get going," are typical thoughts which can be replayed in a person's head, if the Love Light is not allowed to enter the body and spin properly. Interruption of flow forces the person to work by sheer willpower rather than with the ease filled grace of Light.

Complete eight chakra obstruction frequently appears as sluggish daily living. Every day seems to be an effort of massive will. Nothing is easy because of the hindrance the person has created against the healthy energy stream. Every task is a struggle: "I have to do this, I have to do that." It is as if the person has stepped into a huge bubble of protective defense. It is okay living, but it is not a full life using the free flowing grace of the God Energy to its highest potential.

Healing Stories

Over the years I have worked with hundreds of people being healed by the Almighty through my hands. Allow me to share some results that may change your point of view concerning your body's healing potential.

**Lynn had been suffering from migraines for some twenty years. She came to me through a friend, her husband, Mike. I laid my hands on her head and she felt well. She described her healing experience, "I feel as if you drilled a hole in my head. The pressure was relieved and my pain went away." This one powerful experience eliminated her migraines. She has had slight headaches from time to time since, but no migraines to date.

**A four year old girl, Jenny, came to me with massive overall body eczema. We had a few sessions and now her skin is clear.

**Carol, in her early twenties, had been in a terrible road accident and used crutches. Carol came to me with a high quantity of body pain. We discussed her accident. I then did her first a hands-on session. She walked out of the room without the crutches. After a few more sessions, Carol is still pain free in all parts of her body.

** Louisa, a rape victim in her early twenties, was brought to me by her mother. She had been in a full year of rape counseling with little constructive communication or progress. She lived with her mother, could not work or be alone, and generally was very disabled in her life. I sat with her and explained my healing work. I spoke quietly in a gentle, informational tone while explaining the eight chakras and how they can become blocked by emotional trauma. She was quite at ease talking with me. There was an amazing change after the first session, she was uplifted so. It took seven sessions, but she is now living on her own and is a productive, vital young woman once again.

** Bella, a friend of mine, lived in Hawaii where a kitten turned up on her doorstep. Bella was in the process of moving back to the mainland but rescued the homeless cat and named him Pineapple. After settling in San Diego, Pineapple was hit by a car. He dragged himself back to Bella's doorstep where she scooped the tabby into her arms and rushed him to the veterinarian. Three hundred dollars worth of ex-rays later, the news was grave: Pineapple had a broken jaw and pelvis. The vet recommended putting the cat to sleep. Bella took Pineapple home where she tried nursing and feeding him with an eyedropper. All he did was lay in his basket. Bella called and asked that I come to her home for a healing session. During my fourth visit to Bella's there was an astounding change. Pineapple awoke upon my touch, stood up and walked on all four paws to his feeding dish. Bella and I laughed with joy.

**Jacqueline came to visit with severe chest pains. She had tried numerous other medical therapies and finally sought my energy healing. Before I leave a person after a session, I always explain to them that the healing can have far reaching and surprising affects on the client over the next days and weeks. This lady felt much better after our first time together and scheduled another session. She shared that in between these two visits, "Oh, I have had all this black liquid come from my chest. I am feeling good but what do you think of the discharge?" I told her, "You are being cleansed. I do not know all the answers, I admit; but the Almighty does." For three weeks this process continued as her healing energies worked toward wellness. Then one day she said the black discharge stopped. She is feeling great now.

Emotional and physical cleansings take enormously differing avenues. From acne and boils, to crying outbursts and low feelings, to giggles and giddiness, the entire emotional spectrum can be experienced after just one healing session. The manifestations of healing cleansings go away completely, followed by a superior sense of well being which seems to be permanent in most people.

I have read myriad works on reflection, contemplation and spiritual healing. In the next pages I want to share with you some authors whose works I greatly admire and who have helped me heal myself and those around me. Julie Soskins, a gifted meditative channeler, has a wealth of knowledge and advice in her book, *The Cosmic Dance.* She states repeatedly that it is of utmost importance to have stillness, time for reflection. In this work-a-day world with beepers we even take to bed, Ms. Soskins tells us to quieten down and listen to our own musical note, our own tune, so we may harmonize with those around us. Some of us have favourite kinds of music. This means, according to Ms. Soskins, that our inner notes are harmonious with our favourite types of music. She continues by telling her readers that one need not spend

24 hours in solitude, but a little a day will help balance and align God's energies.

Ms. Soskins is another source of the information I related earlier concerning the Thymus Center, the chakra I added to the traditional seven chakra centers to make eight. Ms. Soskins received several messages through her meditations that said the center just above the heart receives Soul Light. It is closer to the heart than the throat and is receiving more and more energy in individuals with the new millennium. I praise Ms. Soskins for sharing her work in *The Cosmic Dance* book because I thought I was reading some peoples' chakras incorrectly. As I do healings I often sense increased energy flows in the area above the heart in my clients. After reading *The Cosmic Dance,* I reveled. It affirms my role as healer and perceiver of energy. Additionally, it is marvelous to consider another area in which we can receive more of God's Love Energy !

I find it comforting to read that other people have received similar messages as I concerning healing and the power of reflection. Caroline Myss, Ph.D., author of *Anatomy of the Spirit*, tells us how to deal with the cultural training we've experienced surrounding 'vengeance' and an eye for an eye. Ms. Myss says that the second chakra (Third Eye, Insight Area) is where we need to focus love when we come in connection with a person who has offended us. Ms. Myss' work correlates the imagery and cultures of three faith systems in *Anatomy of the Spirit* and uses their common symbolism to describe what to do. The white Light Energy from the Deity can be visualized as coming down from the heavens through the crown chakra and into the third eye where one only has to say, "I send you love. You are in my life for a Divine reason and I chose to see that part of you, not the shadow side." Ms. Myss' states that this attitude is "Spiritual Elegance" and a way to make choices and unconditionally love all beings. She suggests that we may be stuck if we keep resenting some one or ANY one in our past. Honour all and our own health will be the reward.

Jesus said, "No healer can be used by the 'Higher Forces' unless he loves all of humanity. Healing is love energy used in the right way."

The more I read, study and assimilate, the more I realize I do not know. I receive information through prayer and meditation, from readings and messages with friends and strangers in letter form and now e-mail. My guardian angels, both in Spirit and on earth, are customized God helpers. I understand the Almighty through these guides because they come in a form to which I easily relate. When we personalize our relationship with the Divine we are on the path to becoming the highest level of human we can possibly imagine.

This is the Almighty's intention: to be one with us.

What is this life all about? In the beginning the Infinite created us in His/Her likeness. In birth we are perfect souls attached to the Energy Force. As children we know our perfection. We then grow, experience life and separate. Out of free will we want to live anew. We have guides who help us as we live on, as we learn new ways to love and re-attain oneness with the Divine. We have the tools for perfection as we work through experiences. We are equipped with the grace of love and free will to make ourselves into the highest individuals we can imagine. The more loving we are the closer we are to the Infinite One.

We are God-created creators.

To develop and craft who we are, our Soul Spirits are set on journeys into this plane of existence. Earth is made for the purpose of souls to experience life in a physical body. We can be anything and any one we desire. In the

Spirit, there is a blueprinting of the life of a soul with choices such as the timing of birth, parents and environmental conditions. There is even a plan for the time of passing off the earth plane. Our physical death is not at all an end but a passage back into the realm of the Spirit, our true and forever home.

Life's blueprint is agreed upon by the Almighty, the to-be-born soul and its guides, angels or whatever you like to call your life helpers. After the planning it is time for the spark of conception—the mystical, mysterious 'energie de vive'. The soul attaches itself to the sperm then becomes part of its mother. Gradually and miraculously over the nine months of development, it receives from the world of Spirit what is needed to live in physical form. From the absolute moment of conception the soul is entirely aware of its conditions and surrounding life plan. The soul's fresh journey comes with the free will to know love and relearn how to love in ever more differing ways.

During birth the soul slowly becomes removed from the Spirit world to begin its creation in a body. We are not puppets and no one is pulling our strings. As we move out of childhood and away from the times when we talk to 'imaginary friends' or speak of what 'I used to do' (during other lifetimes that we remember), we leave our past behind as we concentrate on the present life form. We choose this moving away to advance the soul's discovery of self. It is a new adventure to find out how to love with no conditions attached.

The soul evolves, experiencing the earth setting agreed upon before its birth, and looks for love. The secret to a joy filled, higher level life is living in loving respect for all beings. If we look within we can see a direct correlation between unloving acts and our own disharmony, disease and troubles.

Ah, but this is a time in human evolution when love, respect and gentle kindness are not always there. If we would stick to loving our world would manifest quite differently. Here is when our free will comes into play. We may have decided before birth what will be there to support and surround us in this present life. However, we have freedom of choice. We can choose to be loving as the Divine is with us.

We can choose to love every moment of our existence.

The relationships we establish are the paths to finding out who we are as loving beings. We often are deterred and do not live peacefully. Yet this is what we are supposed to be doing. Loving is our mission. Why else would millions of people be placed on the earth together if not for the purpose of getting along? To live alone in a bubble would not allow us to know our inner selves. We are meant to develop with people, to form ourselves based on loving each other.

We can learn through the opposite of love, too. Must we continually live through unloving lessons to discover the center of higher existence? If we look inside we know the truth: **The center of life is non-judgemental love.** We do not have to be unloving or keep experiencing unlove to comprehend unloving.

The Infinite, through us, is born and reborn to experience forever-love. In every situation there is always another unique opportunity for love, new and fresh yet constant and eternal all at the same time. Each encounter with our neighbours can show the fullness of what love can be. Every soul has opportunity upon opportunity to attain the internal and external quality of total unconditional love.

To be Love,
to do It,

to give It—
to self and fellow man—
is the soul's ultimate goal.

Once the soul has reached this height of wondrous existence, fully realizing itself as a love filled likeness of the Creator, the soul chooses to spin off the earth plane (physical death). The higher soul can become a teacher guide for others, either in the world of Spirit or side by side with the other souls in physical bodies on earth again and again. Each soul's journey of discovery can take hundreds of lives to finally attain its highest mastery.

What is frequently missing in our current world is the teaching of this information when souls are very young. The majority of mankind's babies go about not being taught or shown how to be loving and foster non-judgemental interactions. The Almighty's messages are clear and never conflict with the universality of churches and religions of the world. Our Creator does not alienate people from one another but wishes to bring them closer together with universal love. We are all one with God when loving ourselves and others.

The Infinite created us in the perfect image of Him and Her Self. Perfection is often difficult for us to comprehend, but the Divine is perfection and thus all creations are such. **It is a delightful promise: Our new and fresh babyhood, as perfect as we came into the world, can be reclaimed.** We may again have wellness and healed purity if we desire. If we sensitize ourselves to the Energy Power that is in our body and souls **everything is possible.**

Being a transmitter of the Light Force is my blueprint and life choice. As healer, I beam bright, white light to renew original energies through my hands. I replenish my body too, in every healing encounter in which I participate. My healing process with others rejuvenates my own energy centers. The fresh energy flow beams into every ounce, each cell of my body, mind and soul. Healing is an exquisite team process.

Throughout my experience I have been a messenger of Spirit, both spontaneously and intentionally. I studied channeling and worked with groups to learn more about receiving Spirit messages and information on the art of healing. However, I pledged to focus the rest of my life's work into healing the spirit, mind and body of others, rather than receiving Spirit messages for people, as mediums do. I see that I am best able to help humankind in the singular focus of healing and teaching about the process to increased wellness and high energy flow.

Healing is simple. The Infinite does not cause distress but rather loves and seeks to grow love in us. The Divine wants to see health and love flourish every way we can possibly envision. There is nothing spooky or supernatural, alien or Sherlock Holmes-y about the Spirit. On the contrary, if history has filled people with doubts concerning spiritual healers it is out of their own fears and lack of knowledge. This is why I strive to educate others about healing, so people become unafraid, more loving and ultimately healthier.

Do I know everything the Almighty knows? Certainly not. I profess to the contrary. There are mysteries in life that you and I do not remember, nor can we *figure out* right now. This is meant to be. We have chosen, by free will, to experience this life veiled in forgetfulness. Within this life choice we cannot know it all. If we did we would not live life in its entirety because we would say to ourselves, "We already know it all" and then be unmotivated to learn. We are made to create new ways of learning. It is our life task to learn what we do not know now but already know in our hearts—to love no matter what circumstances arise. Together we are living love and its opposite. We are becoming centered in the understanding of what is love-at-its-fullest and love-at-its-least. We knew in the Spirit and we are now knowing love again as we meditate, pray and encounter with one another. When we arrive back into the realm of complete Spirit understanding we will do so with a whole new vantage point.

This millennium is here and accounts across the planet attest to a higher vibration and a present day higher collective consciousness. There is a new age upon us when we collectively, as an entire world of souls, know that there is more to life than things and doings.

There is LOVE.
We know it.
We are choosing this loving way together.

The dream that more and more people are choosing to love one another, choosing to see the Light and energize each other toward the Light, is the most exciting prospect we could imagine for ourselves and the universe. What a time it is to be alive ! Higher, healthier, closer-to-the-Creator existence awaits us, each and every one.

The following chapters interlace my history with stories of the Divine's power shown to me. I am graced with the goodness of the Spirit every day. Additionally, it is a blessing that you have chosen to take time to learn more about the way to optimal health and a more loving life.

As Neale Donald Walsch has said in Book Three of *Conversations with God*, a trilogy of books depicting an intense five year journaling conversation with the Creator:

"Yet here is the greatest Divine Dichotomy: The greatest complexity is the greatest simplicity. The more 'complex' a system is, the more simple is its design. Indeed, it is utterly elegant in its Simplicity.
The master understands this. That is why highly evolved beings live in utter simplicity."

Neale Donald Walsch,
Conversations with God, Book Three, Chapter 19

We are all here to experience love. And we are in a free will choice about our life experiences and can experience pure, unconditional, nonjudgemental love, or not.

Please read the next chapters with the love in your hearts. It is that simple.

Chapter Four
1946 - 1977
My History

"And thus he who was the learner becomes the teacher… for he has made the one decision that gave his teacher to him. He has seen in another person the same interests as his own."

A Course in Miracles,
Manual for Teachers, Chapter 2, 5:8

In the human experience are events both monumental and life altering—grabbed-by-the-seat-of-the-pants moments. In crafting this book I examined my life with a magnifying glass. What formed the soul 'David the healer' ? I found out countless things about myself.

I realized I relish simple routine, although for years I've not lived a 'normal' day.

I was held prisoner, yet had done nothing for which to be imprisoned.

Were years of my life literally being at the wrong place at the right time or perfectly unfolded according to a higher plan?

I heal with my hands, which I know was meant to be. I understand that what I lived before healing was exquisite training for me to be what I am today, every moment of it, including the hostage days. We may not understand the timeframes in our lives. I have come to know that our experiences move in synchronicity for ideal lesson learning at the exact customized 'teachable moments'.

This is part of our Spirit plan, Karma and the before birth blueprint.

My life is very different but so similar to yours. Commonality draws us to one another for comfort, solace. Uniqueness equally pulls us together out of curiosity (root derivation of unique is **unus**, as in unity). If you do not believe in the notion of your specialness, if you cannot see your common thread with everyone, perhaps Emily Dickinson can convince you and touch your heart.

NOBODY?
I am nobody ! Who are you?
Are you nobody, too?
Then there's a pair of us - don't tell !
They'd banish us you know.

How dreary to be somebody !
How public, like a frog
To tell your name the livelong June
To an admiring bog !

Emily Dickinson

I hope you understand the genuine qualities the Divine has given you as well as the oneness we all share. Why did we show up as embodied souls together on earth in the now here? Why right this moment in this lifetime? Come travel with me and we'll both discover more about the Self.

I came to the earth plane on June 11, 1946 in Dunston, Northeast England. I chose parents with vast emotional pain from their pasts. They set the life stage for me: Mother was the product of an Irish Catholic father and a staunch Methodist mother. They had a host of fundamental religious conflicts in a 1950's societal setting.

These troubled souls joined in matrimony and produced first David, then nine years later, Margaret.

Dad was abandoned by his mother and raised by his grandmother and great aunt, a staunch and strict Victorian upbringing at best. I found out later that Mum honestly married Dad to get out of her homestead of troubles with five siblings and her dictatorial parents. It was a strained manner in which to wed. To their dying days, both never grew through the pain of their youth but rather remained stuck. Ultimately, they each developed cancer succumbing to lifelong, buried individual and combined strife.

We lived in Northeast England in a Sunnyside cottage. Sunnyside town had an active vegetable industry and Dad obtained a farm contract that included rental of the small house. We had electricity but no gas. The kitchen had an open wood stove, a close eating area and a small closet. We shared one bedroom and a living corner with the toilet outside. We bathed in a huge cast iron tub placed in front of the fire with kettles of warm water tepid enough to tolerate. I remember bath water as quite cool to the bum.

My most vivid memory, from about the age of three, was a harsh winter's day. Dad dug a snow tunnel between the house and the toilet, probably ten meters long. I walked through the cloud high, snow walls to the frosty cold loo. I watched the sky peeking icy blue down at me while I did my business.

Mum was one of six: Sarah, Olive, Lily, Joe, Kitty, and Margaret, my Mum. All girls married controlling spouses, except my mother. It was somewhat cultural, those roles. Uncle Joe never married and lived with my grandfather Joseph through all his days. Auntie Olive was mentally disturbed. Every one of the aunts and uncles were desperate for love. I was the youngest nephew and they looked for love in me, vying for my attentions, pitting one aunt against the other. "You love me best, don't you, David? Don't you?"

Dad had one brother and sister both quite bothered in one way or another. My family was like most, born with troubles and needing love. My early upbringing was a good and simple, rural life. I spent much time on my own alone with nature. I was fed and had all I needed. Even the outside toilet was just the way it was; I never minded. At the early age of 4½, I attended primary school after pestering my mother incessantly. I got along well with the usual children's problems that go with making friends. Academically I performed on upper level. Plays and performances became a new hobby and love.

When I was seven years old, we moved to Whickham into a council house that was British government controlled. Not far from Sunnyside, Whickham had houses all the same as the next on basic undecorated streets named after poets; ours was Chaucer Road. This house seemed like a huge heaven to me with two bedrooms and our first indoor loo. Dad switched to coal mining. It was not a choice job but pay and housing benefits were upgrades.

My father was a gentle soul and preferred the simple life. He came home from a hard day's work wanting dinner, the radio, newspaper, and the fireplace. He never went out on the town. Mum, on the other hand, loved socializing, Bingo, dancing, and evening activities outside the house.

On August 22, 1955, my dear little sister Margaret was born. She was a fresh blessing in my life and has been ever since. I looked after her often and enjoyed every moment. With the Whickham move we became neighbours to Mum's sisters. The house bustled with family and I attended Whickham Junior School with two cousins. Mum and my extended family continually pressured me to perform better. I was slight in stature and not very athletic. I recall hearing, "David, run faster !"

and "David, you can do better than that." I was highly sensitive, took it to heart and developed severe asthma. Sharp are the memories of not being able to breathe. With no medications, I simply had to see the attacks through. I missed school and felt as if I were dying, day upon day. I can still recall the tight chest and desperation for a breath. The asthma attacks distressed Mum and Dad, but they could do little except sit with me. We prayed, "Dear God, please give David your breath of life." Looking back, I am certain they felt especially helpless, as did I.

Although my parents did not see eye to eye, they were both Christian and established prayer in our bedroom routine. The prayers together, during asthma crises, were my first meditations. Whenever I could not breathe I prayed extra hard. In a child's timeframe, the attacks lasted forever and I prayed for what seemed like every hour. I succumbed to asthma's frightening, throat grabbing symptoms for years. I grew weaker and have remained small as a man.

My medical condition and hypersensitive nature paved the way for me to feel like a victim. I gave my own personal power away. I see that now. Due to asthma and missing school often I made lesser grades. I did not fit into any one peer group, especially not with those playing cricket or any sport. I felt an outsider. Mum was there and we had much time together, but she was not the kind of mother who doted. I had what seemed to me an immense quantity of alone time. Away from school friends, fighting to breathe, I lacked motivation to learn. I pulled myself to class because my parents demanded it. Each day in school I felt as if I was breathing very thin air. I do not remember ever feeling comfortable.

One day the Headmaster walked into our classroom in his dark tie and signature tweed jacket and asked, "Who would like to learn how to swim?" He was an imposing figure at over six feet as he announced that an outdoor public swimming pool in the next village was to open. Many of us raised our hands eager for the new opportunity. The Headmaster retorted, "Not you, Cunningham—you with the tissue paper chest !" I was ashamed. My face burned as laughter surrounded me. I ran home and told my mother. Immediately the next morning Mum visited the Headmaster and screamed at him. Although Mum never told me the details, she must have given him quite a lashing. Low and behold he came into our classroom the very afternoon of her meeting. I froze in my seat. He said, "David, what I said yesterday you should not have taken literally." To my amazement he appeared embarrassed. Mum's strong will was wonderful that day.

Slowly, as I developed into an adolescent, I grew out of the asthma malady. Looking back, the Almighty answered my prayers. School and life, however, still had its challenges. A particularly horrific moment for an insecure, somewhat sickly lad was in woodworking class. Mr. Greene was a bristly mustached, cane wielding character who ruled the school's precious equipment. Whereas I grew to enjoy and master wood-working, it was not for love of the teacher. Mr. Greene carried two bamboo canes named Ginger and The BumStick. Well, he caught me dropping an expensive chisel. As if by magic Mr. Green appeared at my side. "Damaging school tools is a punishable offense," he shouted and swung The BumStick across my bumbottom. Those were the good old days.

One teenage day I told myself enough is enough. Perhaps it was adolescent testosterone. I was doing better in school and breathing. Maybe it was to get the cousins off my back. Nevertheless, I was a slight, gentle natured loner, who finally felt better. I decided to come out and be me. As I grew ever stronger I found a girlfriend.

At last, I asserted my full self will and left school at age fifteen. This, even in the remote area in which I lived, was uncommon. My folks had not completed school and, although they protested, seemed to understand. As long as I pulled my weight and worked, I was tolerated. School had never been a love of mine; the dramatic plays, my girl, all of it could not hold me in class any longer. It was my first real 'take control' moment and I took it earlier than most boys. I worked in the local movie house, which endeared me to acting on an adult level. I was free to pursue non-school talents. What to do or where, I was not certain, but school course work and even being part of an organized religion were not me.

The local theatre group drew more of my attentions as did surviving financially and making new, older aged friends. At sixteen my first full time adult job paid two pounds ten shillings per week's wage. I kept my expenses low, still living and eating at home with Mum and Dad. They fought all the time, but I paid little mind. I was freeing myself and besides, I had much to do with work and play practices.

I felt like a man, especially when I earned a promotion as keeper of the company ledgers. I'd never had such responsibility. Coupled with my membership in the theatrical society with people I thought were adult I was making my mark. The first performance was *The Music Man*. After my initial need to be pushed out on stage, I reveled in the applause and appreciation. I loved the freedom to express myself.

Just about two years passed.

I grew to dread going home; my parents grumbled and fought. Dad wanted home relaxation and Mum wanted much more each evening. It was for Margaret's sake that I stayed as long as I did. I was grateful that we could talk for hours, comforting each other amid the daily family strife. Weekends were the worst, virtually consumed in arguments. Reared by his grandmother, who instilled old fashioned views, Dad believed women should go out with men, not alone or with other women. Mum went out, in spite of Dad's protests, with our neighbour Kathy. Sunday afternoon tempers rose. Mum shouted, "I've had enough ! I am leaving you and taking Margaret with me !" She stomped off. The bedroom door slam shook the house timbers.

Mum's leaving ! I ran straight out through the fields to the 12th century church in the center of town. I brooded for some two miles. *What shall I do if they split? What do I do without Margaret?* I knelt in a back pew and prayed, "Dear God, do not let Mum leave." When I returned that evening my parents had moved into separate bedrooms and Margaret and I shared one room. Although God answered my prayer for less fighting, the result was a physical and mental separation.

In January 1964, when I was close to eighteen, Mum announced, "I've had enough. I found someone else. I'm moving and getting a divorce." Wide-eyed, my chest squeezed as if in an asthma attack. She continued, "And Margaret is coming with me." *Leaving Dad? Leaving me?* I never thought they would divorce. Never. Margaret and I just thought they'd stay together unhappy forever. I went to the kitchen, had a cup of tea and stared at the stove.

Initially I thought the worst of it was losing my companion, Margaret. Throughout the yelling and arguing we stood strong, united. *What now, God?* I could not even cry I was so devastated. I never gave a thought to how Dad might react.

Shortly after Mum's declaration I came home to a letter on the mantelpiece addressed to my father. Suddenly, every bone ached as I carefully opened the envelope. I had to read it; I sensed massive dread. It said all of what she'd told me a few days before, save how it hit me: *what was Dad going to think, do?*

What should I do? I ran out to the fields—to my friend nature—for comfort and to hide from my father. I kept my distance pacing, standing, watching for him, not knowing how or what to think. I was numb. A fear drenched my body that I'd never known as I spotted Dad walk from the coal mine into the house. I waited longer still, knowing he was reading the letter. I could not imagine what was to happen. Here was a gentle man and homebody. *What would Dad do?* I finally dragged myself into the house and acted as if I knew nothing. His face was white and bleached with grief. He questioned me. I lied. I denied knowing anything about Mum's leaving.

He then went into his room and read the Bible.

I made supper.

Every day rolled by the same. Dad walked around the house not talking or doing anything except working, barely eating and retiring to his room. I heard him late at night quoting the Bible aloud, "THOU SHALT NOT COMMIT ADULTERY ! THOU SHALT NOT COMMIT ADULTERY !"

It was a sad and scary time. Without many friends he kept all of it inside. He grumbled at me occasionally but that was it.

I did my best. I went to work every day and took over all the house responsibilities: shopping, cooking, cleaning, laundry, all of it. I escaped to see my sister and Mum twice a week when I could manage it secretly. Father questioned me regularly. He suspected I was seeing Mum and Margaret. Those times his anger showed, "You better not see your mother or I'll kill you !" My heart thundered in my ears, it was so frightening. Deep down I knew he didn't mean it. He was at his wit's end. She had taken his life away from him. She'd taken his baby girl and my best friend. Although I never spoke of my confidential visits, he knew I was making sure Margaret was all right. He stayed stuck and furious with my mother for ruining his existence.

Life was awful for a young lad. I worked hard, had money of my own and yet was mentally bound to my father. Making sure he was cared for and did no harm even to himself were my daily worries.

Then one day, as quick as Mum left, Dad went out one evening. He turned the corner that night. He went out again. He slowly molded a new way of life. He joined the working man's club and spent many nights there. He increased visiting other members of our family. I certainly felt isolated at this point with my father gone most evenings and I still left to tend the house. I held responsibilities my friends did not have nor understand. Loneliness set in and my life seemed racked with pain.

Then one day I met a young lady and love struck. I was entirely in awe of Pamela. We became inseparable, spending every moment of our time off together. I changed like my father. I mentally left Dad and the homestead behind. I burst out of my shell one special weekend as we set to London with a few of our friends. In the 60's, trekking to London for small town Northeasterners was a breathtaking prospect. Adventure was ours ! We surged with excitement—young, free and in love.

How could I not fall in love with London as well: those lights, the different foods, plays, music, real fun? Upon my return, I approached a friend with the idea of moving to London. We agreed and my life changed. I quit my bookkeeping job. The excitement of living in London even made my good-bye to Pamela easy. I had living to do. London would change me into a man. I knew it.

I told my mother. Her response? "Don't do this, David, it's stupid. You'll never survive there on your own." I guess I expected as much. The look in Margaret's eyes was so sad. She would miss me and I her. I vowed to always keep her close to me somehow. Then I finally broke it to my father who did not speak to me for the rest of the week I was home. He did take me to the bus depot out of town but without a word. I knew he was terribly upset that we had all left him. I could not stay. He was honestly not a part of my life. He was just there, struggling with his own, never interacting with me. I was compelled to really live. In August 1964, on bus route to London, I held just a small bag of clothes on my lap and three pounds in my pocket.

London !

I set out job interviewing and found myself sitting across the agent's desk in my Sunday best answering questions. She sighed and said, "You are intelligent and nice looking, but you've a strange accent which will not help you here." My eyebrows shot up and my cheeks flushed as if she'd smacked me. This was my first encounter of overt discrimination. What she had referred to was my rural background and the *Geordie* dialect. Geordie is not as formal as the Queen's English. It is a Northeastern English regional slang, like the various accents in different areas of the United States. I walked away confounded, stunned that ones accent, ones speech was something judged by others. I felt quite inferior. I realized I had an awful lot to learn.

Ah, youth is such a gift, for I was not discouraged; a bit shocked, yet not deterred from my adventure. As the Almighty would have it, I call it synchronicity, in a few days I found a position with Harvey's Bristol Cream as accounts person. What a wonderful opportunity at ten pounds a week.

My friend, Alan, and I rented part of a house for only five pounds a week each: 77 Mornington Crescent in Houslow. Right down from the Heathrow Airport runway, I reveled in the excitement. I ate out rather cheaply in those days, had a great friend and apartment. Life was fresh and filled with promise.

London was a place of action. I met loads of new people and partied all the time. We were young, single and had no worries. Moving on from Hounslow, Alan and I shared what I thought was a mansion of a home in prestigious, brick laden Cadogen Square. Renting with four other acquaintances we cohabited four large bedrooms, two huge living rooms, terraces, the works, for thirty pounds a week. What London luxury it was, complete with an ivy laced park square across my bedroom window. We walked everywhere drinking-in Chelsey to the door step of Harrod's. It was heady living amid famed places I'd only read about as a young boy from rural England.

I caught a glimpse, the bare beginning of a new me— one of healing. I seemed to draw people close. I counseled, listened to their hardships and always seemed to make them feel better. I was getting to know myself without the worrisome cares of my split-up family. I had the freedom and energy to discover myself. For the first time I truly felt alive with the life I was to lead. My parents' home had been a good one for me, perfect in all of its past security and learnings. I kept connected with them, especially with my sister, but also kept distance from my folks.

Time passed. Alan and I had limited means compared to some of our housemates and could not afford the running up of long distance phone bills and the like in the Cadogen Square mansion. We found a two bedroom flat near Hyde Park for twelve pounds between us. I don't think we ever used the kitchenette; we were in the out-and-about swing of city living. Alan and I regularly experienced spiritual encounters, as I discovered that I had a sixth sense. I had an uncanny ability to sense things others did not. Alan was also intuitive and bore witness, along with me, to things going bump in the night, doors closing and such. We were quite the lads.

Then Frank came into my life. Frank was a true teacher and helped me learn the catering business. During my free time, he taught me the chef's realm at the Rolls Royce Catering Business and Restaurant in North London. I made sandwiches for a breakfast cart which I rolled through a local factory every morning at 5 a.m. for extra cash. I dressed up in a little catering hat and felt ridiculous. Yet I was okay with it all because I was getting ahead, making extra money. The catering trade taught and prepared me to negotiate with any kind of person. As you know from my Baghdad chapter, having been trained in service to others served me in fine stead.

Working and pleasure rolled along until Alan decided to leave London for a job opportunity in New Zealand. It was the first time I was completely alone. I realized I needed a better paying post. With wonderful recommendations in hand, I went to work for Electrolux as personal assistant to the manager. I had an office and secretary with sales compilation and statistical analysis responsibility. I moved near Oxford Street and stayed for two years until they closed their Oxford locale to consolidate with the Electrolux Headquarters in Luton. As I did not want to move out of London, I decided to get another new job near Kilburn down the road from Buckingham Palace.

I was hired by the Society of Motor Manufacturers only a bus ride away from my flat. Attention to details became my forte in directing the publication of the Blue Book of all Britain's Motor Franchises. Another one of my jobs was to organize the London Motor Show where I worked the Society's booth explaining their services. Additionally, I was on a team which set up the pre-opening dinner of the London Show at the Grosvenor House Hotel, Park Lane. This event was attended by some 2,000. At pre-opening night the organizational team's reward was free dinner at the Grosvenor House. It was a multicourse, no holds barred, five star night. I soon developed a love for fine dining in exquisite settings.

I was finally coming of age. To my surprise I continued developing a knack for healing as I sharpened my sixth sense awareness. My accurate psychic ability (see chapter eight) moved me to join a clairvoyance group at the College of Psychic Studies. I wanted to gain insight, understanding and perhaps hone more skills. There I met a truly gifted teacher, Don Galloway, who taught the Monday night classes. After each session along with highly skilled medium students I took the bus home to Kilburn. I distinctly felt a spirit attach itself to me as I got off the bus. It followed me right into my flat ! As I lay in bed the spirit moved about my room finally settling down next to me and snored. *Well, Lord, you'll have to help me here. No matter what I do the spirit is still with me here in my room.* There wasn't a thing to do so I gave it up to the Divine.

One particularly vivid Monday night my eyes bolted open to a rustling in my bed. A huge muscular, rather hairy arm appeared and wrapped around me. *OOOOh, what is going on here? I don't remember anything extraordinary in class this evening !* I swallowed hard and looked slowly from side to side and strained to see the rest of 'who' was holding me—but...

no one

was

there...

just the big, strong arm holding me.

My heart raced wildly.

Then the arm vanished.

Suddenly, a calming blanketed my entire body and I sensed that the arm of Spirit had been sent to protect me. Comforted I fell fast asleep.

Upon awaking I looked back at the midnight vision and realized God was with me and had shown me His arm of protection. He'd sent a Spirit Guide in a form with which I could relate. This made me smile. With ever more inquisitiveness I would seek to understand Spirit. It is a lifelong learning process.

While in the society job I took a short bus route to work down Park Lane to Victoria between 8-9 a.m. weekdays. I usually brought a book with me to pass the time. I kept reading in spite of the hustle and bustle of traffic jams. (I was reading *The Agony and the Ecstasy, The Life of Michael Angelo* and Harold Robbins' works then.)

A loud voice above the rush hour clamor spoke, startling me out of my reading: "David, you will be working there in two weeks." I jumped, swirled around and looked about for the person who spoke. I peered out the window since the bus was stationary in front of 55 Park Lane. Strange. Something happened within a day of this voice: I came across an advertisement for a part-time job in that same rush hour area. When I got to the premises I realized the address was the very one the loud male voice told me about. It was all very odd and I simply brushed it off.

Besides the society's office work, I worked as waiter or host, chef, and bar keep. From 1964 through 1973, the catering or hotel trade was a large part of my life. This afforded the opportunity to meet many, many kinds of people and loads of wonderful friends who guided me along the way. My spirituality grew by bits and pieces.

June 11,1968, London, England   Journal Entry

On my 20th birthday, I received a clairvoyant reading by mentor teacher Don Galloway, one of the College of Psychic Studies' most accomplished mediums. During the reading, Don informed me,

"Healing is your destiny." At 20 years of age, I had no knowledge of this thing called, 'healing'.

I dismissed the reading when, in fact, nothing happens...

Powerfully loyal friends came into my life. We often slept at each other's flats which were mostly in wings of wonderful, vintage London homes. One night I stayed at a friend's and awoke with two spirits' hands around my throat trying to strangle me. I screamed out, "Lord, take these hands off me !" They were removed from my throat. Again I felt calming afterward and fell into a fitful sleep. *Was this what was meant by "Ask and ye shall receive?"*

I then had a dream so spectacular that it felt like an out-of-body experience. By this time in my life I was working diligently at awakening my sixth sense abilities. With Don Galloway's help and education, I was accustomed to spirits present. I was not afraid as much as fascinated.

1970, London   Journal Entry

I awoke within my dream in the backseat of a car driven by two people. (I discovered later they were my guardian angels at the time who took me on a journey across the desert for the purpose of this remarkable experience.) As we drove, in the distance on the left hand side of the road was a figure clad in Arabic dress with long hair and beard. We approached the figure and I looked out of the car window. I could not believe who I saw. I shouted, **"That's Jesus Christ !"** As we drove past I turned to look out the back window to see Him again. Shockingly, the entire back window had become His face: light, bright and shining a smile at me. When I woke, the following three days I could not walk properly, I felt light as a feather. Looking back, I now understand the power of the Spirit's Energy. At the time, I could not figure out what had happened to my walking. To this day that glowing, joyful, smiling face is still embedded in my third eye. I feel His companionship. His kindness and love warms me as I see His face every day whenever I turn my attentions inward for reflection.

One Christmas a group of a dozen friends and I drove down to the Southeastern coast of Britain, Clacton, a favourite vacation area. We pulled into the drive of a friend's home for a Christmas party and overnight. As the host showed us to our rooms we climbed to an unlit floor landing. "Sorry," the host apologized. "That light has never worked since I bought the place." We didn't think much of it, although as I opened the room in the darkened hall I felt an atmosphere of electricity. I didn't say anything, but I knew I felt SOMEthing as I entered and set my suitcase down. Deep into the night, I awoke to knocking at my bedroom door. "Yes, who's there?" The door opened with a loud, slow creeeeeeeek. No one entered. Suddenly all four walls were banged—bam, bam, bam, bam ! The door closed. I'd been getting rather used to Spirit and shrugged it off as a simple ghostly visitation and fell fast asleep.

The next morning I mentioned this to our host. "Yes, no one ever wants to sleep a second night in that room." I nodded with understanding.

During that Christmas respite I did a little thing I'd been known to do with my friends, playing about with my psychic senses in impromptu psychic readings. I sat with one of the guests, an artistic film director, Peter Howard, known for the "Carry-On" movies. During our meditative sitting I saw a vision: numerous people clad in period costume around a grand old estate. "I don't know what is coming up in your future or if this is from your past, but I see a very lavish scene of the Elizabethan era." Peter said it was all very interesting and we parted, Peter deep in thought.

A few weeks after the intriguing Christmas vacation Mr. Howard rang me. "Cunningham, you are a witch !"

"Yeah, yeah," I said, not liking the inference.

He continued, "You remember what you told me over Christmas?" I acknowledged I did. "Well, I have just signed a contract to do a script entitled "Anne of a Thousand Days !" I was delighted for Peter and that my clairvoyance was lucid and correct.

That spring while planning another trip to Clacton mansion I discovered by reading and chatting about the mansion that Lady Hamilton was the previous owner. Lady Hamilton was the mistress of a Lord Nelson a renowned British royal. With an historical perspective in mind, three of us journeyed back to the grand house. After our arrival we perched on the balcony taking in the ocean's mist. Salty breezes sprayed us lightly with the sea. As we pondered life a cloud moved directly and intentionally toward us. We sat dumbfounded as it wafted straight through us and past the open French doors of the dining room. We followed the mist cloud to witness the materialization of Lord Nelson and Lady Hamilton ! They had a little romantic liaison right in front of us and next to the very dining table they'd used in their earlier lifetime. (We'd read in the brochure of the place that it was Lady Hamilton's original possession.) In wonder we gazed as the two intimately spoke to one another. We could not hear what they were saying but it was obvious they were most pleased to be together. Suddenly, Lady Hamilton glanced right into my eyes causing a fright that moved me to run right out of the room !

Within minutes, stranger things happened still that day. The cream enameled, hand painted grand piano in the parlour had been transformed by the new owners into a cocktail cabinet which housed a record player. While we played music the record either stopped, the needle scratched over the record surface or the turntable speeded-up and slowed-down at will. Once three episodes happened one right after the other we wondered if we'd somehow upset the spirits.

Bedtime arrived. While in our rooms set to sleep there came a crashing of glass, doors slamming and things breaking. The following morning we realized the Lady and her Lord had actually broken some of the house hotel's prized lamps. *How was I going to explain that spirits had damaged the owner's property?*. To our surprise, the host shrugged off the breakage saying, "It happens often." Strange.

1972 - Brighton, England
One of My 1st Healing Stories

I visited a friend, Jean Brown. At her house I was greeted by a neighbour and told that Jean was unwell and awaiting a doctor. I stayed with Jean until the doctor arrived.

As I sat with her, a voice above my head said, "Place your hands upon her pain, David." Realizing Jean was in a great deal of stomach pain, I said, "Look, I know this may sound crazy, but may I place my hands on your pain?" Jean agreed and I placed my hands directly on the area in question. Within minutes her stomach pain had completely disappeared.

Jean and I were astonished.

Thus, my healing ministry began in a dynamic manner.

In 1973 I moved to Hastings to the beloved Southeast Coast of England and stayed with a friend until settled. I needed a change and loved the coast. In search of better wages I proceeded through the classifieds and spotted an ad for a housemaster at a private school. The Great Sanders School served fifty boys, ages 8-16 years, who had numerous maladjustments. Donald, my friend, said that most of the boys were abused either emotionally or physically. Great Sanders was known for its high success with such cases. Donald said, "David, that job is for you. You're great getting along with people and listening to their troubles. You would do those boys well."

"No, no," I said without really thinking.

His words rang in my ears all night, so the next day I phoned for an interview. I received a second interview with Great Sanders Schools' two joint headmasters, John French and Hugh Fletcher, near Battle Abbey in East Sussex, Sedlescombe. Out of thirty applicants I ended up being offered the position. Within the contract I had free room and board, a wonderful asset. The more I thought about it I felt I might be of help to the boys. All this went along with my healings to help others.

The Easter of 1973 I moved into the old brick dormitory. As I sat on the bed, it collapsed. *Lord, why am I here? What was I thinking taking this job?* It was far from London, far from much of what I had enjoyed for so long.

I did not have much time to ponder my decision as the joint principals of Great Sanders set me to duty. Generally, I was to ensure the boys were up, showered, dressed, breakfasted, and in the classrooms for their daily lessons. The first morning I was asked to get them in line for classes; it was test number one from the boys. They would not form a line. They stood steady in their shoes as if glued to the flooring. *How was I going to handle them day after day?* Shouting would not go, I knew. Most of them had that back home, if they had homes.

The first night I strained over coming up with a plan. It turned out to be a bit of intuitive psychology. The second day I reported for work with a clipboard and a stop watch. I looked at my watch, scribbled on my clipboard, looked at each of the boys and scribbled again. Without a word they formed a fine line. My calculated, reserved nature served well.

The world of spirit voices was not very active for me in those days. Perhaps I had more than enough tending the boys. One particular night, however, I did have a sixth sense event. My bedroom was directly above headmaster Fletcher's Mum's quarters. After lights out I awoke exactly at 2 a.m. per my alarm clock. I saw Hugh's mother come up through my bed and suspend above me. She said, "David, please tell Hugh that I am all right. There is nothing to worry about."

"Oh, okay," I said simply. She vanished. I sensed she was on her way to the world of the Spirit and I fell back asleep. Remember, I was used to that sort of thing by this time. At breakfast many of the boys were distressed, some cried. Hugh said, "David, I have something to tell you."

"Oh, Hugh, I know. Your mother died at 2 a.m." Hugh glared at me in disbelief. I continued, "She came to me to tell you not to worry. She is just fine." Everyone in the room sat very still looking puzzled.

I must have been doing something right in the staff's eyes. Within the first week of my employ I was left alone to put the fifty boys to bed, while the masters and teachers went out on the town. I managed the younger ones to bed right on time, 7 p.m. The older chaps had a routine of television after their homework hour with bedtime at 9 p.m. Come around 9 o'clock I called, "Time to settle down in your rooms." No one moved a centimeter. "Fellows, this is my first week and I don't want to get in trouble right away. You're listening to me during the day, why not now?"

"We want to watch the end of this program."

"Okay, just thirty minutes more." I went back to the office by the TV room.

9:30 p.m. "All right now, lights out and into your beds," I said firmly.

"We want more time."

"No, come on boys, it's time."

They sat with not a budge among them.

No way are they getting the better of me. I unplugged the television and rolled it into the office and locked the door. That created friction but bedtime was finally enforced.

I worked as a housemaster for two years from 1973 through 1975 and honestly reaped wonderful relationships. The boys gradually learned I meant what I said and that I was not a tyrant, but simply doing my job. In the process I realized my own capabilities. The boys tested their new housemaster in myriad ways and forced me to figure out how to behave and gain respect and control over each situation. I grew to trust myself and my instincts.

One of the older boys, a fifteen year old bully named Len, set out to prove he was in charge. I walked down a corridor where he pounced and threw me to the floor. Instinctively, I placed my fingers in his ribs and tickled him. On and on I tickled. Within a few minutes he was laughing and rolling over the floor. The atmosphere of aggression changed. From that day on we were the best of friends. He became my young assistant in many activities over the two years.

During a camping trip not twenty minutes had gone by upon our campsite arrival and one of the younger boys fell out of a tree breaking his arm. I was grateful for my relationship with Len, for I'd no choice but to leave him in charge of the two dozen campers. "Len, I have to get Stephen's arm fixed at the nearby hospital. You are the senior man and in charge while we're gone." Len's grin said it all. I knew he'd be up for the challenge.

Four hours of driving, ex-rays, consults, and casting the arm kept us away until well past dark. Frantic, I screeched the car to a halt and carried Stephen inside the cabin. Comfort blanketed my very core when I saw that Len had organized all the gear, fed everyone, cleaned up, and had them in their sleep togs ! *Praises to relationship building, Divine One.* The rest of the week was uneventful, meaning no more accidents. I learned as much as the boys did about hiking, the different flowers and fauna and nature at a whole new level. I'd never been on a trip like those school campouts.

A second significant healing with my hands was on Len. While he was jumping on the school trampoline he fell, dislocating his knee. Instinctively, I settled him down, placed one hand on top of his kneecap and the other under his knee and gently straightened his leg. The pain was gone. Amazed and grateful to have helped him, I slept satisfied with my job that night. *Could I heal many others on purpose and at will?*

Over time I read every student's file, especially if I'd had a negative incident during the day. Reviewing history helped me to understand why a boy did what he did. Even though my childhood was far from perfect, I never witnessed such horrific family conditions.

One Sunday a youngster was due for a visit from his mum. I barely got him dressed and through breakfast; he had ants in his pants with excitement and anticipation. He stood by the front wall promptly at 9 a.m. in great expectation, waiting patiently. Tragically, at 9 p.m. that evening the lad was still by that wall waiting. His mum failed to show. My heart tore in two. Darkness fell and I finally peeled him away, put his nightshirt on and rocked him to sleep. It took me days calming him down, getting him to accept small comforts. Inside he tortured himself. Incidents tore at my heart-strings throughout those two years; I realized how grateful I was for my own life.

The school was close to the coast where we planned a swimming outing for eight of the boys as a reward for good behaviour. Always trying to get my goat, the array of culturally mixed students surrounded me on the beach and shouted, "Daddy, daddy buy us ice cream !" I got attention from them all right. This greatly interested the standers-by who stared at Mr. C., a young blond with eight multicoloured offspring.

Later that day there was more. Nigel was eight years of age, only four feet tall and frail. He drew in the sand with a stick. *At least one of them was safe and busy.* All of a sudden, Nigel jumped up, dropped his pants and attacked the sand sexually. "My God," I shouted and ran to him. Stunned, I realized the sand castle was shaped like a woman. I cradled him in my arms, covering his slight, bare body. How those boys had lived. Nigel's file revealed not only a sexually abusive birth father, whom his mother divorced, but the same from the stepfather. The poor little mite had no idea what was true, real love.

The Great Sanders housemaster position taught me about life and appreciation of my background. It wore on me though. I relished my day off every Sunday. It never failed, however, that I was detained from my getaways by a little one. Anthony came from the west country of England and was also a mightily abused soul. He frequently sought me out for long talks. Just as I drove off to Sunday time out, little Anthony would turn up missing. The headmasters insisted I find him before my free time.

Anthony always ran away to his favourite hiding place in the middle of a field nearby. The routine never changed for the year since Anthony joined Great Sanders. He'd stand right in the field waiting for me to find him. I'd call out, "Come Anthony, come back in the car." He'd hear me and scurry off. We'd play cat and mouse for hours ! He obviously did not want me to leave the premises for any length of time. Just as he counted on me I could count on him to make me half a day late for my personal plans.

A housemaster had more time and responsibility than even the teachers. I played mother and father to those with no family reliable enough. I learned the biggest lesson of unconditional caring and non-judgementalism by master teacher Paul. Young Paul was a rounded lad of twelve. We got along famously unless it was a full moon. On the night of our first full moon together, Paul was one minute as pleasant and jovial as he could be and the next, he brandished a 12" butcher's blade ! Paul transformed into a foul mouthed aggressor bringing the kitchen knife within inches of my heaving, fear-stricken chest. I instinctively folded my arms across my chest for protection and spoke quietly, gently, while some of the boys got behind Paul and me. The witnesses understood that this was not their everyday Paul. They pulled the knife from his hands and we helped him through the full moon night. The next morn Paul placed his arms around me in his normally huggable manner, "Good morning, Sir," he said as his usual.

I replied, "Good morning, Paul, are you all right?"

"Of course, why?" he asked.

After discussing the event we realized the poor youngster had no recollection of the knife or the attack. He shook his head embarrassed and troubled by his actions. "But I love you, Sir !" Paul's file revealed he had an older brother about my age. Perhaps I reminded Paul of him in some way. It was something about the full moon that brought all the negative experiences with his older brother out to the surface for Paul. I was just a scapegoat. I understood that it was as simple and humane as that. My boys could not help how they acted sometimes and I knew I was helping. It was hard, taxing, good work, but often most unsettling.

Hastings is a coastal town near the boys' school. I drove the older boys into town for some time out, food and the slot machines. I usually dropped them off, setting a meeting time for a couple of hours later. I then hiked to a favourite rock in the middle of splashing waves and the thunderous churn of the sea. I sat for those hours wondering. *What do you want, Lord? What is this all about, this working with the boys? I've learned a lot but their lives wear on my soul.* I was distraught and cried, shouting to the ocean, to the Almighty, "What am I going to do with the rest of my life? I love the boys but something's not right. Help !"

Divine will placed me in London the second summer of my housemaster position. I fell in love with London all over again. I relished being with people my age, old friends, drinking, partying, going about the sights. It was captivating. I phoned in sick and lied to the school secretary. I stayed in London the first full week of September, opening week for Great Saunders. I was brimming with uncertainty about another year of solitude among disturbed children. Being in glorious London, away from the boys' hardships, accentuated the stress of my work.

Finally I returned, having missed their first whole week of the new school year. The drive back depressed me— until I saw the boys. They came out of nowhere jumping on me, surrounding me with hugs, pats on the back, and smiles galore. "Where were you? Why weren't you with us?"

With a lump in my throat I mumbled, "I've been sick," and quickly dismissed myself, escaping to my room. In the solace of my quarters I cried my heart out. The weight of guilt completely covered me. It hit me how I had let down the boys when they relied on me and cared so very much.

I had to admit I cared, too.

The 1975-76 school year had begun. Thanks to the affections shown by my welcoming committee I felt more self assurance in my work than the previous first trial-by-fire year. We took the boys to town weekly as we'd done in the year past. I sat on the rocks of the shore, contemplative but happy with myself in many ways. The sea and its reassuring movement surrounded me with peace. I knew I was doing a good job and my relationships with the boys proved that day by day.

Change was brewing. In Sedlescombe, where The Great Sanders School called home, I met a new friend. Charles had retired from the chairmanship of a large corporation and owned an antique shoppe in town. We met on one of the boys' outings as I browsed around waiting for them. I loved talking with Charles and fingering the fine antiques in his shoppe. He said, "What do you fancy yourself doing one day, David?"

"I always pictured myself in the catering business," I said. "I've managed many food service experiences in London. It's fun, exciting, challenging, great foods, although a lot of toil."

"Did you know there is an old restaurant for sale here in the village?" Charles asked.

Food for thought. "Really?"

"Would you like to go have a look?" Charles asked. A connoisseur of vintage items it sounded as if he'd already considered the building a find.

"Hmmm, I'd love to see it !" I chimed.

We obtained the key from the agent and met for a tour. The structure was built in the 14th century near Battle Abbey, a famous scene of The Battle of Hastings in 1066. The Abbey had been home for centuries to a Catholic order of monks. The Tithe Barn, the name of a later restaurant, was indeed a barn where the monks stored grain. As tithe or taxes grain was paid to the Abbey to support the monks' services and town expenses.

The building was cobweb heaven and shabby as we stepped through leftover rumble and decayed floor planks. It had served residents and tourists as a tea shoppe then an Italian restaurant after World War II. The place had always been boarded up since I arrived in town for the school position, some two years now.

Well.

The Tithe Barn's history and the feeling of lives past surged those walls and flowed into my veins. I was hooked as the spirit of the Barn enveloped me. Mesmerized, I explored room to dusty room. *It just needs loving care.* I envisioned future oiled oak beams, gentle, warm fires in the cozy brick fireplaces, and shiny polished tables welcoming diners from around the globe. There was even a garden at the rear. My heart raced. *This was my new home.* I just knew it.

"Wonderful, " I gasped. "Charles, how might we work this out?"

"Well, David, I want to take a chance on you. I shall obtain the building if you'll manage the restaurant. We'll split everything between us after that," Charles said. His grin was broad and sincere. My mind ran. *Be my own boss? What an opportunity !* I hadn't said anything to Charles; just nodded my head affirmatively trying to look mature, serious and business like. *Yes ! Yes !* My mind shouted.

"Yes," I boldly said aloud. We shook on it.

Christmas was just a couple of weeks away when I convened with the headmasters. "I have learned and grown here at Great Saunders. I love the boys and I think I've done them well. However, I have an offer that I cannot pass up. I have always wanted to be my own boss and this restaurant is my chance."

"We hate to see you go. We understand. Living here, working with the boys morning, noon and night, is good, but difficult," Hugh Fletcher said. John reiterated, nodding, "The boys will sorely miss you."

I didn't move very far, just a few kilometers from the school, right before the holiday. I felt so guilty about leaving the boys, I simply slipped away. I could not say good-bye. The boys stopped in now and again as the Tithe Barn was right in their village. It was awkward at first but they grew to understand and seemed to love the restaurant.

Charles gave me a spare room in his house while we worked readying the Tithe Barn. It took six months with most of the kitchen facilities old and tatty and needing replacing. Modern health codes warranted major overhaul of equipment. We added new French windows, a few partitions and a pantry/utility room. We took great pains to preserve every bit of antique wood, re-staining, oiling, and polishing to refurbish the valuable ambiance inherent in the building.

Bone tired work it was, but every night that I washed and plopped down on my bed I felt lucky. It was as if every single thing in my life pointed me toward Sussex and managing the restaurant. All of my relationships and understanding human character would suit me well in pleasing the clientele and paving the way for success.

My spirit life was changing as well. One night I stayed up late after the carpet was installed, tidying things. I loved the 600 year old place and enjoyed being alone in it. By then I lived there, literally. After remodeling the plumbing and upstairs mezzanine, I made one of the extra rooms a bedroom and moved out of Charles' house. It was best. We felt more secure with someone living on the premises in light of the expensive investments. It gave me privacy which I relished after living at the school. As I swept I suddenly felt a thick, weighty presence moving around me, then it went away. *What's up, God?* Wondering, I bathed and flopped into bed exhausted. I was aroused by a great heaviness across my legs and feet. I awoke unable to move. There was a huge, fat monk sitting on me ! With a cowl across his face I could not make out his features. I did feel the piercing of his eyes staring...

He stared right into my soul.

There was a monk on my feet.

What to do?

Innocently, I said, "Hello." I struggled to sit up and gain composure. "How can I help you? What do you want?" I asked.

Silence.

He peered straight at me as heavy as a mountain on my lower extremities.

Poof, he vanished.

Just like that.

Honestly.

That was the beginning of the haunting of the Tithe Barn.

My room backed up to the mezzanine where the oaken bar was located. Many a night I heard tinkling of glasses, bottles and rumblings when there was no one there save me, myself and I. On the first few occasions I jumped up ready to secure our investment from burglars. No one there. After numerous nights of interrupted sleep I stopped getting out of bed. He appeared a friendly monk so I learned to sleep and live with my new Spirit friend. He only helped himself to a dram or two.

Final planning and touches relieved my physical weariness. It was time for work in mental fun and games: what menus to choose, what crockery and cutlery to purchase, to give the feel of our old-yet-new establishment of fine cuisine? Days were consumed with interviewing, hiring and extra training. I certainly was not a master chef—not yet anyway. Teachers were obtained from a local catering college to give me crash courses in management and flambé. I knew I had to do a top notch job. From exquisite food to the atmosphere, it all had to be relaxing, inviting, efficient, and fun right from the start. Building a fine cuisine reputation was paramount.

Grand Opening night arrived following an inviting advert in the local press. We were jam packed ! The press even came with photographers. An article in the paper summed it up well, "The new Tithe Barn has relaxing, beautiful surroundings which create a warm, old-fashioned atmosphere...". With thirty-two seats completely filled, customers waited, filling the mezzanine top level and enjoying high-profit drinks at our fine antique bar. If I had had a moment to stand and take it all in, as a client I would have thought that it was most enchanting. But it was so very busy, I only sensed the joy of it. That night certainly set the next few years of my life on fire.

** see actual article from SUSSEX EXPRESS & COUNTY HERALD in Appendix

Mr. Spirit was a bright monk and quite a trickster. After just a short time he knew the names of all the new staff. They'd tell of little incidents when their names were called as they set the tables or stocked the utility. It seemed to always be a voice up on the mezzanine calling down. The stories came to me separately and thus a 'monk pattern' formed. Upon every thorough search no one was ever found up there. Mr. Monk kept us on our toes.

My cheeky friendly monk ghost had loads of fun. One evening in particular I recall locking the door for the night after what I thought was the last customer and tidying up with the night crew. We often sat for coffee or brandy together as we were very close knit and enjoyed each other's company. Sitting at a dining table I noticed a man walking back and forth jostling the bathroom doorknob. "May I be of assistance, sir?"

"I'm just trying to use the toilet and then I'll be on my way."

"Certainly, sir, but we're the only ones left in the building. The loo is free."

"I have tried. It is bolted tight as a drum," he stated, frustrated.

I dashed to the door pulling and pushing. It was solid locked. I knew on the other side of the door was an old fashioned bolt at least twelve inches long. It would have taken someone a heck of a long time to jimmy open, if one could. Furthermore, there were no windows into the bathroom. No one could leave the loo with the bolt still in place. "Well, sir, it looks like a practical joke. I'm sorry." Knowing full well as I showed him to the staff restroom it surely was our friendly monk. The next day I called for help to unhinge the door. No one was inside. Through the days Mr. Monk was a comfort to me causing familiar little noises that made the Tithe Barn home. Because I loved the Tithe Barn, I enjoyed the monk living with me in that grand vintaged place.

Grateful was too small a word to say in my prayers. The decisions Charles and I made paid off right from the beginning. An example was the apprenticeship program we'd arranged with the Hastings Catering College. Ever since opening night we had on loan, young, vital, energetic, and highly professional graduates from the college's two-year catering and chef's certification program. They presented their best professional feet forward with silver linen service amid the relaxed, antiqued atmosphere of dear, old Tithe Barn.

I practically flew through the next weeks and months on an adrenaline high. Tired? Yes, energized, good, hard working tired. It all paid off handsomely when we obtained an Elon Ronay # 1 which is the highest, most prestigious class in England's restaurant classification system. This excellent rating was the tops and an enormous feat for a new restaurant. My joy and energies seemed boundless as we realized customers came from far and wide to dine with us. The Tithe Barn was an event, an outing. The entire Tithe Barn family felt elated. Wonderful comments referring to our chef's creations, food, presentation, and ambiance as five-star abounded; all crafted from a bunch of wooden rooms and a large Spirit.

Time changed the boys from the school as they grew into young men. I shared food with them when they came and knocked on the restaurant windows. We'd chat and I realized that they were fine without me and liked the new housemaster just as well. I took pride in their maturing.

Challenging work continued. To not miss a single customer we opened seven days weekly deciding to serve luncheons, afternoon teas and evening meals. Sunday night and all day Monday our growing in infamy chef Peter had time off. I pitched in with newly acquired flambé skills developing a short, modest, ever changing menu for Sunday and Monday suppers. I kept the place open and had great fun cooking at the tables. It was a chance for me to show off my theatrical antics. I'd have carts of food set to prepare four or five special entrees. People did not mind the wait as they watched other foods being prepared right before them. I kept my arms flying and the flames high—a bit of dinner theatre.

The first Christmas we decorated the entire restaurant in the local foliage from the town woods. We sprayed some with gold and silver making a unique, inexpensive winter wonderland. Christmas Day the customers packed the Barn. We gave out hats, party popper streamers and rallied to the wee hours together.

Two years into the restaurant I flew to New York for a birthday holiday, in June of 1977. Damian, an associate I knew from long ago, met me. As a treat I stayed near the hub of NYC action, The Plaza and Central Park.

Just as I stepped off the plane and placed both feet on American soil a voice said loud and clear, "Welcome home, David !" I was reminded of the same, clear voice on the bus at Park Lane, London. As way back when, I jumped, turning around to see who was talking to me. No one was there. *Well, that's strange, "Welcome Home, David !" when I'd just arrived in America for the very first time.* The voice rang in my mind as Damian and I caught a taxi. *Home?*

Seeing "The Big Apple" caused my heart to jump with joy. There was no time for worrying about some voice. As I entered the city traffic New York engulfed my senses. The skyscrapers and every last sight thrilled and comforted me. I could not wait to see it all, every square block. I wanted to experience all of the great New York.

The voice repeated itself. *Welcome home. Welcome home.*

Maybe it was just that I loved big cities. I knew that from my London days. Intrigued about the voice in my head, I decided I would have a clairvoyant reading back in England to see what Spirit had to say. I arranged it on my return flight home.

With the voice, the comfort level and the fun, I fell in love again with this new, most gigantic of cities and city life. Only all of this was in the long dreamed of America. The lights, the excitement, the culture, the people were totally different from the small town environment I'd been living in during the past four years as housemaster and Tithe Barn manager. The NYC lure caused me to ask Damian if it was easy to live and work in Manhattan. "Can a person get a job here in short order?"

He replied, "Why don't you give it a try? Of course, you'll have to get a green card, working visa and such, but it's worth it and I know an attorney."

Again the guilt over my old world and the dream of fresh prospects heavily weighed on my heart as I flew back to England. *What should I do?* I questioned and prayed. *What of that voice telling me I was home in America?*

I saw the London psychic after I landed. The medium stated emphatically that I had been an American fighter pilot in World War II, shot down in the war over Germany. Since I was born in June of 1946, in this life, it became obvious that my time between reincarnated lives was very short. And there I'd just been, back in America, only thirty years since the war. I recalled how comfortable I had felt from the absolute first day of my arrival in the US. According to the reading, I realized I was visiting a past home.

Interesting.

It seemed like a signal; I knew it all meant something. *What?*

I returned to the Tithe Barn and came clean with Charles. While having a spot of tea I explained, "You know I am grateful beyond measure with all you have done for me. I achieved far more than I'd dreamed. I am ready to tackle a larger restaurant or hotel situation. I've fallen in love with New York and want to give a go of it there."

Charles was upset. He was rather furious. "What of all of our plans together, our hard earned future plans?" he cried. He understood, I was still young and he was retired and wanted to stay put. He reluctantly agreed.

Changing things after only the second year in operation truly shook up the Tithe Barn family. Fortunately, I'd been training the head waiter to ease my schedule. "Robert, our head waiter is certainly up to the task of managing the restaurant," I told Charles. I also agreed to stay on one month until Robert was fully prepared. I desperately wanted to make it right for Charles and help the Tithe Barn's success not miss a beat.

So, just as I had done in 1964, my adventurous soul (similar to my Mum's spirit, come to think of it) grabbed my attention and relocated my body, mind and spirit to the big city.

Chapter Five
My Story ~ 1977 to 1990

"There are no accidents...Those who are to meet
will meet, because together they have the potential
for a holy relationship. They are ready for each other."
A Course in Miracles,
Manual for Teachers, Chapter 3, 1:6-8

New York, 1977. The Divine has always helped me
along my path, this time through Damian, who housed
me until I found a small studio apartment. I became a
sandwich maker near my new, very small, but my very
own New York City flat. The shift was 6 a.m. to 5 p.m.,
but it was catering work and a ground floor start while I
became acquainted with the famous Manhattan.

One evening Damian introduced me to Hugo Rali,
the general manager of Tavern on the Green in Central
Park. I was presented as the founder of a five-star
restaurant in England. In the 1970's, Tavern on the Green
was *the* restaurant in which to eat and be seen. The food
was exquisite; the movie stars and famed clientele
sparkled everywhere I looked. Jackie O., governors,
senators, nobles, and aristocrats were regulars. The
operation was impressive, especially Mr. Rali's 'Hollywood
History' tour of The Tavern. Hugo was to reference Charles
about my Tithe Barn work and thus my Tavern application
would be complete.

In a couple of days Hugo offered me the head waiter
job to start. In due diligence I virtually lived at the Tavern

showing off my knowledge of the business. I studied the staff memorizing their names in one day by learning about their favourite things. This was an endearing trick I'd learned and was a way of connecting me with people instantly. I organized supplies and increased efficiency while saving staff energies, a winning morale booster and team builder technique. To top it off, I personally kept tally of the turnover (the number of parties a table serves in a day). Increases were impressive and I intended to share these figures with Mr. Hugo as soon as appropriate. My maitre d' routine was well underway when the restaurant manager was dismissed, although I did not know this until late in the day after his discharge.

I reported to work the next morning and to my surprise, my superior sent me back home with instructions to wait by the phone. *What had I done wrong? I thought my work was more than adequate and was even liked, from all outward signs.* I paced my studio apartment wondering and praying. It took hours.

Finally, the general manager called. "David, Hugo here. Will you see me right away?"

I suited and readied for a formal I-didn't-know-what. Hugo shook my hand, sat me down in his office and said, "David, we'd like to offer you the job vacated yesterday: restaurant director of Tavern on the Green." My eyes popped wide open. Trickles of perspiration drenched me as my heart skipped.

"I'll take it, thank you, sir. You will not be disappointed, I assure you !"

Only in New York about a month and I was restaurant manager of one of the world's foremost restaurants? Thank you, Divine intervention ! I couldn't sleep for the excitement and opportunity to make my mark in New York. There was a mountain of work in managing 200 plus waiting staff, some twenty chefs, with three main dining areas, and several private rooms. Energy surges guided me through those long shifts from 8 a.m. through closing at 2 a.m. or so, depending on the celebrity of the late night party goers. VIP satisfaction was paramount. Always I presented myself in British upper crust manner and verbiage. This served us all well as business grew steadily with return clientele. My energies ran so high that sleep did not matter.

The Tavern was one of the largest and most famous restaurants in the world with turnover of 1000 served mid-weekdays and 1500 diners on a Saturday. Oftentimes we catered private invitation only affairs, a lucrative, guaranteed income. It was my job to ensure that the people attending each specially catered affair had, indeed, an exclusive invitation. This was The Tavern silver service guarantee and fundamental to our five-star reputation.

During one private reception a tall, distinguished gentleman stood beside me as I received guests taking their invitations. "Sir, how may I be of assistance?" I asked.

"I am here for the party."

"Oh, certainly sir, may I have your invitation?"

"I don't have one," he replied.

"I apologize, sir, but this is by invitation only." Just then Hugo moved me aside and coolly addressed the man, "Good evening, Governor, how may we help you?" I had no idea ! Embarrassed beyond belief I apologized with a bow. The governor laughed graciously. Fancy the new Brit on the job. I immediately studied and memorized the guests as I met them, asking the local staff for details to bolster my memory when needed.

One thrilling event was the opening of *Saturday Night Fever* with John Travolta, celebrating his first major motion picture hit. Tavern on the Green hosted the opening gala. That day after the luncheon shift we closed the restaurant in preparations. The movie's producer, Bob Stigwood, arrived to oversee the prep and proper seating arrangements. We were polished right down to our cuff clinks and tuxedos.

After the premier the guests limousined to John Travolta's perfectly attired tables in the Crystal Room, which were cordoned off with red carpet and two guards. Famous faces graced us, from Elizabeth Taylor to the Bee Gees. The press flashed cameras adding to the sparkle of the evening chandeliers' candlelight. Time after time the small press contingent requested to see Mr. Travolta. I had instructions to refer all to Mr. Stigwood. John was not only having a fine time but was a bit nervous and overwhelmed. I double checked with Bob, "The press wants an interview with Mr. Travolta. Do you think it would be all right?" Bob agreed and asked for a quiet, secure locale. *Fair enough, the manager's office would do the job nicely.*

I secured transfer of John through the throng and into the office. Just when John moved out of the Crystal Room the crowd swarmed. We literally had to drag him out the back door with guards posted. Bob and I watched behind the closed office door as the unnerved John settled into a leather winged chair. He turned and faced the wall, staring at the wallpaper. *Oh, my God, now what?* Bob encouraged, "Come on, John, you can do it. They want to talk is all. It won't take long."

Silence.

"The press is waiting." Bob shuffled his feet. "John," Bob kind of growled, "you wanted this fame, now smile."

In an instant, John swung the chair around and pasted a large grin over his face. "Fine," Bob said, "Let them in."

I bowed and opened the door. Only a few moments, a couple photo ops was the very least Bob allowed. The press was dismissed. Next was the challenge of John's safe return the oh so few meters from office to his table. I do not know who they were but the legions of people moved us ! It was as if there were no controls to our bodies, the mass simply rolled forward together ! Afraid for his safety, I placed my arms around John's waist and pulled him to his seat. By the time John sat down his face was glued stiff with shock. Although he thanked me kindly his eyes were glazed wide open. Such a handsome face on a man who was as scared as a pup. I bowed my farewell and dismissed myself, leaving security to the Travolta bodyguards and I to serve his guests.

Late that night Bob appeared. "John wants to exit as discreetly as you can."

Exiting infamous guests of honour was always a logistics challenge. We organized the limousine around to the glass door behind John's table. A half dozen waiters were instructed to stand in front of John, creating human camouflage. He escaped with few noticing he had left. The party carried into the wee hours without the guest of honour ! John Travolta's first night of legendary fame was a success and he'd had some fun, I believe. The Tavern did our utmost. I hadn't spoken to John until I was in London six months later. I knew he was in town so I rang him. He accepted my call and thanked me for a memorable premier gala. Moments like those make service to others very gratifying and rewarding.

A similar party was arranged for opening night of Liza Minnelli's "The ACT". Hundreds of happy Hollywood celebrities, politicians, and royalty enjoyed the star studded eve. Hugo instructed, "You have got to look after this lady in a big way. Stay next to her at all times." That was part of the job in such an establishment as The Tavern. His command stirred up my nerves, however. I inhaled a couple of large breaths and dashed to her side the moment she arrived. I had no idea what Ms. Minnelli was like but she was served in royal Tavern fashion: from flambé drinks and delicacies right down to the orchestra playing each of her requests. I stood near, never hovering, yet keeping people at bay. She turned around and asked, "Who're *you*?"

"I'm at your service with the Tavern, David Cunningham, restaurant director. I am here to take care of you."

"Well, bug off. I don't want you standing here," she grumbled.

"It's my job, but I'll move farther away, Ms. Minnelli." She glared at me.

Between 2 and 3 a.m. Liza partied on with a handful of friends tinkering on the piano and stage instruments. I was flabbergasted at the incredibly talented singer and performer as I watched their astounding, impromptu concert. She sang her favourites, one right after the other, in spite of the hour—what strength of talent. Liza caught my eye, "David, I want another drink." She was drinking Sambuccas, a drink set afire. I bowed and brought the silver tray with her flambé beverage. In a merry state Liza shouted, "I don't want that friggin' drink." She swatted it with her arm and the enflamed liquid saturated my hands and jacket setting me a blaze ! I ran for the ice bucket. At last steam emitted from my body and I was safely doused out.

Of course, she realized her mistake and wanted to treat me to a drink, inviting me with a huge apologetic look and her big beautiful eyes flashing. Patting myself dry as I licking my wounds—how could I refuse—I said, "The only place open at this hour is Studio 54. Let me call Steve Rubel." We customarily visited each other's places when not working. "Look, I'm bringing over Liza Minnelli, will you watch for us and get her into The Studio safely?" Steve was pleased to oblige.

A dozen or so party animals piled into limos for Studio 54. It was 4 a.m. and I'd been on duty since 8 a.m. Liza provided my drink as promised and disappeared. I wondered about chatting with Steve. He was overwhelmed tending the Minnelli party. I drank my drink alone, on my last legs, exhausted. That one drink went right to my head.

As I walked to the rest room I lost my footing and fell straight down a full flight of stairs. *Enough already, I'm going home.* I went to the front desk and called a cab.

** See Appendix article RE: Liza Minnelli SUNDAY MERCURY TIMES, Dec '77

Riding home I felt blood dripping and pulled up my trousers. A monstrous gash on my shin oozed. At 5 a.m. I showered, bandaged the leg and anointed the flambé burns. I crawled into bed dreading, for the very first time since I came on to The Tavern, that I had to report at 8 a.m. The famed Tavern job with only an hour or two of rest between shifts could get old.

Upon my arrival back to work Liza's messenger brought complementary show tickets for myself and a guest with a nice thank you note. I smiled; she soothed me through the next triple shift. *When would I have time to go to her show?*

Christmas magic, 1977. Every tree surrounding the Tavern was frosted with tiny, glistening white lights. I surveyed guests in the Crystal Room admiring the beautiful holiday finery and watching the workers decorating Central Park. If you don't know the Tavern, the Crystal Room is a sparkling glass structure completely fashioned in floor to ceiling picture windows overlooking Central Park. I watched the cherry picker lift the electrician as the lights were strung. Suddenly there was a wrong move.

The lift swayed closer...

...closer... straight toward our walls of glass !

My God, what is he doing?

In what felt like a slow motion movie I bolted for the disaster. The lift thunder-crashed through the glass, showering slivers, flashing and piercing all in sight.

Oh, my God, is anyone dead?

The cherry picker swung back with the man unharmed. I sprinted to the table directly under the gigantic crystal hole. Snow, fibers of glass and icy wind tornadoed about. A party of four senior women froze, with slivers in every crevice of their finery, silver hair encrusted in broken shards. "Madam, please do not try to move. Let me help you get the glass out of your hair." I took a mammoth deep breath and went to work collecting the glass splinters in linens. One lady sat still and stared; I worried of shock. She finally spoke, "You know, David, the last time I was here the waiter spilled soup on me."

"Madam, I am sure we will be able to compensate to your complete satisfaction." I smiled, thanking God that I didn't have one dead person anywhere. Miraculously, save a few scratches, there was little blood. My fingers numbed with the winter wind and icy shards. The staff teamed together and cleared everything in time for the next shift's seating with the window boarded against the night's bitterness.

Countless incidents happened at the Tavern—as I am sure transpires in all establishments accommodating thousands per diem. Bittersweet restaurant stories were my jokes of the time. I watched candle wax from lit chandeliers drip onto bouffant hairdos and the inevitable spillage of ruby red wine over pristine white, luxuriant gowns and tuxedos. Piles of finery were destroyed by the powers of gravity mixed with heavy dinner plates. I thrived, rescuing damsels by valeting to the local dry cleaners.

Untold numbers of celebrities entered The Tavern. One of my favourites was world renowned artist, Buel Mullen, a vibrant woman in her eighties, with a few work-hampering health problems. She worked with pieces of flat steel, some ten to fifteen meters in height and width. She had her materials-to-be-art installed in lobbies of banks and other prestigious Manhattan buildings. I was in awe watching as she stood on ladders, drill-in-hand, crafting glorious pictures and patterns in steel. Once she completed the metalwork she painted-in the grooves. She was utterly amazing to me.

She was a regular at The Tavern and shared the pain of her work hampering health problems. Eventually, I mentioned that I'd done some hands on healing with my friends. A marvelous Spirit filled friendship and healing relationship developed between us. I went to her on my days off and gave her healing sessions. We were quite a healing team, as I helped make her artwork pleasurable by relieving pain and she allowed me to watch her craft when I had time. Buel was grateful for the release of pain my hands seemed to alleviate.

One day she said, "I want to throw a party in your honour, David." I must have looked surprised and even apprehensive. She continued, "Don't worry, I'll make sure the right people will be invited. You are a blessing and I want to share you with my friends."

Her affair was a lovely black tie dinner for twelve at Buel's home. Her gracious toast brought tears to my eyes. I sat next to Ms. Mullen and a new acquaintance, Lois, who was part of a prominent Californian family. Lois and I hit it off straight away, privately arranging a meeting the following day, which I took as a sick day. We attended the theater, went out to supper and back to her place. We grew close and romantic and within weeks we became engaged.

Through Lois I learned to take some time for myself. I met influential people: we lunched with GeeGee Getty and dined with Roger Horchow. The love affair was a heady experience for a small town Englishman ! I flew to California for a few days break and stayed in one of her houses in Palo Alto. It was breathtakingly good fun with California, a new adventure for me. Lois played tour guide in the great state and, of course, the Pacific Ocean was a delight. I'm not sure my heart ever beat normally during our entire relationship. I flew back from California, as if on my own wings, back to my wonderful job at The Tavern. Within the next few days a few things I had not considered came to light about Lois. I saw that our union was not for me and broke off the engagement.

Coming down off the relationship I realized it was almost a year that I'd been in New York. Every Sunday afternoon since getting the Tavern position I practically propped my eyes open with matchsticks, the hours and work became so long and grueling. Amid the depression of the fallen courtship, I felt as if I could not last much longer. After a year of high performance, being almost dead on my feet, it seemed the Almighty wanted me back home in England. I needed time away.

What to do?

I loved Tavern on the Green. Warner LeRoy, owner of Tavern on the Green, was a master teacher in my life. Bedecked in tartan suits especially designed by his public relations department, Mr. LeRoy was exacting, punctual and demanding. Lessons abounded at The Tavern with Warner and Hugo at the helm. However, in 1978, I broke the news that I was compelled back to England. Again it felt as if my life forced me to say good-bye. Life at The Tavern was deliciously wonder filled and my healings with Buel were amazing. I made sure everyone knew how grateful beyond words I was for their kindnesses, exciting times and treasured moments. Indeed, I am who I am due to the rich New York relationships. I closed my beautiful little studio apartment packing what I could fit in my suitcases, even leaving some of my collections for the next tenant . I flew back to London and the only home I still felt I had, The Tithe Barn.

London, 1978. I telephoned Charles and told him of my exhaustion, broken engagement and exceptional experience at Tavern on the Green. "Look, I know you're upset with me but my things are still at the Tithe Barn. Would you have me back, Charles?"

"Of course, let us see how things go."

I took what was left of my life and memories of New York and moved back to East Sussex. Oh, it was good to see the old place, even the friendly monk ! Going back there made me realize that I had moved on mentally. I'd managed over 200 employees at The Tavern and felt the smaller scale Tithe Barn's challenges were over for me. Rather than upset the applecart I worked on staff at the Tithe Barn. They had moved on without me, too, and I certainly did not want to strong arm anyone, especially Charles and his new management.

I worked religiously every day with Charles but set my sites on a hotel management job where I'd have a good deal more responsibility. Fortunately, the Lord took care. I met a gentleman, Ray King, who owned a country house hotel and the biggest nightclub in Eastbourne, England. He was scouting for an inn manager when I mentioned my Tavern on the Green experience. He hired me on the spot. My post was assistant manger with food and beverage responsibility. This man owned plenty of opportunities for me. I accepted the challenge enthusiastically and shook his hand with the strongest, manager style shake I could muster. Charles watched, saddened, but understanding.

I arrived at Mr. King's beautiful country manor set upon lovely green acreage. I breathed in the country air glad for the new adventure. It was a subdued life, managing only part of a small hotel with a tasteful dining room which seated a hundred, compared to the New York lifestyle. Yet there was plenty to accomplish as standards had been lax and things needed sprucing up. Change seemed my middle name and I went about it happily.

Ray King lived in a separate house from the manor with a wife, children and a controlling mistress named Heather Cunningham (no relation). Heather lived and worked in the hotel and was an extremely difficult woman with which to get along.

One day the inn was hired for a huge, lavish function in honour of the local sheriff. His Royal Highness Prince Charles was invited and expected to attend. We excited the staff to create a grand impression by getting new uniforms which were in tip-top style, fresh linens were pressed and every room was splashed with bright garden flowers and special occasion touches. The gardens were tended that morning, the lush green grass manicured to perfection. Then it was time to tend to my personal appearance. Prince Charles was due in late afternoon so I had ample time to catch a hairstylist and change into a tuxedo back at my Eastbourne flat.

In the 70's, perms were the rage. I had one that I thought needed touching up for the Prince. The stylist did a quick perm rejuvenator and I dashed by to my flat. Sweating to make it before the Prince's arrival, I barely looked in the mirror until my last cufflink was fastened. I looked like a mop that had gone wrong ! The perm clumped my ultra fine hair. I frantically tried sticking, gelling and spraying it back away from my face. I could not do a thing with it. Time ran out and I hopped in the car looking like an unkempt gollywog.

Not one person mentioned the hair but you know how one's hair makes for higher confidence level. I breathed in deeply and grabbed all the composure I could as I welcomed the numerous dignitaries and officials arriving before Prince Charles. Harrowing to be sure, I desperately tried keeping my hands out of my hair.

Standing at my post when the Prince's helicopter arrived I was indeed pressed and ready to bow. I surveyed the manor; it was immaculate as the helicopter approached. I noticed, though, that the remaining grass clippings from the morning's manicure flew about as the blades of the whirling aircraft whirled ever closer. Then a grass hurricane developed and the world went green ! Poshly attired officials with their elegantly gowned ladies in crowning touch chapeau's were blanketed with grass clippings...and not a thing was to be done. Nature and man's machine had taken her course.

Royal protocol dictated that each person in the welcoming line keep his or her place once the Prince was in presence. Ladies with brightly coloured lip polish pursed their lips delicately blowing off the grass shavings. If a lady wore gloves touching her face would have soiled them. It looked as if we were conducting a spitting contest.

Dear Prince Charles is a seasoned helicopter pilot. As he neared the welcoming committee he burst into laughter. The first lady to greet the Prince was the wife of the high sheriff of East Sussex. The Prince joked in a great teasing tone, "I've gotten you this time !" He kissed her gloved hand and the remainder of the welcome was replete with giggles and merriment. By the time His Highness got to me, I bowed, speechless. He smiled greatly looking straight at my coif. Lord knows what he thought. The mood was light and good-hearted thanks to Prince Charles' humour.

The party atmosphere was well underway when I was summoned to a bedroom. I opened the door to find numerous men in black suits polishing their guns. "Who are you?" I questioned.

"It's not really for you to know. We always arrive unannounced." One of the men spoke while packing a gun into his coat holster. Another replied, "We protect Prince Charles and secure every nook before he sets down." They held hand radios.

The secret police had obtained a list of staff and guests while I was having my hair destroyed. They asked several questions before I got back to my duties at the Royal reception. We disbanded off to our respective posts. I wasn't used to armed security and was a bit uneasy but realized it was all in the Royal protocol.

The lawn was the cocktail time setting, still flurried with green. As I approached the bartender I scanned the trees and grounds. The lush green became speckled with men in black ! Prince Charles moved into the tented area and champagne was served. One of the corks had apparently given the waiter a tough time. When it finally popped, the noise was gunshot loud. I spotted a secret service man walking straight toward the man with the bottle, gun cocked. *Oh, dear Lord, someone is going to get shot !* I eased toward the bar keep, "You better pop them noiselessly or bullets will fly." The poor man was all but crawling under the table with embarrassment.

The safety of the evening was riskier still as we had to ensure the Prince's exit to spend the evening at Ray King's nightclub. As a surprise, Mr. King had flown Prince Charles' favourite modern rock group, *The Three Degrees*, in from America. The Prince sat with the performers supping and having fine fun. The concert was beautiful and particularly memorable when Prince Charles joined them on the stage. This was before Princess Diana's time. She would have been proud if she knew or saw her Prince this night. A member of the royal family in the 1970's simply did *not* go on stage dancing disco with three black women. It was an incredible evening of fun as we thrilled witnessing Prince Charles in a most human light.

After around a year at the country hotel I went to see my Tithe Barn cohort, Charles. My roaming spirit was restless as I'd mastered the country inn management and wanted to learn more somewhere else. It was good to see old Charles with his 5' 8" teddy bear body and somewhat thinning hair. His smile and heart of gold to tolerate me all those years warmed me right to the toes. "Charles, what can we cook up together?"

Charles smirked. "We've already had a restaurant. You've had your hotel experience this year. What is it that you want to do now?" I shrugged.

In Eastbourne there was a well-groomed, elegant section called The Meads with glorious Georgian Manor homes. It was the most exclusive area around. Charles and I met in The Meads and took a surveying walk, chatting. "What is this little custom shoppe area missing?" After discussion of possibilities, walking the cobblestone lanes several times, we came up with the best one—a premier fresh flower shoppe.

It was decided. We remodeled an elegant, oak adorned Victorian building and called it 'Bloomers'. The business papers were being processed with what we thought was a unique, trendy name. Coincidentally, British actor Richard Nightingale's character on a new television show ran a florist called 'Bloomers'. No one objected legally, so we a took the good stroke of luck and ran with it.

We hired a top florist who lived in the area, Jenny, and opened our doors with full intentions of being the ultimate floral house. Our reputation grew rapidly thanks to Jenny's artistry. Bloomers was chosen by representatives of the Queen to fashion a delicious bouquet. Queen Elizabeth was to visit Eastbourne in dedication of a special building. It is British tradition that anywhere the Queen or royalty goes flowers are presented by the townspeople. Often local children are the floral bouquet messengers. Upon notification of the honour we were informed that the Queen's favourite was white flowers. We were beside ourselves with nerves. As a new shoppe our future business was held captive in one prominent white bouquet. The Eastbourne town officials got wind of the event and soon residents were a-buzz with interest in Bloomers, another stroke of luck. The Almighty works through all sorts of people often in delightful ways.

The town's reception committee made an appointment to obtain the bouquet at 7 a.m. in anticipation of the Queen's arrival at 9 a.m. You'd have thought we served breakfast that morning, with locals popping in and forming lines to watch Jenny's magic. Her hard working, skilled hands shook as she crafted the bouquet. At last Jenny gave the fragrant nosegay a final misting and off the Queen's men went to deliver our treasure.

It proved to be a celebration of a sunny fresh Southshore day in spite of all the raw nerves and long hours. The Queen's messenger sent word that out of the flowers given to the Queen that day Jenny's bouquet was the only one kept with the Queen in her car.

The royal news spread and our business took off running. What fun it was gracing weddings with floral decor. With pleasure we filled orders for weekly arrangements in numerous homes. Most of the hotels requested regular deliveries of huge arrangements for their foyers and reception areas. Like the Tithe Barn, Bloomers was a hit founded on hard, honest work, fine quality service, and goods with personal customer relationships always our specialty.

The summer flower show in Eastbourne was our next chance to boast. Bloomer's floral booth theme was 'From Birth to Wedding to Death' displaying a full array of artistic creations. We won first prize ! After the wonderful award and just a year from our grand opening, Jenny opened her own place in the next city. Fortunately, she had taken care and trained a colleague and me.

We'd do fine, I remember thinking, but it was harrowing. It was one thing having an expert directly instructing and clearly another experience to create on our own. We were apprehensive but managed to develop a unique-to-Bloomers artistic flair. Another successful year passed. The twist of arranging the bouquets myself was incredibly rewarding and a creative highlight in my life.

One day, in early 1980, an agent from London rang. He asked, "What have you been up to the past couple of years?"

"I've been running a business with my friend Charles."

"How would you like to run a hotel called the Maiduguri in Northeast Nigeria?"

I shook my head at the thought. "I don't think I want to go there."

"I'm not taking no for an answer until you hear the details. Come up to London and we'll talk."

I was happy at the shoppe. Money was good; Charles and I had solid assets.

But my gypsy blood surged with curiosity. I arranged time off with Charles and drove to London to interview with the hotel agency. It did sound exciting and the foreign assignment wages were excellent.

On the way back to Eastbourne I once again felt the weight of a new decision clashing with my present business arrangement. I adored challenge, although remote Nigeria seemed an adventurous opportunity. Still, I was thirty four years old and I wanted more. To my surprise, when I broke the news to Charles he said he'd been pondering retirement. Charles was looking for a lot more peace at seventy years of age. We sold Bloomers, Charles retired and I had a small return on the venture.

July 1981, on Prince Charles and Princess Diana's wedding day, I boarded a jet bound for Northeast Africa, neighbour-to-the-Sahara Nigeria and another adventure.

There were no long distance telephone lines in the Nigerian hotel. My agent had not called ahead to inform the new manager which flight I'd taken. I, however, was on my new quest, no dampers, nor obstacles would bring down my spirits. I landed in Kano.

I looked about.

My hands turned cold.

What on Earth have I done with my life now?

Northern Africa, especially the outskirts of the bush, was a dog fight getting through immigration. I had no guide or local hotel representative to grease the country's entry wheels for me. It was awful with walls of people rushing off the plane shoving passports at the customs official— just to get a little old stamp. I drew in a deep breath and entered the throng; hours passed until I received the blessed seal-of-entry. Further on I waited for a local plane to Maiduguri. Some fifteen hours after I first boarded the plane in England I landed at my destination and secured a taxi to the hotel. Later, I found out how I'd overpaid even the taximan, unaware of the currency or proper charge for the airport hotel shuttle. The new European guy in the land of Nigerians was taken for a ride, literally.

At last the Maiduguri Hotel was in sight: a fresh, white, bright, and lush place with gardens manicured and water from an on-grounds water tank. A posh oasis amid the desert and just the size I wanted to work with a couple hundred rooms. I stepped to the reception desk. "Mr. Michael Carr, please. I am the new restaurant manager."

"Welcome, I am he ! Let me help you get settled." This 5' 10", thin, very British young man immediately took my bags and chatting thus making me feel at home in a land far from it. "This is my wife, Judith."

"How do you do?" Judith smiled warmly with a British charm so demure I could not help but beam. Judith wore a crisp linen suit and was a finely groomed young English woman. I enjoyed these bits of British familiarity. Michael gave me an historical tour. "We've been running the Maiduguri Hotel for two years and are eager to have a restaurant manager since the last one left months ago. We'll be showing you the ropes as soon as you are able."

What relief that they were well versed with Nigeria and the town of Maiduguri. I would not have to start from scratch obtaining goods, supplies, etc. Judith and Michael were very amiable. Then Michael's words rang in my ears. "What do you mean: as soon as you are able?" I quizzed.

Michael placed a knowing hand on my shoulder. "Everyone who sets foot here has stomach ailments within three hours of landing." I glanced at the clock and realized I was long overdue. Momentarily I was sick as a dog and had not a drop of their water, either. It seemed just breathing the air gave a person diarrhea. Fortunately Judith had medicine. From the moment I set foot on Nigerian ground it had been an ominous beginning at best.

After a couple of days the cramping ceased. New world, new challenges await as I could see when I finally felt more myself. I moved into a staff house on the hotel grounds about a three minute walk from the hotel office. I shared a reasonably nice house with another assistant manager. We stayed together there for six months then he transferred abroad and I had all the quarters alone.

The remote hotel was amazingly busy with guests from Europe and Nigeria conducting business. Countless deals were sealed in our midst such as gigantic rice and oil agreements. We were the best accommodation around and the restaurant was the only upper crust one in town. There was an excellent, moderately priced Chinese restaurant next door to us, that was it. The European staff gathered at the Chinese place every so often for an evening. I valued spending good, solid time with my new workmates.

The restaurant's good reputation and the service standard needed upgrading. I retrained the dining staff to full silver service and refined the environment with new lines. Team relationships grew. Judith, Michael and I got along famously as they learned to trust me. When they traveled I stayed in their house and looked after their two Dalmatians.

Life in Maiduguri was unusual but I fell into a good, dependable routine. I ventured forth to learn about my surroundings on the Nigerian border. There were four major tribes in Nigeria. According to the Nigerian culture of the '80's the Southerners were less cultured than the Northern two tribes. In my growing experience the

Northerners were also more honest, which I learned to appreciate as a wonderful quality in my close knit staff.

Maiduguri's population consisted of Nigerian, Ghanaian and European, mixed together with Muslim and Christian religions. The poor were absolute dirt and lived on the streets. Begging was their way of life. Desperate mothers broke the limbs of their babies and gave them no help in healing properly. This created children who grew deformed and were far greater, more successful beggars for their families. Outside the hotel environment one could not walk far without being swarmed. Never could I give enough to suit the need and I realized that the Nigerian world view made my past look like a king's. Gradually, as they grew to recognize me as a local businessman and not a tourist, the locals let me be, ceasing the begging toward me.

Apart from the hotel gardens Maiduguri was barren of vegetation save scrubby shrubs or an occasional desert tree. Temperatures averaged 100-120 degrees daily. The rainy season was cooler and only four weeks in duration. It rained from 4-5 p.m. daily like a time piece. We planned around the rain for the roads were quagmires. No one passed through except in four wheel drive vehicles.

There were sand storms called Hamatam that blew off the Sahara and brought even higher heat and clouds. When sand storms arose all commerce halted while everyone headed for the air conditioned indoors to breathe.

Maiduguri is an official State within Nigeria with a separate governor and politicians. When the European regime left, back in the 1960s, the organization went with it. Those remaining moved in for the kill, financially and power-wise. The politicians and property owners wielded enormous power and were above any law.

The owner of my hotel was Al Haji Mai Deribe, a Muslim, married with four wives. He flew to England to shop for anything he wanted. He ruled his domain in North Africa. He owned numerous houses outfitted by Harrods and other top stores in the U.K. I befriended him immediately for political reasons, having been briefed by Michael and Judith.

Africa is a massive dichotomy. Imagine the destitution of Nigeria and walking a muck road after the rain and stopping short at Al Haji Mai Deribe's compound walls. Beyond the walls were his opulent palaces in the center of barren desert sands. One palace was for each wife, servants, Mercedes limos, and dozens of children. Mai Deribe's life was pure, unadulterated opulence.

His mother, however, lived in a mud hut behind one of Mai Deribe's estates. She had not one utility and zero amenities. Mai Deribe's mother supported herself by obtaining empty cement bags from Mai Deribe's building companies, cutting them into squares, cleaning them and selling the paper to meat sellers for customer packaging. This son, with enormous wealth of countless kings, kept his mother in destitution. Life was staggeringly unfair in Nigeria. My relationship with my own mother was heavens better.

Michael and I teamed up to help the owner's mother as we developed our relationship with Mai Deribe's over the months. Time gave us an opportunity: "Your mother lives poorly and you have so much. What might we do to help her?" I asked.

He said nothing. We did not carry it further.

Later we found out that Mai Deribe strung one wire with one lightbulb from his house to his mother's so, the reasoning was announced, she could have more light to cut more paper to make more money for herself.

Awful.

Time marched on and I grew increasingly pleased with my staff. Made up of the various local tribes, it was a real melting pot of culture and communication challenges.

I sorely realized how they cherished the money they earned with us. It was high wage indeed given the setting. I worked hard training and refining the boys and gals who were all in their teens and twenties. The brightest were appointed head waiters. Achievement and mutual respect grew between us and they became my Nigerian family.

Michael took me for a drive one day. To my surprise we parked next to a gigantic construction site. Michael informed me that it was Mai Deribe's second hotel. The plan was for one hundred rooms to capture travelers on the main road and airport clientele. The new land was closer to the airstrip than our hotel, only ten minutes. Then Michael said something fortuitous. "Judith and I are recommending you as the general manager of this new hotel." Michael smiled broadly. Once again, the Almighty displayed His helping ways. My eyebrows must have touched my hairline with shock, my mind raced. *What are you up to, God, dropping me into this place and giving me a brand-new hotel to manage? Am I up to the task?*

I could say nothing but, "Thank you, Michael." I shook his hand gingerly.

So it was.

Owner Mai Deribe agreed with the Carr's recommendation. From that point on I was the new hotel overseer charged to supervise its completion in addition to my restaurant post.

New energies abounded. I liken the experience to giving birth, starting a hotel from the ground floor. I planned and created the hotel of my dreams, within limits, that is. Judith helped immensely because she knew the region so well. We purchased materials, combing the open air markets. This was not easy; Nigeria was not Europe. Residents did not have draperies or curtain rods. We literally installed thin pipes for drapes in all the rooms. When in Rome...

Mai Deribe owned warehouses with treasures from deals and collections in anticipating the opening of more hotels or another palace. Walking into one of his tightly guarded warehouses was like walking into Aladdin's lamp. The contrast between the multitudes living in the austere conditions and the golden storage buildings was earth shaking to Judy, Michael and me. Mai Deribe could have furnished numerous hotels without importing another single item. With lorries we transported our finds to the almost completed hotel. I even negotiated a few pieces for my house in the bargain.

Hiring was my next step and completely new to me. Michael's staff was already in full swing when I'd first arrived. Fifty plus waiting staff, cleaning crew and reception people were required. There was no need for barkeeps because there was no alcohol allowed, per Muslim policy. I was instructed to interview with Mai Deribe's personnel manager. He was in charge of the final hiring. As a European, I did not understand the nuances of Nigerian customs: only certain tribes and levels of people were hired and men only for most positions. A few women were allowed for maid level work but not for serving guests, another Muslim tradition. Nigerian women were truly second, perhaps even third and fourth, class citizens.

At last, we correctly acquired everyone to keep the peace with all of the tribes and training began. "Young man will you get the cutlery?" I asked to begin the on the job teaching. "I would like to show you the proper manner in which to set the tables."

"What is cutlery, Sir?" The lad asked innocently.

"Cutlery is just another word for forks, spoons and other serving pieces."

"What is a fork or spoon?"

Oh dear Lord, I believe I have enough challenge now. Send help!

A calming voice went through me: *Now David, this is a wonderful experience. You know where these boys come from and how they live. You must start from scratch and your teaching will benefit them greatly.*

> "Therefore do not wrong the orphan, nor chide away the beggar; but proclaim the goodness of the Lord."   ~ The Koran

There was a mere month to opening day. I prayed, swallowed hard and fell back on basic, step-by-step instructions. All was detailed: foods on the menu, restaurant routines and presentation with full silver service; repeat, repeat, instruct, and repeat. By opening eve these natives, who had never set foot in a restaurant before, could serve with the best of the five-star crews. They listened carefully and took all that I said to heart. They were eager learners and mastered things swiftly; it was an amazingly rewarding time.

Opening day, 1982. As a manager I loved viewing the guests and delighted in watching those boys dressed to the nines allowing few, if any, mistakes in presenting our menu. Their genuinely sincere attitude aimed to please customers made the difference. We were successful and quite booked from opening day forth. How could our combination miss? The new structure was just minutes from the airport. With a hundred cooled and beautifully decorated bedrooms and baths, a luxurious restaurant with five-star chef and meeting rooms with gourmet catering, we were an oasis in the 120-degree sun and desert.

Blessings multiplied as my staff grew ever more efficient. After a life of no-sitting-down jobs, I found myself with long afternoon breaks between luncheons and dinner hour. What a treat in the Sahara where 120-150 degrees is common place. A peaceful routine formed as the hotel hummed. We served breakfast when my job was to make sure every guest was welcomed. I chatted, forming relationships and enjoying the coloured people who came through our doors. We then prepped for lunch and dinner. Luncheons were served in the dining room and meeting rooms. Dinner was formal silver service with full and fine linen set-ups. With my well trained and bright assistant manager, Mr. Sing, managing the afternoons, I took siesta time at last. I was most satisfied with my life not being bone tired and collapsing when home. Nigeria's new hotel world made for a lovely life.

October, 1982. Siesta.

Gunshot !

Tanks rolled outside the hotel gate just past my kitchen window. Bang. Bang, BANG !

"Help !"

The hotel security guard pounded the door and shouted, "Trouble, sir ! The police are firing at civilians in the next village !"

"Please, get yourself, the other officers, any guests, and staff secured !" I ordered. *Thank you, God, this is the hotel's quiet time.* (Most of the guests had gone on business midday.)

Then I remembered: no telephone. I had no way to contact Michael and Judith. After a year in operation, telephone lines between our new buildings and the outside were incomplete. We only had an internal hotel system from room to room.

Isolation seeped into my heart; we were ten miles from a civilized town.

What to do, what to do...Lord, no man is an island, I need your help.

I listened.

The shooting lulled.

The Assistant Commissioner of the Police was also a guest who'd been relocated for duty in Maiduguri. He rushed into my office. "I have been informed that the

Muslims in the village are dealing in black magic. Ritual ceremonies were performed right in the hotel's neighbouring bush. While the Maiduguri police went in to sort things out, they were attacked."

"How many were hurt?" I asked. My heart was beating so loud the assistant commissioner could surely hear it.

"Only one out of the six officers escaped back to police headquarters. Reinforcements went in and now this." He gestured toward the tank that sat outside our hotel security gates.

Nigeria was a primitive outpost. As long as one was walking or driving down the watered and manicured lanes inside Mai Deribe's hotel compounds things were civilized. However, just a few kilometers away was a tribal village with no toilets or water and many cultures and religions I did not understand. I walked out of the hotel foyer. Through the gate I saw bodies laying askew. I closed my eyes in disbelief and overwhelming sadness. *How will I protect ANYone?* (Please refer to the 1999 article on Nigeria in the appendix.)

The main road was police blocked. No cars or jeeps were allowed to pass and thus I had a skeletal staff and a mere handful of guests. (Little did I know how well this would prepare me for the hostage imprisonment in my near future.) Evening fell. No one moved. We served food to those inside and waited.

Silence crawled along.

There existed astonishing silence on a once busy, busy roadway.

It was eerie, chilling and unnerving.

The 5' 8" somewhat stout, impeccably groomed Assistant Commissioner of Police had been issued a battery operated walkie-talkie and gathered updates. I invited him for coffee and information, instinctively trusting him. I had no one else, did I? As witness to events I did not understand it was a blessing to have this well educated man, whose forte was armed conflict.

"One group of Muslims slightly different from another was practicing Black Magic," the Assistant Commissioner began, his English exquisite. "When the police went in the Black Magic leader stood with his arms firmly folded not budging. This is what the young escaped soldier told Commissioner Cam Romembich." The Assistant Commissioner was shaken. I poured the strong coffee. He continued, "As the young policemen fired at the Black Magic leader—he brushed the bullets away without a scratch !" The Assistant Commissioner shook his head. "Once they spent their ammunition, the leader beckoned the officers with an extended right arm and index finger. The policeman who escaped said it was like a trance. One by one each officer went directly to the Black Magic Leader."

Dear God, I need your guidance here. I poured the Assistant Police Commissioner another cup and drank-in the conclusion. "Those highly trained men were as lambs to their slaughter." He swallowed a big gulp of hot java. "They hung each officer by their feet and slit their throats." Grief and sadness melted over me.

"Then the Muslims drank the policemen's blood." He shook his head back and forth, back and forth. "I am an educated man, David, but I do not know what we can do. Bullets seem powerless. We are forced to stay far away from them." He stared into his cup.

"We're venerable here. How might I help?" I began to sweat. "You are highly trained police, but our guards have bows, arrows and muskets from World War One ." I swallowed my coffee slowly and intentionally, trying to calm down.

"We can do nothing but hope they don't invade the hotel. You should vacate the premises."

I felt like a prisoner as I got up and shook his hand. "Better get some sleep, Assistant Commissioner." He nodded. I checked on the dozen staffers and guests and locked up. I rushed nervously back to my house on the hotel grounds. The silence was deafening. I hadn't realized how I enjoyed hearing guests having a good time. Now my hotel was a lavish prison with savages beyond its gates. It would be a long next few days. I barricaded myself, thankful for the steel doors Michael had wisely installed. I dropped into bed and prayer. *Show me the lesson here amid my fear.* (As we know now, Kuwait lay ahead. Nigeria was a kind of training ground for my own Baghdad imprisonment.) Like countless other times in my life, sleep came as a wonderful escape. Sleeping, in even turbulent circumstances, was a grace for which I have always been thankful.

The next day I mustered strength and walked through the gates to the main road. The bodies were gone. The dusty empty pathway was the closest to a war zone I'd ever known. The heat waves rose as I looked toward the town and police barricade on the horizon. I squeezed my eyes closed to block the sandy gusts and the image of the dead, whose blood was slowly being erased by the Saharan winds. I shivered. We were a defenseless island if some tribe decided to attack.

I felt completely deserted and alone.

The chief of hotel security shouted, "Army car ahead ! Armored car coming !" My archery clad guards escorted me outside and stood by my side. A tall, well educated Nigerian army man jumped out and in perfect English demanded to know who I was.

"I am the hotel manager."

"You are in grave danger and must leave immediately."

"I have no means of leaving and am responsible for the staff and the guests trapped here."

"The army insists. We have taken over for the Maiduguri police and will conduct a clean out campaign of the bush village adjacent to this establishment. There must be no civilians near, especially whites. You must leave by dusk." Impeccably uniformed with glimmering rows of medals, he was not the type to accept no to one of his commands.

"I understand. But I have no transport or exit plan." I wiped my brow.

"You must go this afternoon."

I rang Michael at the main hotel. Miraculously, the line worked and within the hour, God sent Michael in a fine, four-wheel drive. He had passed the military barrier and agreed to transport the hotel occupants back to his hotel immediately. We secured outdoor furniture, doors and dust storm shutters, then gathered guests and staff. The guests had arrangements with their respective corporations and promised they were leaving immediately. The Assistant Commissioner left word that he'd gone to Police Headquarters. My native staff had mixed feelings regarding their departure. They held a dual allegiance to their village tribesmen and their jobs. Therefore, they felt safe enough to stay, promising to stand guard. Mohammed, my assistant now, claimed they had protection because they were locals.

My heart grew heavy with fear for them. Michael pulled me away as I hugged every one farewell. As we drove along we were stopped by drunken policeman demanding money, food and drink from us. As they searched the car we explained that we were managers of Mai Deribe's hotels and friends of Police Commissioner Romembich. Their posture changed when they heard the name Mai Deribe and they let us pass. At last the main hotel was in sight—a building never looked so wonderful to me. Judith welcomed us with food and settled us down. Suddenly I realized, I had the food storage key with me. Fingering my key chain I screamed at Michael, "I've left the guards with no way to obtain food ! I must return !"

Michael shook his head, "No way, David."

"But…but I'm their manager !"

"Well, then, I say I am your manager and giving you a direct order: you may NOT leave this hotel, period. "

"I know you're protecting me. Look, you have a wife, I'm single. Please. I cannot leave my friends without sustenance." Reluctantly, Michael negotiated that we'd both go. Unhappily, Michael and I waved to Judith as we drove off to fulfill my obligation. Michael thought his presence, having been there some two years, would keep us safe.

You must leave by dusk. The army's command rang in my ears as we raced through police barricades dropping Mai Deribe's name. We had an hour window to return the keys before nightfall. Between the road blocks Nigeria's desert remoteness engulfed my body, my mind.

I wish I could talk with my sister Margaret right now.

The golden late afternoon light darkened as we clouded through the mute desert. Nervously, we sped around the hotel's circular drive where I hopped out, gave the keys apologetically to the guard and jumped back in Michael's vehicle. We raced back into Maiduguri, with Mohammed and the boys who'd chosen to remain, flashing in my mind's eye; their faces smiling, standing guard on their hotel drew tears to my eyes. My heart ached that their jobs seemed more important than their lives. Did I even understand this country, these people I worked with day in and day out? The ride back seemed interminable but at last, Michael's hotel appeared and Judith in her classic navy English businesswoman's suit ran out to us. Three dusty Brits embraced madly. I was far from England but a spot of home was there nestled in the midst of our friendship. The stars appeared and nightfall was a welcome relief, now that we were united.

Gunfire !

We flew into the elevator to the top floor and onto the roof. The eight story high panoramic view of the flat-lined Sahara flashed with sparks; the black horizon was electric with hundreds of gunshots peppering the sky. The morbid fireworks ignited blazes and engulfed the bush in minutes. The night became a shocking, gigantic inferno. Who was dying?

Who had won, if you could call this winning?

The air was sick with burning humanity. Michael, Judith and I hugged on the roof top. We knew the fight was not with us and that the police murders were unacceptable. But what of the innocents? The grim night weighed massively on our hearts leaving us speechless and sleepless. I was only grateful that we had one another.

The following day's reports told of the murderous black magic leaders impervious to military law and gunfire. The Nigerian army took over the police outpost and invaded to gain civil control. Flame throwing tanks burned all villagers alive. Any of the Muslim tribes thought to be black magic followers were targeted and completely consumed. A mass grave was dug for the entire village to be buried in the bulldozer hole.

After two days of peace I forced myself to drive back to my hotel. The patch of land where the village once lived was smooth, leveled and as pristine as a fresh spring garden. Shivers up and down my spine resurfaced at every thought of the massacre. Eerie nighttime darkness engulfed me as I journeyed down the dirt road. The villagers' spirits loomed, thick with angst. My gut shot pain straight through me as I drove past the thicket of wretchedness. I approached what I thought was the hotel, but the pitch black confused me. *Lord, am I seeing things?* I caught a flashlit smile from one of the windows and waved pointing to my quarters. The light went out. I knew they knew I was there. Mohammed and the guards dared not turn on more light. Exhausted and scared out of my skin, I ran from my car to the little house, bolted my steel door and soon dropped into a deep sleep.

The next morning brought the rest of the employees back, banging on my door. I was elated seeing each person alive and, though we had only a simple bit of food, it was a grand reunion filled with celebration. Reunited, we vowed to keep the hotel open together and collectively breathed a sigh of relief.

Middle Eastern travelers returned and life moved into working machine order. We served customers with an urgency that could only be attributed to the recent events just kilometers from our windows. We could not openly discuss what hung over us because it would have frightened our clients. When I allowed myself to think and pray over the massacre, it consumed me. Gradually and privately, the boys revealed the harrowing moments during the military invasion. Some had lived in the torched village but escaped, telling of and finally releasing their terror. The details painted nightmares for me but were therapeutic and bonded us.

Life rolled on carefully.

War flashed between Nigeria and Chad and the Nigerian Air Force confiscated our hotel ! It made perfect sense to them being ten minutes from the air strip. They had the cash which turned the massive conflict into very good business for Mai Deribe, our owner. In fact, the Captain Commando always had a pocketful of money to flash around. He commissioned little extras such as custom laundering of uniforms which we struggled to provide for a dear price. Weeks of teamwork yielded the finest meals and service to the Nigerian air soldiers and military commandos. We were the Nigerian 'USO' comforting troops day to night through awful skirmishes. Through this arrangement we became rather close, sitting with the soldiers, sharing food, tea, and conversations; we were akin souls, working far from home with no vacations. The opulence of the hotel could not mask the severity of our situation when we received word that a plane was shot down. It was as if we'd lost a brother when our soldier guests never returned. Some days the dust storms brought a sea of sadness with their winds. This was a classic paradox in my life: collecting high rates for the rooms with not one complaint during the devastation of war. Mai Deribe's high priced service paid off in other ways as the soldiers were appreciative of our service. We were never attacked with military living among us.

After eight weeks the air force moved out. As fast as they came, they left, leaving the facility no worse for the wear. With the increased income we'd actually refined our facilities to upper crust. Word traveled fast that we were no longer booked and our five star reputation for businessmen flourished. Telephone lines were reconnected and I finally called my family and friends. Oh, how good it was to hear their voices ! The mail system was renewed and I received a batch of backlogged and loving letters. Post war routines emerged; life was fairly normal and even satisfying, teaching and caring for my staff family again. We came up with a siesta rotation between us, to give everyone some time off during the scorching afternoons. We focused on the good around us.

Things became almost boring. I played cards and even devised a Ouija board to pass the time. One day I asked an assistant, Peter Jamison, who'd joined us after the skirmishes for hotel training, if he had seen a Ouija board in action. "No, I haven't," he said, seemingly intrigued.

I had few distractions besides reading and went about showing off with my makeshift Ouija letterboard and drinking glass message finder. It was fun communicating with the Spirits. I was excited at the chance to show Peter how adept I was at connecting with Spirit Souls. I did not consider myself a full fledged medium, just a fairly sensitive clairvoyant. For example, a friend of mine in South Africa passed on in a drowning accident. He came to me frequently as I played Ouija, telling me what he was doing in the Spirit realm as I spelled out his messages. This comforted me because I had been in such sorrow with the war around me and then hearing of his death. He became a Spirit guide helping me through my desert days.

Peter was mesmerized by the messages under the glass. "I am Charles," the board spelled: "I died in my room. Worried about pup. Help me, David."

"I don't understand," I said aloud. "Charles is in Eastbourne and well after selling Bloomers and keeping his Tithe Barn going," I continued. My face flushed with panic.

"Let me prove it," the board communicated. The board spelled out the details of the Tithe Barn safe and where Charles' will was and what it said. All of this information was privately known only between Charles and me. The Ouija board was perfectly accurate. I told Peter I had to telephone to see if Charles was all right. He left and I dashed to the telephone, only to find that day, the outside lines were not working again. *God, how am I to take care of Charles' dog if Charles has passed on when I'm in Nigeria?*

For the rest of the afternoon Charles' Spirit remained with me. I went back to hotel duty where I reminisced incessantly about Charles and the good life we'd led together. Later I became somehow grateful, as the entire day proved phone-less and the memories and Spirit of Charles kept me company. He filled my mind all through the night and into my dreams. When I arose at dawn I got a line out to England and rang Charles.

Charles answered.

"Charles?" I was shocked. "Ch...Ch...Charles?" I stalled, not wanting to tell of my Ouija board. "It's D-D-D-

D-...David." I breathed in deeply. "I was just checking to see how you are." He was apparently fine. We conversed for some time. I then put down the phone and stared at the wall, most confused.

The Spirit communication said he had died…

What's going on?

I went over and over again what the Spirit had spelled out on the board; how the Spirit told of things only Charles and I knew. In my mind it was Charles' voice loud and clear yet he was still on the earth. Was this a haunting?

By whom? I dressed for work and stayed confounded and confused all day until siesta. I went back to the Ouija board. I spelled out, "Who are you?"

It answered by spelling out through the glass, "I am Spirit killed by army. I was burned to death."

"Why do you claim you are Charles? What are you doing?"

Then I felt laughter—loud mocking laughter as the Spirit answered in my head rather than on the board, "You stupid, bastard !"

Fear rained into my soul.

A surge of terror energy raged through me. I ran outside and smashed the Ouija glass into a million pieces and burned the board. That was the last and final play on any Ouija board—in my life. I prayed for relief from my fright but never slept well in Nigeria after that.

Later, a clairvoyant and I did a healing together and removed nine negative Spirits from the massacre from my Soul. They sensed that I was sensitive to Spirit and had hovered over me, attaching themselves to my Spirit. Some souls are not ready to go back to Spirit and stay within their old life for a time. For deep-seated reasons they linger unsettled, confused, not forgiving nor seeking peace; they may be upset about how they left that life or who they left behind. They had, according to the medium, attached themselves to me because of my sixth sense openness.

At the end of 1982, still shaken from the war, the killings and that Spirit imitating Charles, I asked Michael for a vacation weekend. I ventured down to Lagos on the southwestern coast of Nigeria. Acquaintances through the hotel had invited me to their home and had even arranged for a car at the airport. I felt like a king.

Lagos was a whole other world compared to Maiduguri.

The car my friends sent proved not a luxury but a necessity I soon found, as we approached the expansive decay in Lagos City. The roadway was lined with abandoned vehicles rusting in place. The sheer mass quantity of beggars staggered the mind. Coming through center city the driver said, "Make sure all is locked and closed. They'll rob you right inside the car." I lost any trace of security; Maiduguri seemed like Gotham City with Superman compared to Lagos. Swarms of people flashed knives, pounding and thrashing the limo's darkened windows. The driver continued, "Tourists have made the mistake of placing hands on the window ledges. Thieves grab and chop-off arms, stealing jewelry from the dripping, severed hands." Horrendous, deplorable visions I could never imagine, I witnessed. No seaside spot was worth what I saw. I did not rest the entire weekend.

Maiduguri seemed an advanced civilization upon my return. I relished living in the hotel world, an oasis in the uncertain African desert. I clung to my routine, keeping peace as the order of days. Prayer, sleep, teamwork, and food were my priorities as I lived out my job contract. I knew of nothing else to do to keep sane, until one day two guests asked what my position entailed at the hotel. I explained to which they replied, "We're with Sheraton and are going to build a hotel in Lagos."

I remained coolly professional as I thought of our successful hotel trade. We didn't need competition locally. "We have a couple of hotels here, quite sufficient for the travelers," I stated.

"We've been watching your caliber of service. If you'd like a career change, when we get back to England we'll call and fly you up for a chat."

You could have knocked me over with a feather. The Sheraton was up there in the ten star category of hotel organizations. I agreed to take their call. *Thank you, Lord !* I could not help but marvel at the perfect timing in my life. I needed a change and one with an established company could give me career security.

July 1983. I decided the Sheraton interview was, at the very least, a way to transfer away from Nigeria eventually. After training and serving the required Nigerian-Sheraton time, I would be in a corporation which afforded myriad international opportunities. Desperate to get out, see my family and put the recent months behind me, English green beckoned as I landed at Gatwick and was driven to Sheraton Headquarters in Denham, Middlesex. Margaret and Mum drove down for a visit with Jim and my little nephew David. Increasingly, I saw this was going to be the right move. I wanted to easily to fly back and forth visiting my family any weekend I chose. A long term Sheraton job would afford me this freedom.

Subsequently, I was offered a managerial position for the future Maiduguri Sheraton restaurant, a notch down from being manager of a brand-new, full-size hotel, but a step up in the corporate world. No more worries over a private owner such as the Maiduguri Hotel's Mai Deribe with his shady wheelings and dealings. The corporate pay and benefits were great as well as being on the team of a hotel industry leader. Life grew to fever pitch as I realized this was the chance of a lifetime. No more wars for me ! I was jubilant shaking the interviewers' hands all around.

Then I mulled over telling Michael, Judith and my staff as I flew back to tie things up. It seemed that I lived on 'Planet Paradox' during each career change. I breathed-in deeply, landed, taxied, and had a talk with Michael on the way from the airport. "Of course this is a tremendous opportunity for you, David. Congratulations." The new Sheraton was not to open until 1984. I could well complete my commitment to Michael just after Christmas of '83 and then report for Sheraton corporate management training in London in January 1984.

Jonathan, one of my senior boys, came into my office the day before my Nigerian departure and said, "Mr. Cunningham, you are not allowed into the hotel coffee shoppe today. It is out of bounds for you." His smile was broad, his eyes twinkled with mischief.

"Mm," I played pensive.

"No entry until we come for you."

"Okay."

I had my suspicions entering the sea of employees— every single person employed in both of Mai Deribe's hotels was there including Mai Deribe, Michael, Judith, and their dogs ! *Lord, who was taking care of the guests?* They guided me to a special seat and read original letters and poetry. What gifts ! Judith held my hand, crying. I had all I could do to fight back my own tears. Never in my life had I such caring been shown toward me. I had no earthly idea the depth of our relationships. One assistant was so upset he'd locked himself in his house and wouldn't come out. My old companion guilt set-in heavily that last night.

I had a dawn flight and planned a solo ride with my driver, Mohammed. We loaded baggage and drove to the gates where he promptly stopped the car. I looked at him in the rearview mirror. He looked back at me. I looked at my watch. "Mohammed, please, my plane shall leave without me."

I searched in the mirror to see his face. He was crying.

"Mohammed?"

"Mr. C., you are our father. What will we do without you?"

I could have died.

I thought I might get out of my car and stay.

I could have.

No, David, you know it is time. This was good but enough. It has been three years of service through civil wars and death. It's time to go. The voice was right, again.

I squeezed the handle of the door, got out and hugged Mohammed. He then drove forward in silence. As we approached the little airport, I saw the entire hotel staff standing by the hotel shuttle van, all waving, crying and smiling, sending me on my way.

My God, who is working the hotel?

I loved those people.

I cried as I flew back to my homeland. I was brimming with trepidation. Did I even want to go back to Nigeria after the Sheraton training? I celebrated a late Christmas, chuck full of personal plans before my life change with Sheraton. I saw Margaret and Jim, Mum and Dad, aunts, uncles, cousins, and friends. I then flew to Houston for New Year's 1984 with Texans I'd met during their Maiduguri business trips. I'd never been to Texas and needed the R & R in somewhere new and absolutely safe and secure.

10 p.m., New Year's Eve, 1983, Houston: we were gathered around the television, champaging and waiting for the Times Square ball to drop. The news flashed: war ! The Nigerian civilian government, headed by President Shagari, was overthrown by the Nigerian military.

In the first days of 1984 my former hotel was taken over by army and all employees were put out on the street. Grief, deep and abiding, waved over my very core. *Thank you, Lord, for saving me, but what of Judith and Michael, Mohammed, Peter, my boy staffers?* How I mourned for the marvelous souls I'd come to know and love. The list of names I prayed for every day seemed endless.

I received word that a Swiss-English friend of mine, Nicholas, was in the wrong place at the wrong time, too, and was imprisoned by military in Keri-Keri. He remained for what was to be three years. I had letters smuggled to him through the Red Cross. Eventually I heard from him, receiving bits of his plight on toilet paper smuggled back through the Red Cross. Grateful he was still alive, I'd share the scraps of news with our British circle of family and friends. He was imprisoned in a cell meant for only ten people, along with 27 Nigerians. The things he went through. I was amazed he had not died. Prime Minister Margaret Thatcher journeyed to Keri-Keri in 1987 and obtained Nicholas' release. He was a perfect example of strength-in-will-to-live after all their torture. He was never the same, but he did get home.

Nigerian warfare has a living nightmare to me.

January 10, 1984, I started my Sheraton training. My living base was the Heathrow Airport Sheraton and I worked in the Sheraton Skyline, London, training for the Nigerian assignment. The Maiduguri Sheraton was still under construction and certainly with the war the project was delayed. I was informed of their plan: after training I was to go back to Nigeria and supervise the building project while working in the Lagos Sheraton. Lagos? Surely that savage place was never where I wanted to be stationed, but I remained committed to the Sheraton team by holding my tongue—a rare quiet for me, but an intelligent decision for the time.

First day to report a lovely, blonde Sheraton Heathrow receptionist's smile glowed. "Oh, Mr. Cunningham, welcome aboard. We have a nice room for you. Let me help get you settled." The young lady continued, "My name is Suzanne Fitzsimmons and if I may be of any assistance to you, do please feel free to call." I had a wonderfully, warm feeling about Suzie—or was it just the excitement of being out of Nigeria and back on homeland soil?

That old voice inside me said, *THIS is the one.*

If it wasn't desert fever then it was surely love.

On a bright sunny April 12,1984, Suzie and I were married, preceded by a whirlwind romance amid the lights and modern thrills of Londontown. I look back and feel as if I had chemicals (of love?) in my system. I was almost drugged those first three months of 1984 back in London, dating, dining, partying in the safe feelings of homeland again.

We were married in Northeast England. Suzie's background was Czechoslovakian by her mother and she had never met her biological father. Suzie's Mum left during WW II, traveling to England where she married a local Englishman. They had a son, Mark, Suzie's half brother. Wedding attendees from Suzie's side included: her Mum Susan, Les, Suzie's stepfather and Mark, the only ones who managed the flight from London to my childhood home, where we held the Whickam Methodist Chapel ceremony. The reception followed, a sumptuous five-star buffet at Lumley Castle, a 12th century retreat, with a band and lush, gilded decor for a hundred family and friends.

I began the celebration, as with Margaret's wedding, nervous about Mum and Dad being together with their respective new spouses. Unfortunately, I'd not seen my mother since her own cancer diagnosis; her gray pallor told of the advanced condition. We managed a delightful stay, inclusive of each relative, warts and all. For the wedding party transport from chapel to reception, I hired a fine jet black and canary yellow 1930's Rolls Royce for Suzie and me, with two sparkling white Rolls for the bridesmaids and their families. My little Northeastern

English town was a-flutter, when we came chugging through downtown Whickem ! It was a glorious day concluding with the wedding suite upstairs in the castle, all roses and romance. After a full, luxurious day with family following the wedding we drove down to Eastbourne where I still owned a house with my old friend Charles.

After we'd settled in Eastbourne for the honeymoon stay we went driving. A series of strange events happened. First, a young boy ran smack in front of our car. We screeched to a halt and discovered that he'd just fallen over and the car had not touched him. We checked him out thoroughly. All were sorely shaken but fine.

We resumed the journey to a coastal vista called Beachy Head with a lovely view of the sea, where tourists watch a large expanse of God's British coast. Suzie'd never been to the area just outside Eastbourne, which was one of my favourites that I wanted to show off to my bride. The cliffs, the frothy, pounding sea, the mist, and the hiking were sheer exhilaration for me. We thrilled in climbing and breathing the wonderful ocean breeze. Then…the woman hiking right in front of us jumped off the cliff.

Suzie and I froze. Strange honeymoon event number two was upon us !

As witnesses we were trapped, with no entry or exits allowed from the 'crime scene'. We stayed until the police picked up the poor woman's smashed remains. In an hour's time our honeymoon took an awful mood swing from near-death to death experiences. Chilling. At last, the officers released us.

Back at our house that evening we stared at a comedy on the telly, exhausted. A hilariously popular comedian, Tommy Cooper, was doing stand-up at the world renowned London Palladium. It was marvelous relaxing together being newly married and laughing right out loud, especially after our jarring afternoon.

All of a sudden, Tommy Cooper collapsed on stage. And he never got up.On live TV, in front of our very eyes, Tommy Cooper died.

Three major incidents occurred on the first full day of married life. Suzie and I felt a bit like doomsday. I still do not understand what it was all about. Were they omens of life to come?

Back to work in London Suzie and I acquired a small flat near the Sheraton in which we both were stationed. It was a lovely life of daily, happy, safe, and secure routine living side-by-side. I reveled in it, feeling as fit as I'd ever been.

June 1984, I was called to Sheraton Headquarters in the Denham area of London. A director informed me, "With the seriousness of the Nigerian military situation in both Maiduguri and Lagos, your original Sheraton management team is disbanded."

I sighed audibly. *Thank you, Lord.* He continued, "Consequently the job for which you were hired is no longer. We will pay you for the training time, but I am sorry to say you are relieved of your contract under events beyond control."

"Excuse me Sir, is there no job at any other Sheraton worldwide? I would move to work for Sheraton." He shook his head and my hand and lead me out the office.

Now what, God?

I could not believe my life: 1) I left a beautiful, wonderful position in Nigeria, 2) war had broken out and continued raging, 3) I was safe, 4) I'd met Suzie and married, 5) the very reason the career decision I'd made with Sheraton was taken away.

I barely breathed as I phoned Suzie with the news. We both broke down.

I job searched for anything in London, in all of England, almost anywhere. The only offer that came around was managing a small holiday hotel on the Isle of Wight, off the British coast. "Well Suzie, we have to pay rent and the mortgage on the house in Eastbourne." She agreed I had to take the post. She stayed with Sheraton, London and I packed my bags again.

The island hotel owner picked me up in a shiny Rolls Royce. It was a luxurious ride on the car ferry to the Isle of Wight until we drove up to a tattered, seaside inn, its whitewash in the midst of faded glory. I was asked to wait in a room while the owner went next door. There, not six inches behind the thin, plaster wall for my ears to hear, the owner sacked the existing manager. While I awaited job instructions my new boss boomed recriminations to my predecessor. This was not a good start. Keeping busy looking about the room, while the poor man cleaned out his personal affects, I was disappointed at the one or lower two star condition of the establishment. I sighed, envisioning loads of crusty work ahead of me.

The Isle of Wight Inn was a tourist place offering week long, low priced motel packages. Families rode the ferry on buses, off-loaded in a stampede and stayed for a week, thus a complete turnover occurred each Friday. It was challenging for a time as I'd never dealt with this type of inn. Suzie ferried over on her time off but our married life seemed destined to be strained with extended separations, given my lack of luck with Sheraton.

There arose another problem when I realized, as the English north winds blew, that the job was inherently seasonal. When the weather changed tourism ceased and I was laid off, forcing me back into the job market until the spring. Future imprisonment on the Isle of Wight was not desirable, thus I interviewed with the intention of full time employ. I secured a year round position at the San Pierre Park Hotel in Guernsey, a spectacular five-star business. I was manager of one of several top notch restaurants. It wasn't hotel manager, but status be damned, I needed the money. Forced to leave Suzie again to live on the Island of Guernsey, my saving grace was that it was lovely surroundings right on the fresh, crystal clear waters. Suzie spent days off and finally Christmas with me. Great fortune came when the San Pierre manager, Keith Martel, offered Suzie a personnel position. He reasoned it would be best for business all the way around if a married couple were together. I thought him an incredibly sensitive boss. Lady luck was changing, until I found out Keith had a mistress, Dorothy, who was the personnel manager. She had started as a maid for the San Pierre and literally worked her way up to manager. Keith had not consulted Dorothy about Suzie's personnel position, a grave error for us.

Talk about jumping from the tourist fire of the Isle of Wight into the frying pan at Guernsey. Dorothy controlled Keith and resented Suzie for being there without her express approval. With Dorothy's snippy tone one day and snide comments the next, Suzie and I decided to avoid her boss' moodiness by keeping out of everyone's hair. We were on a second honeymoon and happy with our day-to-day togetherness in a gorgeous hotel. Dorothy didn't like that we didn't play her 'game' so to speak, letting her control us. Ultimately, her dislike of Suzie's hire boiled into hate and she turned against us. After just nine months Dorothy had Suzie fired through Keith; then they fired me. I don't know if Dorothy was jealous of a happily married couple or if it was only Dorothy's fanatic need for total control. What a pity, for we had let our London lease run out and shipped our belongings to the island. We did look for other island positions but there was nothing.

The spring of 1985 was our first anniversary and we stood back on ground zero.

We telephoned Suzie's mother with the discouraging news. Susan sympathized, "How awful, ov course you stay vith us until you get on your feet." It was generous of her really. We piled furniture and treasures into Susan and Les' small house; it was everything and everyone on top of one another from the first day of our unemployment. Suzie and I had her old bedroom next to her parent's. If Mum-in-law Susan needed something, she'd walk straight into our bedroom with no warning or knock. We had to live there for nine long and stressful months, in conflict with Suzie's Mum. A married daughter living back with her Mum was less than a perfect solution to our job woes. This definitely motivated us to seek employment post haste.

Suzie, fortunately—or perhaps unfortunately for me— got a job straight away and then she was never home. I combed the daily papers, called agents and interviewed to no avail. Suzie ventured home around 10-11 p.m. daily and I on the other hand was home each live long day and night. Thankfully, Mum-in-law Susan worked outside the house as a high powered manager with General Biscuits. Les ran a tavern and wasn't home much, especially evenings. Mark was young, went to school activities and bedded mid-evening. We often played chess and got along well for the short time we had together. But I was going out of my mind.

Thus by default, I was left with Mum-in-law for too many hours of those 300+ days. Susan was a controlling person; nothing in her house was done without her permission. She came home from her boss job still wielding her power. If a person was watching TV, she'd switch it off. No question, no option, the telly went off because she hadn't turned it on. Good Ol' Big Czech Mumma whose comment upon meeting me for the first time before our wedding was a growl, "David, I love you, but if you harm my Suzie I'll kill you." Ah, very nice then Mrs. Mother-in-Law.

Often during evening Scrabble time Mum-in-law told me about her awful day. I resolved to get along with her by not confronting or arguing with her, just listening and nodding my head. Admittedly, she was not my mother and did not grate me like she rubbed her daughter every wrong way. I appreciated Susan's background and tried keeping it in focus. Her family had escaped from Prague and walked the entire way to Vienna. Looking at a map I didn't see how that was humanly possible but I believed Susan had had an awful personal history. During the exodus, she'd been captured by Russian soldiers, raped and one eye put out. She lived the pain of her past every single day.

One dinnertime while Suzie was working, Susan, Les, Mark, and I ate while tolerating Susan's verbiage as usual. That particular evening Les spoke up. We all looked up from our plates—hearing his voice was that uncommon. Susan dropped her knife and fork and said, "Did I give you permission to speak?" Well. Mark and I looked at each other, grinned and buried our heads in the meal. We dared not glance up again for fear of laughing aloud. Lord knows what Susan would have done then.

Another night I sat in the living area in just my stocking feet. Susan came in from work and commanded, "Where are your slippers? You vill put them on now." I jumped up. "Yes, Susan." I suppose I felt guilty being unemployed. There I was in my forties behaving like a little boy…or was it a great excuse to run and hide in my room? Susan probably was an effective boss at work, keeping every single living being in proper order. She had that talent all right, but it was used to excess at home.

At long last six whole months into the latter part of 1985 I obtained a contract at the Londonderry Hotel as general manager of the Le Privè nightclub, with management responsibilities in the hotel, a five-star environment once again. I was most confident in this kind of business and felt I'd earned the position already after hours of waiting for my interview. I was tea'd and newspaper'd for some three hours, kept on the edge of my seat to meet the almighty and powerful Londonderry Director, Mr. Michael Day. While reading the countless items fed to me by Mr. Day's secretary, I watched a large flamboyant character flash by me every so often and then finally leave the premises. David Northey, the assistant, apologized, "I am terribly sorry for your interminable delay, but Mr. Day was summoned elsewhere for an emergency."

Desperate for a job and a way out of my in-law situation I said, "I shall wait, thank you." David Northey smiled, my sincerity impressed him. David interviewed me right then and there and welcomed me aboard with Mr. Day's final approval. Sweet hotel luxury plus the opportunity to unveil a brand-new nightclub—what a delicious challenge. To think I did not have the potential of any war time gunfire outside ! I was happy, secure and saw my dreams materialize once my wife and I got our own place. Northey began scouting apartments for us and has been a close friend ever since.

The Londenderry Hotel was introducing its nightclub with engraved invitations to London society in hopes of obtaining permanent, high caliber members. The Barclay twins, David and Frederick, owned the Londonderry and spared no expense creating a posh, sleek, nouveau interior with Mr. Day's Hollywoodesque direction and persona. Its sparkling black and silver coordinates, flashing lights dance floor and bar with servers wearing spotless black tie tuxedos were a London tourist's delight. Valet parking provided by top coat and hat doormen welcomed impeccably dressed guests. The modern, black granite entryway housed hostesses dressed in top-of-the-line gowns.

The boss twins were identical with only hair as their discerning difference. I was thankful I did not contend with keeping the two straight, mostly working with Northey.

Within a week I hired and trained staff and auditioned musicians and DJ's. It was a busy time planning the gourmet dinners accompanied by live music and after dinner dancing. At midnight a disk jockey took over the nightcaps and brandy crowd until 3 a.m. Days began at 3 p.m. for the hotel check-in hours then I took over the nightclub every night save Sundays. I loved it but the hours were hard on a marriage.

Unlike in Nigeria, liquor was the profiteer in the Londenderry operation. Wealthy hotel guests lavishly spent entertainment cash on expensive champages and caviar. Profits were more than I'd ever imagined and I was duly well rewarded. I was allowed to party with whomever I liked and enjoyed my own chef's food and drink as I politicked with clientele. In positions past I rarely had a moment to sit down. In the Londenderry Nightclub part of my job was to woo and charm the hotel guests into becoming annual exclusive, nightclub members. I lavished attention and conversation on every customer and was immensely successful at it.

I seemed to please all of my bosses: the German hotel manager, Dirk Grote, a strong, controlling figure reminiscent of Mum-in-law, the Deputy General Manager and friend, David Northey, and the Director assistant to the Barclay Brothers, Michael Day. I received a commission for bringing in scores of nightclub members.

Pleasing these men was not always easy. Michael Day reminded me of LeRoy of Tavern on the Green fame—a 60ish, party-hard, cigar-smoking powerman. He was extremely well spoken with a beautiful English-Irish accent. Impeccably dressed, (no tartans like the Tavern's LeRoy) he commanded a room in his tall, rotund stature bedecked in designer suits. Michael Day, being the number three man in power at the Londonderry and having an Irish Catholic ancestry, firmly believed he was the

British Pope. He wore a gigantic ring always to show everyone his attitude and position.

An example of his Pope-ishness was how he reigned over the employee parking lot. For security purposes there were large iron gates. Employees drove to the gates, tooted car horns and a guard opened the gates. One afternoon I arrived in my falling apart BMW and beeped. Nothing happened so I tooted again. Out thundered Michael Day who opened the gate, sashayed through it and walked around assessing my car. I rolled my window open and said, "Good afternoon, Mr. Day."

"Good afternoon, Mr. Cunningham. What do you want?"

"Well, sir, I want to park and come in to work, please."

He looked at my car and then into my eyes and said, "We're obviously paying you far too much." He turned on his heel, closed the iron filigree and went back into the hotel.

Good, God, what had I done?

I gently repeated the horn toot as my shift had begun. Mr. Day appeared again. "Yes?"

"Mr. Day, please sir, I need to get parked. My shift is to begin."

He walked to my window and stuck his huge hand with famous, protruding ruby ring right in face. "If you kiss the ring the gates of Rome will be opened to you." His bellowing laugh echoed against the hotel back quarters, reverberating inside my little vehicle.

I kissed the damned ring, parked and went to work.

Life. Boring? Routine? Never seemed mine.

The hectic work schedule increased during all holidays and special occasions due to extra parties; I did not get home until 4 or 5 a.m. after those. The job was actually normal for David Cunningham the single man. It was not so great for Suzie and me as a couple. Suzie arose at 7 a.m. so we didn't see each other properly until

Sundays and the few smidgens of mutual moments off. The routine gradually became grueling. I'd never such a tedious commute; with London traffic it amounted to an hour's drive either way to Susan and Les'. I functioned on two or three hours of sleep but the money seemed worth it. At long last, we found a London house via Northey's help, which was mid-way for both jobs. We moved out of Susan Mum-in-law's daily life for good, we hoped.

December 31,1986—a spectacular Londonderry extravaganza, New Year's Eve. The Barclays partied high with their wives and top management, including Mr. Day, our exclusive members and Suzie, her Mum and father. Suzie wore a luxurious evening dress from Harrods, all black velvet and very regal. Finally, we had a couple of days vacation when the Londonderry Nightclub was closed as London nights were notoriously quiet over the holidays.

Mr. Day called me into his office along with David Northey, my first day back in January of 1987. "David, the Barclays decided to close the Nightclub." My eyes fixed on his gaudy ring, glistening in its obnoxious extravagance. He continued, "We'd like you to come over to the hotel full time as assistant manager." I swallowed hard. Pure, unadulterated, never-saw-it-coming shock, drenched my body. It was worse than Dorothy in Guernsey. At least there we knew the evil Dorothy hated us. At the Londonderry I'd no idea—especially being offered such a demotion. I was speechless.

Finally, I rasped, "Have I done anything incorrectly?"

"No, the Barclay boys just changed their minds."

I sighed.

"We have a week to close the club building. Tell your staff." Lucky me, I had that pleasure left to do. I dragged myself to the club, depressed. Sitting in my office I rang up two Americans I'd befriended at the Londonderry. They were frequent hotel guests and brandied with me regularly. We had a wonderful friendship, Kathy, Mark and I. "You'll never guess what just happened…" And so I told the story with special emphasis on my undeserved plight.

"We'll talk with you tomorrow; perhaps we can help."

I rang Suzie at her work and of course she was mortified. "How are we to make it? We've a mortgage and Christmas bills." She wept.

That day was endless. I convened the staff, telling young and old alike, that although they were well trained and fabulous at their services the nightclub would no longer exist, or need their services. Happy New Year.

I re-rang Kathy and Mark in Carlsbad, California, as soon as the time zone allowed, the following day.

"We've got an idea. Let us send you a ticket and you can investigate this yourself," Mark said.

Thank you, God, your timing is perfection. I thanked them and said I'd fly out on the weekend after closing the club. I phoned Suzie. "No, I shall not leave my job. You go, it's all we've got." I wanted her to come, knowing my bride should not have been left behind, but she had her job.

I fell in love with California. Kathy and Mark sent a limo and there I was in Los Angeles, good ole America once again. A catering business was for sale with a million dollar pricetag that Kathy and Mark were considering. "If we purchase this firm we would like you as manager." Graciously, they set up an appointment with the owner. It looked like a wonderful opportunity for us all and they decided to buy. Next I went into training to assure the transition was smooth and we did not lose any customers from the current owner's excellent reputation. I drove Route 101 and combed LaJolla hoping to find a flat. My diligence paid off and I signed a lease for a place right on the Pacific. Everything was up and running, with just the final paperwork for the business purchase to go. In the interim, Kathy, Mark and I flew to Lake Tahoe where we had a little holiday learning how to ski and playing the slot machines. The lake and the mountains were breathtaking. Life was tremendous and marvelous at this new turn, save missing my wife. Kathy and Mark put me up for three months until my flat was ready. They graciously allowed me to call Suzie every single day so we could plan our future together. One day Suzie called, "Your father is not well, the doctors think it's cancer."

Dear, gentle Dad, no...

Suzie said something else. I re-focused, "I also found a lump in my breast."

"What?" I absolutely panicked. "I'll be home tomorrow." I informed Kathy and Mark that I must tend to family business for a few days. What gems these friends had been, even giving me a plane ticket to get the family crises under control.

March 1987. I flew to London and met Suzie at the physician's. Fortunately, all of her tests were clear. *What a relief, thank the Divine.* We then packed the old BMW and drove Northeast to be with my father. I brought Dad a cross as a gift to wear. Sitting with him I looked closely at our relationship. Sometimes silence can be profound. We never spoke much, nor then either, yet somehow I knew I'd never see him again.

Unfortunately, some aspect of our work on earth does not move very far along; Dad and I never grew close during this lifetime. Soon the day came when I had to close the catering and apartment deals in California with Kathy and Mark. Suzie protested vehemently. The thought of breast cancer had drained her and me, as well. Along with my father's illness and impending death, I was compelled to stay in England and cancel the plans in the States. I called Kathy and Mark with the bad news. Ultimately they never closed the deal with the caterer. A missed opportunity for which, it seemed, I had little control.

As fortune would have it, again, there was a nightclub located in a Kensington Hotel in South London needing a manager. I interviewed and received the post to run The Bank Nightclub which was part of a four-star hotel. Suzie and I were thrilled we could be together side-by-side, day-to-day, in the same country.

Our expectations coupled with my success let us down hard. The Bank became staggeringly popular with yuppie Londoners. Joan Collins, movie stars and pop groups thrilled the wealthy patrons. But the night life nature of a club manager separated Suzie and me even though we lived in the same flat. When one mate goes to work at 7 a.m. and the other begins at 3 p.m. there exists little time for couplehood.

On June 9, 1987, two days before my birthday, Dad passed into Spirit from overwhelming cancer conditions. I wished I'd known him better. I cannot say I had even a relationship with him. The funeral was awful as I felt so guilty along with an inner sadness I could not shake. Suzie and I continued our lives together but apart because of work. Deep down I felt sadly alone.

Summer,1988. Two finely dressed Englishmen enjoyed a cocktail at The Bank. I welcomed them, chatting about the club performance schedule and asked what they did professionally. "We're part of the scouting committee for The Dubai Country Club in the Middle East." Most people in the hotel and restaurant industry knew that Middle Eastern and third world assignments were highly paid. I was familiar with the wage levels, but also the climate in Dubai, which was some 100-120 degrees with uncomfortably high humidity. All this fleeted through my mind along with the negative feelings left over from Nigeria, as one of the gentlemen asked, "We're searching for a general manager. Would you be interested?"

"Lovely opportunity, of course." *Boy, could we use the money, but that climate.*

"We'd like you to visit the committee." I bowed.

They called within a few days and I agreed to interview at least to see what the job entailed. "Suzie?" I called her at work with the news. "I do not want you to go. I want you in London !" Suzie surely had inherited a controlling streak from her Mum. I proceeded to get time off, rescheduling with another colleague at The Bank and drove to the interview without Suzie's approval.

I arrived at the posh London hotel for the introductory meeting, where I was presented to several of eight country club board members. We sipped tea around a gorgeous rosewood boardroom table as I answered scores of nerve-quaking questions from the many potential administrators. This would prove another fresh experience, as they explained that the appointment to the Dubai Country Club included working for eight bosses, all of equal power. One boss was always more than enough. I was excitedly apprehensive as they crowned me Dubai Country Club manager.

Suzie was pleased about the salary only. I was concerned about many things as I fulfilled The Bank contract with enough time for Suzie and me, along with a friend and her baby, to take a small holiday to Portugal. It was a delightfully romantic beach pleasure and sorely needed togetherness for Suzie and me. In a few short days I was leaving her again for a job in another country. Although this club was exclusive and not in a barren wasteland as Nigeria had been, I was set to go with a bit of lead in my shoes.

We arrived back home from Portugal on a Friday night. I repacked Saturday, flew to Dubai on the Saturday red-eye, was met at the airport by one of the committee, and given a gorgeous suite until I found my own accommodations. BOOM, I was The Dubai Country Club Manager and countries away from my wife.

July 1988. Change is the fuel of the soul, for me anyway. The Dubai Country Club was a membership club for European, Asian and Arabic expatriates with a lush, manicured golf course bordering the desert with squash, tennis, several swimming pools, a gourmet cabana restaurant by the pool, a lovely clubhouse with fine wood bar in a comfortably elegant lounge and lavishly ensconced main dining area. Staffers were most often Asian, as Arabs did not work in that sort of club environment due to the alcohol served. It is against their religion and cultural belief system.

I convened with all eight committee members to change the menu, upgrade the cabana decor, acquire new uniforms for the staff, and generally move the club into a formidable five-star plus standard. I conducted my own replacement staff interviews and began retraining to provide premier silver service. I decided on a black man as my restaurant manager. Upon review of my work the committee objected to the choice of a black manager. I stood by the man, for out of the people from whom to choose he was the best of the lot. This was the first of numerous prejudicial experiences with the committee that often set my blood boiling.

The Dubai Country Club was extremely busy, beginning with dawn's daily exercising by expatriate members to dining and drinks anywhere on the grounds. We planned affairs in-house and catered off-ground business meetings and parties as well. The thriving commerce kept us challenged and refining our planning procedures as we grew to be an efficient team. The operation hummed and I finally obtained a house, just outside the club grounds, rather than living 24 hours at the club. It was extraordinary: a complex with four bungalows, a swimming pool and two servants, an Asian lady and her brother, who took impeccably good care of it for me. My lifestyle was now so pleasant I could not wait to share it with Suzie at Christmas. My goal was to convince her to stay. Over her holiday we job searched and found a Sheraton in Dubai where she was brought on as their personnel manager. This was a terrific change of events: to keep her benefits and have her join me in such luxurious surroundings. I prayed that our strained marriage would now be released of the pressures of separation. She moved in the first week of the new year, 1989.

Disconcertingly the committee and I were always at odds. Not one of the members had hotel or catering backgrounds and their micro-management meetings were comprised of doubts and second guessing my professional, well reasoned decisions. Some members even changed things without my knowing, commanding me to do that with which I disagreed. I was manager but felt more their slave. My year's end contract was up and I did not renew.

July,1989. In meeting with the committee I blamed my health and the heat (100-120 degrees with 100% humidity morning, noon and night) for the non-renewal of the contract. For a couple of months I'd been dog tired, falling asleep at odd times if I dared sit down and my feet pained me 24 hours daily. I was also plagued with frequent trips to bathroom, more than I cared to count. My afternoon siestas had not helped my condition as I arose feeling worse after rest. The committee handled it well and I burned no bridges by saying anything awful to the misinformed, arrogant committee members.

In spite of the heat I even tried to obtain another Dubai job, for Suzie loved her post and did not want to leave. Nothing was available. I networked with people and connected with a long time friend who offered me a job back in England. I flew up for the interview feeling quite ill, but was successful in landing the job. I flew back to pack and share my job news with my wife. "I am not going, I love my job here," Suzie said. *Why must our relationship be faced with such strains, such hardship?*

It was a long and uncomfortable limo ride to the plane back to England. I kissed Suzie good-bye and walked into the Dubai terminal. The voice above my head that sometimes blasts me with accurate information said, *You will never see her again.* I spun around and looked for a face to go with the voice, as I always did. It repeated screaming, *David, you will never see Suzie again.* I waved at her, drinking in her beauty, her blonde hair flowing in the hot desert breeze.

I have not seen her since.

Three months into my new London position, Friday, the 13th of October, 1989, I received a telephone call: Suzie was divorcing me ! I subsequently found she had been having an affair with an Arab bank manager at Barclays' Bank in Dubai. This was why she did not want to leave. I was desolate but not surprised.

The voice had warned me.

That voice always seemed to come to fruition.

Alone again.

The North London country hotel I was working in proved disastrous. I had full responsibility, but upon my hire they neglected to mention I'd be sharing an office with the owner's daughter. She was a spy who appeared wherever I was, taking notes, questioning my work and reporting back to her father a la her own personal twist on my actions. It was dreadful and irritating; I quit not three days after Suzie's call and packed my things to move out of hotel.

The apartment Suzie and I had was subleased because for our contracts in Dubai, so I was homeless.

I was jobless.

I was wifeless.

Now what, Lord?

With nowhere to turn I forced myself to call Suzie's mother. Susan was up to speed with our divorce and was gracious. "Ov course you may stay as long as you need, David," her thick accent actually sounded comforting right then. I stayed some three months. It was bearable considering my lack of alternatives.

An old colleague of mine, Yan Peacock, and I had worked at Sheraton Heathrow. Yan was food and beverage director for Harrod's. I noticed this while job hunting, reading a catering magazine. I rang Yan. "Any chance of work at Harrod's?"

Yan said, "Funny you should call. We're researching a catering arm for Harrod's. Why don't you come down and we'll talk over the feasibility studies."

I agreed and met Yan the next day. We proceeded to discuss focus groups for assessment of the potential catering business. Yan hired me as a consultant for three months and gave me an office. We went over Al Fyad's goals, detailing the target markets and the number of outside catering units. The plan was to use the best chefs and brand name Harrod's on everything right down to the uniforms of the servers and their signature silver. The idea was exciting and a sure success, given Harrod's impeccable reputation. Yan and I finalized a polished business plan with our marketing survey results for presentation. Al Fyad was ecstatic and approved Yan hiring me as Harrods' Catering Business Manager. My salary was to be very high, with 33% discount shopping at Harrod's plus a new company car. Elation washed over me, mending my shattered life as I looked toward a far brighter future in the year 1990. The position was to begin after the first of the year. I would not get a London flat until after my Harrod's work began so I drove to Northeast England to visit my family for Christmas. Mum, who was very ill, managed to enjoy time with Margaret and me. In spite of my divorce it was a celebrational time sharing career news with loved ones.

After Christmas I drove back to London, dropping by Yan's to finalize my starting date and receive initial job instructions. I was met with news that there had been a row between Yan Peacock and Al Fyad. Yan had resigned. "What of my job and Harrod's catering business?" I almost screamed at Al Fayed's assistant.

"There is no job for you and the catering business is off."

January 1990. Coming from a Christmas vacation, rested and well loved, I was filled with promise one moment and crushed in 60 seconds of conversation. My whole life was dashed against the rocks.

I was almost finished, my devastation took such hold on me. I was still officially living in my divorced wife's parents' house with no job, no home and nothing in my future sights. I was lower than I'd ever been. My mother and my sister both said, "Come home for a while and let us take care of you." Margaret lived around the corner from Mum; both had small homes but it was better than ex-Mum-in-law's. I reluctantly agreed and stuffed my car with all possessions to stay in a bedroom at Margaret's. I had a lot of clothing, suits and tuxedos for my line of work. They simply did not fit at my sister's so half of my life was stored at my mother's house around the corner.

Upon seeing Mum again I realized my journey back home was meant to be. She was on death's door. I spent more time than I had since her leaving my dad. Things between us were strained but I was glad to have tea with her every day.

Off and on I looked for work in England or abroad. No one was interested in me. I poured over a food servicing magazine one day and read an advert for manager at a hotel in Kuwait. I sent my curricula vitae and received word for a London interview. I drove down and interviewed with the Kuwaiti Hotel's General Manager, Ammed Al Injibar. After an impatient week of waiting I was notified of my post in Kuwait.

I was over the moon ! After half a year out of work, living off my families, both former in-laws and my own mother and sister, I needed to be on my own and earning a living. To top off my situation I'd received no communication from Suzie since autumn of '89...until my birthday in June 1990. "Happy Birthday, David," she said when I answered the phone.

On June 11,1990, just prior to my departing for Kuwait, Suzie telephoned me with an announcement. I was diagnosed with diabetes. This diagnosed disease would save my life, though I didn't know this then.

We continued talking and I realized that made sense. My condition in Dubai was: dreadful thirst, painful numbing of the extremities, overwhelming sleepfulness, and excessive urination, all symptoms of diabetes. I'd thought it was Dubai's climate, even way back I thought it might have started with the Nigerian climate.

Now my challenge was to get healthy again and fully regulated on medication before I left for Kuwait at July's end. It was the first week of July.

Lord, I need your support. I have a marvelous new job opportunity, but my health is at odds and Mum is dying. She's begging me not to go out of the country. My life is in your hands.

I talked with Margaret daily, struggling for answers. On the television there came reports that Iraqi troops were lining up on the Kuwaiti borders. I telephoned the Kuwait Plaza's general manager who assured me that soldiers did that sort of thing all the time. "It is perfectly safe, David, I'm here aren't I ?"

I rang the Kuwait Embassy. They asked, "Do you have your visa in order?"

"Yes, but what of the soldiers?"

"No problem. This has happened for eight years or more."

"Well," I told Margaret, "it seems everyone in proper authority says it's safe in Kuwait. You know I need to work." Margaret understood. Mum did not. During a farewell dinner in London with friends, the conversation, quite naturally, came around to the Iraqi-Kuwaiti news reports about conflicts. One of my friends joked, "I hope you have a helmet with you, there is obviously going to be some shooting down there !"

"Don't worry, I've spoken to the hotel and the Embassy. All is right as rain."

At dawn I boarded the British plane for Kuwait with my life in luggage. I was ready for what I thought would be the most exciting career opportunity of my life.

DAVID'S LIFELINE

1999	USA	full-time healing consultant, USA; Certified Minister of Healing, USA; biography written
1998	India	visit to Sai Baba Ashram
1997	County Cork	David marries hypnotherapist Petra, his soul mate; move to Ireland
1991-7	UK	Certified Spiritual Healer. David travels as professional healer, England, Germany & Ireland; His Hale Clinic office opened
1992	Coventry	Human Shield party for Hussein hostages
1991	Kent	1st Healing Counselor position, Dartford Hospital, England Alt Medicine Unit for AIDS/HIV
1991	March	David's mother passes away from cancer
1990	October	David is freed from Saddam Hussein and returns to England
1990	August	David is taken hostage by Saddam Hussein's soldiers
1990	Baghdad	Manager of the Kuwait Plaza Hotel
1990	June	Suzie announces divorce
1989	London	Harrod's catering consultant
1989	London	David & Suzie separate
1988	Dubai	Country Club Manager
1987	London	various hotel and restaurant management positions
1987	NE England	David's father dies from cancer

1984	Sheraton	met & married Suzie
1983	Nigeria	war begins, David leaves just before it breaks out
1980	Nigeria	Manager of Maiduguri Hotel and restaurant
1979	Meads, UK	Bloomer Florist Owner with Charles
1978	Eastbourne	Country Inn, met Prince Charles
1977	New York	Tavern on the Green Manager, David meets John Travolta, Liza Minnelli, Governor of NY, GeeGee Getty, Mary Higgins Clark, and Roger Horchow
1974-5	Eastbourne	Tithe Barn restaurant opens with Charles
1973-4	Sedlescombe	Housemaster for boys school... The Great Saunders School
1964	London	1st move to big city, various jobs, moved into catering
1964	NE England	mother moves out, takes sister; parents divorce
1961	NE England	Quits school, begins theatre group and bookkeeping, attends meta-physical courses at College of Psychic Studies under Don Galloway
1955	NE England	Margaret, David's beloved sister is born
1946	NE England	David is born to Margaret and Lawrence Cunningham

PHOTO SECTION

David and his Mum, Margaret
1985

David's Dad, Roly

David with his Dad, Roly - 1950

Great Sanders School, Sedlescomb, E. Sussex - 1974

The Tithe Barn, Sedlescombe, E. Sussex - 1976

Tavern on the Green - New York - 1977

Maiduguri Hotel - Patrick, Michael, Judith, David, Hotel Chef
1981

Hotel staff members, Nigeria - 1982

David & Suzie wedding - April 1984

Isle of Wight - David with two staffers - 1984

David with Jim Davidson, Famous English comedian
Dubai Country Club - 1988

David's return from Baghdad, Nov 1990
Ruthie Lee and friend

Hostage Birthday Party for prisoner John
hosted by the soldiers at the Baghdad bomb Plant
Fall 1990

David and Hayley Mills - 1996

Plane to India - Dec 1998

Jeanne Brown,
first healing with David - cir. 1970s

Dan - during
healing sessions,
Ireland - 1996

Indian boys to assist David - 1998

David in India at Deepak Chopra Retreat
October 2000

David's home in Ireland

Linda Ratto's husband, David
David Cunningham,
David's brother in law, Jim
Newcastle, England

David's nephew's wedding, Durham, UK

David, sister Margaret, and her daughter, Lynsey

David, sister Margaret, and Jim

Chapter Six
My Healing Decade
1991 ~ Present

As far back as 1882, professor William A. Hovey was conducting research on what was at that time termed *supernatural powers.* Interestingly, the Society of Psychical Research was the early version of London's College of Psychic Studies, which I attended under Don Galloway's tutelage in the early 1960's. Professor Hovey and his colleagues conducted countless experiments well document in *Mind-Reading and Beyond,* published in 1885. These studies are worth reading if you are interested in historical research on the field of extrasensory perception and such. Professor Hovey's premise is that no one is supernatural. What is shown in some individuals as highly developed senses is actually all part of nature; nothing is abnormal but all a part nature's processes and therefore not to be feared. This was important work because often people fear something they do not understand. As far as we've come in over a century, there still exists fear of the subjects in this very book.

* * *

July 1991, the Kent Inn that offered my first post hostage position was part a hotel consortium by the BransHatch Racing Course. I was charged to manage the thirty intimate and elite rooms at the Inn. I drove onto the circular drive of an ivy ensconced, rustic brick manor nestled on twelve acres of woodlands. The exclusive

BransHatch Racing Club had a regal feel and membership list.

Healing crossed my mind as I pulled my bag from the trunk of the taxi. *When was my healer's life going to begin? I can be a successful hotel manager but what of my Baghdad pact with the Creator?*

In prayer I was guided to go and find healing work while managing the Kent Inn. The Bible quote, "Seek and ye shall find," rang poignant in my mind. I skimmed the daily job adverts in the caregiving field. The work at the Inn was steady with good people so I was grateful for it. And I worried about changing career fields; I knew the hotel trade and little of the health system. I resolved to let the Almighty steer my healing life. I had nothing to lose. I was working, had income and was my own person again. I found the patience to begin interviewing while at the manor.

Every newspaper was replete with articles on HIV; the AIDS crisis had just been discovered. In fact as luck (or God's perfect timing) would have it, the healthcare industry was in grave need of caregivers. Overwhelmed at the numbers of victims' stories and the horror of the disease, I was compelled to find my place to help. Working and conversing at the inn, I watched and listened for those having healthcare connections. One day I was introduced to Dr. Paul Key, Director of AIDS-HIV Unit in the Dartford Health Authority, Kent. Our mutual interests became clear and we agreed to meet.

At the hospital we had a congenial three-hour interview in which we discussed hands-on healing, counseling and complimentary medical techniques. With no traditional medical cure in sight, the AIDS population could benefit from alternative care. Dr. Key often investigated out-of-the-mainstream techniques because of the ravages of AIDS and organized the Complimentary Medicine Unit at Dartford Hospital. Our meeting culminated in an astounding turning point in my life. Dr. Key stood, placed his hand on my shoulder and said, "David, I'd like to offer you a job as counselor for the HIV-AIDS Unit of the Dartford Health Authority."

At once I was both drawn to and afraid of the prospect he proposed. I looked down at my feet not knowing what to say. Dr. Key patted my back and told me that he'd listened intently about my experience serving and counseling people, even in the horrors of Baghdad. He thought I would be an asset to his patients at the alternative care unit where acute daily care was administered. What a compliment and vote of confidence in someone he barely knew. I must have looked worried for he continued comforting me. "Don't be concerned. We'll make sure you get the necessary HIV-AIDS training free."

Going back to the inn felt oddly foreign and not nearly as important as the first day I'd arrived. Life shifted as I realized the power of will and that I could make my choices happen. I was in the midst of accomplishing my Baghdad promise to heal. I made a conscious, consistent effort to move into the healing field; yes, it had taken over a year since my release, but it was at my doorstep. It is often forgotten that every single aspect—even our trials and tribulations—have manifested by our experience choices, our free will. At that moment in autumn of 1991, Dartford Hospital was the choice for me. Although AIDS and HIV were unknowns in my life, counseling and caring I knew well. At the crest of a fresh and long-awaited path, I flew through the last days at the Kent Inn walking on air. I left BransHatch after just three months, ready for my new career.

Dartford Hospital day one of living as a healer. I saw vividly that morning, there are no accidents, everything fit. No longer was I the victim of circumstance but a chooser—a man of free will choice and I was living my new life as healer, just as I'd promised ! I was given a trainee nametag and paperwork to complete and although I had always been frightened of medical needles, I knew somehow I'd learn what was necessary to help patients. In the past, I fainted at the sight of blood. Determined to be a healer I elected to not have that happen any more. I *was* a healer, I would do what it took to be a part of the hospital team. I passed all classes and even became a phlebotomist ! On April 1992, I placed a white counselor's coat on my back, pinned official credentials in place and joined the sexually transmitted disease team at Dartford Hospital.

Godspeed ! I'd been reborn but in the same ol' David Cunningham body.

As Dartford's introductory counselor I greeted patients initially as they walked in the door, complied an updated history with immediate ailments and concerns, took blood, received lab results, then educated and counseled patients and their loved ones. I watched other Dartford caregivers to constantly refine my methods of presenting negative lab reports or other sad news, always with love. AIDS patients' need was gigantic and my healer's call to love my fellow man, unconditionally no matter what, was tested with each patient family. In spite of long hours and very ill patients I was energized day after day in my new job.

The Complimentary Health Center was an arm of Dartford Hospital where patients received a variety of therapeutic procedures: massage, aromotherapy, reflexology, and hypnotherapy in conjunction with the budding AIDS-HIV medical treatment available in those early years. At that time physicians were at a loss for effective treatments so alternative regimes were highly desired and nurtured. Dr. Key was a visionary in the care of AIDS patients. Thank the Lord for his work and the incredible learning I gleaned from his hospital.

In May of 1992, at Coventry Cathedral, I was honoured in a special service for Hussein's freed hostages. The party launched a book on the experience entitled: *The Human Shield.* It was an amazingly uplifting ceremony. I felt as if my family, friends and countrymen honoured my Baghdad experience and recognized my career as healer. Seeing some of the former hostages healed me and moved my life full circle. I did not realize how important the ceremony was at the time. However, after reading the book *The Human Shield,* which detailed the hostage ordeal, I was publicly vindicated. Once again I was astounded by the blessings of the healing circle I lived within—my dear sister Margaret, her husband Jim, Lynsey and little David, Mum and my new colleagues at the Dartford Health Authority. These souls anchored me with care. As I met more patients my own support would help me help others who were often in excruciating circumstances. I felt wonderful and a new man !

I developed a healing session procedure (see chapter three) for Dr. Key's referral patients. I used a room with an examination table at the Complimentary Health Center where I did healings. With more help needed I began private healing session appointments in my flat. It was a rewarding time seeing patients smile after our work together. For all of my adult life I'd simply counseled and healed friends spontaneously. Now it was intentional and it seemed that I had only just begun the real David Cunningham story. At forty something years of age I was awake at last.

I knew more.

I felt more.

I looked forward to each day and was energized through the help I extended.

God has a plan for every one rang in my mind, heart and soul. I was living His plan, my pledge and felt my fullest potential. Daily events manifested into my life with ease, grace and love.

Wendy, a Dartford colleague and senior nurse counselor of our unit, witnessed numerous healings with me. The energy healings were very affective in helping HIV patients maintain their HIV status and often delayed full-blown AIDS. Wendy was moved as she began understanding my work and shared it with a close friend, Dr. Sam Browne.

Dr. Browne telephoned, "David, Wendy told me about your healing and counseling. I believe very deeply in spiritual healing. Traditional science cannot affect everyone to the point of cure and I understand that your complimentary approach is helping many. Is it all right if I refer some patients to you?"

"Wonderful, Dr. Browne !" I don't think you could have scrubbed the smile off my face that day.

The healing work grew leaps and bounds after connecting with Dr. Browne. Within days I received my first patient with Dr. Browne's referral letter explaining her condition. Dr. Browne's patients and our healing successes together formed my first independent professional healing practice. Life was busy, pleasurable and I was the healthiest I'd been in years.

It was immensely sad, too, working with those who were full-blown, being close to the families. Often the disease had taken a stronghold and our sessions did not stop the condition. Patients died. I struggled with this aspect of life even though I understood. However, I knew our time together helped them pass into the world of Spirit (or heaven or whatever you like to phase it) in peace and harmony. This was my purpose for those who passed on. I held their peace within me as I shared and cared for the next afflicted person.

One of Dr. Browne's long time patients, Fred, came for an appointment with his son, Mike. Father and son ran a backstreet repair garage and were quite the characters. I referred to them affectionately as Jack the

Lads (an English expression meaning street-wise fellows). They visited me because Dr. Browne prescribed it; Fred was not well with several maladies and Dr. Browne felt I could help him. Son Mike, in particular, was skeptical of what I did, but obeyed his father's doctor nonetheless. While Fred and I discussed his case and began the energy healing Mike waited, watching. Fred sat up at the close of our session saying he felt much better. Mike stared at me, his face blanched. "While you worked I felt something like electric heat go right through me !" Fred and I looked at each other smiling. Fred had just experienced God's energy and Mike discovered it right along with his dad. This made their visit extremely powerful and Mike more believing than when they first arrived.

They returned every few days for further treatments, always together. Mike grew actively interested and positive in his father's healing treatments. In the third session Mike mentioned that his mother-in-law was ill with asthma most of her life, especially in the current season. Did I know how she felt having suffered not breathing as a child.

"Let's take a look at her chakra energy," I said, pulling out some paper. This was an opportunity for Fred and Mike to learn about absent healings. I wrote the mother-in-law's name on the paper, drew a matchstick person and the locale of each chakra energy center. "Now I'll use my pendulum and see how her energy flows from the top of her crown to her base." Fred and Mike were fascinated. "The energy in most of her chakras is blocked," I stated. I then concentrated my thoughts and energies on her with my hands on the paper, just as I would if she were in the room, freeing each energy chakra into swirling clockwise again. "Please let me know how she's doing," I said upon completion.

Mike decided to give his mother-in-law a ring right at my place. She talked excitedly, "It's funny you should call and ask me that. This hour I've suddenly felt wonderful—

better than I have for decades !" Fred and Mike were awed, as was I. I have enjoyed watching the Creator work through me in absent healings over the years. I focus on a photograph if I have one or a basic drawing as I did with Fred and Mike. It is inspiring to all the family and friends involved.

Mike always accompanied Fred, both true healing believers by then. He waited patiently watching his dad and me work. As he sat he'd look around especially at a painting of Christ hung on the wall. Mike continued to feel the warm, glowing energies generated by our sessions. After we'd finished one particular healing Mike remained seated, staring straight at the Christ painting. His eyes grew wider as he exclaimed, "The beams of light from His chest and the angels at his feet...they glowed...and the hand—Christ's hand waved at me !" Fred and I looked at the painting and tried seeing what Mike had seen. We couldn't, but the look on Mike's face convinced us.

Mike confided another time, "Sometimes I know exactly what's going to happen before it happens. What is that all about, David?"

Mike was awakening spiritually ! "This means you are a psychic sensitive, Mike. You have a sixth sense and an awareness of the Spirit dimension of life." Egged-on by our sessions with his dad, Mike began reading and studied healing and clairvoyance.

Word of mouth through Fred, Mike, their garage clientele, and Dr. Browne's referrals positively grew my reputation. Healing times were booked every day at the flat. In the Kent area, I was known as the one people went to after they'd spent years trying to get well. From full body covered eczema and chronic back pain, to chronic iritis and chondromalcia, we teamed together—client and healer—and attained complete healings with continued remissions. Some individuals went out of their way to tell others about our good healing results, bringing a friend or colleague in for healing. Still others never admitted they'd been to see me. Modern cultures are puzzled by successes using spiritual energy healing. In this age of science healings cannot be fully explained. Medical doctors often refer to complimentary medicine when modern science appears in failure and people who become healed are at times afraid of what their friends, family and colleagues would say if they knew about their spiritual energy sessions. Such is the paradoxical acceptance of a healer's work.

During my first year of practice AIDS patients were the most distressing. One year I met an eighteen-year-old man who was far along with AIDS, and I counseled him almost daily at Dartford. He shared with me, "Yeah, I go out every night having as many boys or men as I can, all unprotected sex everywhere in London." My counseling skills were challenged with this young soul. I listened as I always did, but hated saying good-bye and knowing he was out there every night between his hospital treatments and my counseling trying to commit murder. I struggled and prayed. *Should I try talking him out of his destructive behaviour?* I decided to seek my superior's advice.

"What am I to do, call the police?" I asked my boss.

"Nothing. You can do absolutely nothing. We are not here to judge, only to listen. We do our treatments. We counsel. It is his life and we cannot live it for him." With that he turned his white coated back and walked away.

How disappointed I was at such a callous sounding attitude. However, his words were the brilliant pearls of the wisest of counseling lessons. I knew my job. I knew I could not judge but listen, educate and heal. That was the lot of it. My boss was correct and I suddenly saw counseling in an all important new light. I chose my words even more carefully trying to make every sentence count after that shocking advice.

Oh, how I mourned for the boys and men this chap met in the coming nights.

In spite of my varied client base and increased experience, I always took to heart the AIDS patients. They seemed so far gone into dis - ease. Their personal and spiritual troubles were almost untouchable, it seemed to me. I reached a low point in lack of effectiveness with some people. As with my mother and father I could not understand why some people did not heal nor could I reach them. I surmised it was for God to know and the patients' free will in choosing the life they led. I struggled with that disease. My mind knew I had to find a way to live beside these devastatingly ill and often careless individuals. They lived on the same planet as my loved ones. *How do I cope? How do I face this awful sickness day after day?*

Then came a thirty-three year old man, Maxwell. The Dartford counselors recommended he have daily sessions with me, if he chose, for he was deteriorating so rapidly. Issues of guilt and anger over his past lifestyle involving frequent visits to bathhouses in LA and San Francisco came up in our sessions. He had lived a flagrantly unprotected life with untold hours subjecting himself to countless men. I listened with absolutely no judgements but loads of praying. I unblocked his chakra centers, counseled more and his pain diminished. Each day we surfaced evermore anger and guilt and his painful cycle would spin again.

October 1992. Maxwell was moved to intensive care with chest problems. AIDS patients were isolated on one floor but Maxwell had been moved to a ward with general patients of all kinds, still in a private room. He needed critical attention besides the AIDS. No other patients knew exactly what was the cause of his ailments of course, due to confidentiality. "What am I doing in here with everybody?" Maxwell growled at me. "I am responsible for AIDS being passed around the world and you brought me here to finish me off?" His anger was massive.

The following weeks were cut out for me. "Maxwell, this room is so we can give you the best care. The breathing equipment and intensive care nurses are right here for you." He was loud, abusive and filled with grief. I listened. The normally festive time before Christmas was consumed with Maxwell. For example: Maxwell was mistakenly given silverware in place of the 'plastic utensils *only* order'. Maxwell approached me with a knife set to stab away, screaming obscenities. I settled him and myself with hour upon hour of quiet counseling.

I prayed, meditated and communicated with God morning and nighttime. I asked the Lord for guidance for I was completely at a loss. *What were the right words?* I felt ineffectual with Maxwell. I struggled with the lack of morals and ethics often fogging my days. Maxwell had done this to himself and I was not to resent his illness, simply care for him as a living, ailing soul. It was gut wrenching work.

God answered my need. I began receiving help through an odd form: letters from people who meditated and were given messages addressed to David Cunningham ! These people did not know me, yet remarkably found me by Spirit and angel guidance. They transcribed the messages and found ways to connect with and send me these important pieces of Spirit guidance. Excerpts are included below to share with you what I consider Godsends through a horrendous period in my healer's journey.

Message from the Spirit world from Joshua through Kathy (whom I do not know):
November 8, 1992 - Message for David Cunningham

May I ask wisdom for a man who is called David Cunningham, whom I know nothing about?

We can offer you information for him: This person is a man who has many opportunities to progress into the realm of the Light. He has many helpers beside him at present; he has the ability to become a medium of great distinction and will endeavour to enlighten many people's souls.

Those who seek David's wisdom will respond to his words and they will be able to accept the journey that we all have to take. Our destinies are already marked for each and every one of the Earth plane. It will be a natural progression for David to be a leader in the realms of Spiritual Guidance. He will become a beacon of light for all to obtain the knowledge they seek in becoming the Souls of Light.

Many will need much understanding for they are not so evolved (in the Spirit) and so David will enlighten these people so that in time their journeys will become less painful.

Wisdom is like a song sung by the followers of Love and Light, it is given freely to those who search and ask. David must continue to be aware of this potential he has and use it wisely and not allow his head to rule his heart. There have been many opportunities for him to be a master of many trades but he has put before him barriers. Now they must begin to be removed, from this will spring many avenues of opportunities that will enable him to experience the true David—the David he wishes.

So my Daughter, give these words of wisdom (to David), it will enable him to see how we can all accomplish the heights we set ourselves, provided we truly wish it to happen.

After I read this letter I fell to the floor shaking. When I woke the next day I felt stronger and more loved than ever. Wendy, my patients and now even strangers were helping me understand how to love and heal myself along with others. I absorbed new energy as I healed and counseled at the hospital. On a particularly sad day, I re-

read the letter for strength after I found Maxwell crawling on the floor licking it and all the trash cans repeating over and over, "Maybe I'll finally get enough germs inside me to die !"

I pulled him back to bed and went into my focused hospital care routine. Using traditional, old-fashioned syringes I drew Maxwell's blood. Like a slow-motion movie I watched his eyes as I moved the lethal vials out of reach and off to the laboratory. "Now Maxwell, you wouldn't want to hurt me?" He grinned. Until I had the syringe secured I felt like Maxwell's hostage. I was never sure if he wanted to take me to death along with him.

Christmas Eve, 1992. Maxwell was semi-consciousness during the day while I tended other patients. I returned to his bedside after Christmas eve dinner where I found him with his mother and sister. As I approached, I realized he was frothing at his nose and ears with blood and his mother was dabbing it up with cotton. I rushed to the head nurse and explained, "We cannot tolerate bleeding all over people. Maxwell must be tended to at once !" She looked at me. Rattled, I said innocently, "Something has to be done. This is dangerous." Again, she looked long and hard at me then picked up the phone, ringing one of my colleagues. A doctor was on the way she said. I went back to be with Maxwell. Within a few minutes a fresh, young resident arrived. "Mr. Cunningham will you clear the area please?" he whispered. I nodded and did so.

Time passed and I finally walked back from the waiting area where I'd been counseling Maxwell's mother and sister. The doctor whispered, "He is too far gone with the disease. He's passing now." I rushed to bring Maxwell's mum and sister to his bedside. The baby-faced doctor stood against the wall, pulling me back and giving room for the family to speak their love. Maxwell passed into the Spirit filled with peace—a condition I'd never had the privilege of seeing in him before. I closed my eyes fighting tears.

A senior staff member arrived, "Are you all right, David?" I nodded. "Will you take Maxwell's mother and sister home?" I nodded again. This was Christmas eve, of course I'd give them a lift. After I dropped them home I went back to my flat realizing how much I cared and how much of me I had spent trying to help Maxwell. This patient did die in peace, I knew, but I felt drained by his struggle. I opened a bottle of wine and got drunk.

Christmas Day was to be spent with Dr. Browne and his family. I heard knocking—Dr. Sam ! I managed to get myself up and dressed, surely looking the worst for wear. Dr. Sam asked, "David, what happened?" I told them every detail on the way to their home. Dr. Browne understood so well, having been in the profession of healing for some fifty years. "David, don't worry about a thing. We're taking care of you for a couple of days." Dear Dr. Browne knew. Death was inevitable but it still was sad when the process was slow and painful. The AIDS epidemic really hit home, devastating me. In a way the AIDS patients' suffering was as harsh and cruel as Baghdad.

I could not shake it.

Maxwell.

AIDS.

The HIV plague.

What are we to do, Lord? I drank more than I should have that Christmas. *What are these awful diseases— AIDS, cancer?*

January 1993. I carried on. Such a dichotomy, being an HIV-AIDS counselor, yet being obligated to keep all my work confidential, almost forced to stuff the sadness inside. It was a stressful time in healthcare history with the discovery of how AIDS was transmitted. I kept peace within families, yet counseled members of those families through gut-wrenching emotional and physically violent pain. Untold stories of unimaginable lifestyles consumed my waking hours. I had to keep everything secret between families, between friends. There was massive fear everywhere, in all factions of the public.

My managers did not want to hear of it either. On several occasions I attempted to discuss my growing depression amid the AIDS tragedies. The reality was that most medical personnel were taught to hide behind a wall of protection against feeling for their patients. They shrugged their shoulders at personal distress. I finally went to my friend Wendy. "I need a formal counseling session with you. I am in great depression."

Wendy was kind and skilled. She listened. I was comforted that she knew the hospital unit's circumstances. She, too, worked under the disturbing, often futile AIDS conditions. Ethics, morals and personal values were tested—along with personal limits of patience—every day. I broke down in a torrent of tears in her office.

Wendy said, "This profession can either make or break a person. You have time-off coming?" I quivered and shook my head yes. "David, save yourself and take the time. Go somewhere beautiful with good friends and place your work aside. It is the only way to survive the healthcare industry." I hugged her farewell for the day. I knew the AIDS counseling days were numbered for me. I could not see myself 'hardening' to people's troubles.

My long needed vacation plans took me to Kidderminster in Worcestershire, Midlands, U.K.. Rustie Lee, a friend and television star I'd met at a cabaret show working in Dubai, put me up. I stayed in a gorgeous little hotel overlooking the Seven River in Bewdley. Marty Kyle, a so-called American millionaire, was also there with his entourage. Rustie knew him and said, "Oh, he's known for his wheelings and dealings, David. He is very wealthy. I'll introduce you for fun."

In relaxing over the next few days Marty and I got along well. He asked me what I did for a living; I explained that I was a spiritual healer and counselor. By his comments I learned that he was familiar with energy centers and healing.

"I have always been interested in your area of expertise. I wouldn't mind setting up a healing centre here, if you'll come down to manage it."

"I'll think about it," I replied.

I flew to my room and prayed for guidance. In spite of Marty Kyle's flamboyant reputation, he seemed sincere. My own clinic would be an answer to my prayers and a graceful way out of what I saw as AIDS caregiver burnout. My one year hospital contract was almost up. I decided to write Dr. Key a letter of resignation.

I did not have a contract with Marty, but on good faith and my desire to have my own full time healing practice, I closed-up my life in Kent. Mike, Fred's son, had become an understudy of mine. He'd developed a high degree of sensibilities and some healing energy transference. I was worried about my patients. *Who would I turn to, who would care for them?* I prayed over this and Mike was my one answer. I called him upon my return to Dartford. He came over, eager to learn whatever it was I had in mind. "Mike, I am taking this opportunity to open up a healing center with an investor."

Mike looked down in his lap and swallowed. "David, I don't feel right about your move. Please don't do it."

"Mike, I'll be fine. It is a chance to practice my gift with even more patients." I appreciated his concern. I continued, "Mike, I need your support. My clients here need you to carry on healings for them." Mike looked surprised. I kept on, "I know you can do it. You've shown sensitivity and healing energies already. I am going to now transfer the Divine's light energy and skill to boost what you already have inside you."

Mike's eyes grew wide as I placed my hands on his shoulders. "Dear God, please energize Mike to carry on my work."

I chose the new clinic path, in spite of Mike's uneasiness. Within a month he was healing my patients and more ! I asked Dr. Browne to give me a recommendation letter which I share with you below.

Dr. Samuel E. Brown - Professional Recommendation Letter
RE: David Cunningham, Master Healer   1992 London

To Whom It May Concern:

In the hope that other doctors may be interested, I would like to record my experience of referring patients to a healer, David L. Cunningham, for treatment of various health problems.

My first referral was actually my own daughter who on her return from a skiing holiday was crippled with an acute exacerbation of chondromalacia, which was not helped by intensive physiotherapy or orthopaedic consultations. Two healing sessions (with David Cunningham) completely relieved her pain; as a skeptic beforehand she was particularly impressed by the tremendous feeling of heat radiating from the hands of the healer. Even more dramatic was the experience of a trainee doctor in our practice who was losing three days per week from work because of severe chronic iritis, which was not responding to treatment at Moorfields but which was completely relieved by two sessions of healing and has remained in remission since.

Other patients treated included a man of 22 with chronic severe eczema who had complete relief as did his mother with recurrent asthma. A man of 70 who was house bound with a stroke recovered enough power in his affected arm and leg to allow him to do his own shopping. Another patient who had been unable to work for a year with severe lumbar disc problems was able to return to work after two sessions.

Results like these are difficult to credit but observing the healer at work one is aware that something meaningful is happening to the patient and that a powerful source of energy is being channeled through the healer's hands.

It is well worthwhile to refer any patient for healing particularly if they are not responding to normal treatment. It was made easier for me to make the first referral because of what I still think is a minor miracle which happened to a friend and patient of mine three years ago. I had tried every treatment I knew for her severe post-herpetic pain of two years standing including acupuncture, local steroid injections and deep hypnosis without effect. She referred herself to the healer who produced a permanent cure in one half-hour session.

Of all these patients the most abiding memory is of my trainee lady doctor crying with the pain of her iritis despite heavy doses of steroids and the next working day happily smiling in her morning surgery.

Dr. S. E. Browne, 1992
Kent, London
United Kingdom

I sold my furnishings and moved from Kent to a marvelous suite provided by Marty Kyle on the River Seven. All I had was my clothing and a dream, but the suite was wonderful accommodation and soon I was booked with healings through to July. As I lived there, I got to know Marty, who seemed an odd, unpredictable duck. On the surface he was more than amiable, yet there was an underlying current we could not pinpoint. Margaret more than agreed when she and Jim came to visit. Margaret, who is very intuitive and psychic said, "David, watch that man. Something is not right with him." Again I told yet another someone that I would be fine. Margaret knew it was a chance at what I'd been looking for—to heal more people—however she did not have confidence in Marty. I forged on, tending to my healings, making terrific healing progress with my clients.

There were signs though. Marty's entourage lived in half the hotel including Marty's daughter, various financial advisors, his girlfriend, and 'hangers-on' or 'groupies' in the lingo of famous folk. I heard hotel staff grumblings that his bill was mounting to tens of thousands with not even a down payment. The hotel management I'd befriended was suspicious and I was leaning that way as well. Marty was supposedly covering my suite financially. Would I have an unplanned expense soon?

One weekend in July, 1993, the hotel was completely reserved for a wedding, so we were required to move out for three days. The entourage had arranged rooms for everyone in an alternate hotel. Marty's girlfriend came up to me that morning and said, "Since we have to go to another hotel for the weekend Marty asked me to ask you, David, if we could borrow your credit card."

Bells rang off in my head. "I do not have a credit card." I then practically ran away from her, hopped in my car, drove to Rustie's and told her the scenario. Rustie agreed I needed to get away. I called the hotel manager and told her what I knew. "I must move. Please have my extra bills ready, I will be there this evening." I would stay the weekend at Rustie's. I went to Marty and gave him my termination letter. I was honest and explained that I did not feel right about things. I thanked him and we parted, shaking hands.

Within one week the Fraud Squad investigators of British Police Force had invaded Marty's Midlands offices, arresting Marty and his girlfriend. Marty had a draft in his possession worth 3½ million pounds. The illegal bank note was in the confiscated papers along with my departure letter. It didn't take long for the investigators to reach me.

"The department has followed Marty Kyle for years. The hotel and his office telephones were monitored." I thought of the warnings from Margaret and Mike. *Dear*

God, how could I not have listened to these trusted souls?
In that one decision though, I had learned so much, so
quickly. The detective continued, "When we spotted the
recent illegal bank transference we pounced. Kyle is one
of the most wanted financial con men around." I informed
the police that Marty was to cover my hotel suite and that
he'd paid me directly for healing sessions until we got
the clinic under way. Fortunately, I paid my extra bills such
as telephone, before I moved out of the hotel and proved
these actions with my receipts. The police had no
problems with me and we parted on good, clean terms. I
found out later from the newspapers that Marty was jailed
for five years, then would be extradited to the States. Marty
owed that one hotel some $ 40,000. Blessings that I never
had a credit card to loan him. I've not seen him since.

Thank God for friends. Rustie had a house she
shared with her friend and son. The house did not have
room for a fourth. I was generously welcomed and stayed.
I knew it was not for long for we found an unfurnished
house owned by Rustie's friend. I loved the Midlands and
the new little house, but it was unheated and I knew the
English North winds. I lived through the autumn anyway
because it was my best and only choice.

Healing work was next on my agenda. I'd gone so far
in healing, I didn't want to go back to the hotel catering
trade. Thus, I went on public assistance and received 35
pounds/week for expenses and rent. During my
healthcare job search, it was evermore clear that my
reputation was in tact, but it was back in Dartford. *Now
what, Lord?* At least in Baghdad, I had rice, cucumber
and tomato; during this period I had all I could do to feed
myself.

I look back on those days as a perfect example of
the paradox that is life on earth. There I was in Bewdley,
Midlands, on the Seven River. One could not ask for a
more beautiful setting in which to live, yet my lovely

cottage had no heat. I possessed a fine reputation and a good living paying my bills on time, but it was all back in Kent. Healers advertise only by word of mouth, but I had to see clients in order to build a word of mouth business in the Midlands. Paradoxes abounded. I cinched in my belt and set out meeting people, my old stand-by technique. I had a few healing sessions, word passed on and I was asked to do a radio interview. Then I read about the local Spiritualist Church's healing services on Thursday evenings.

Seek and ye shall find. Ask and it will be provided.

I went to the church the very first week I rented the house and offered my services in their healing group. I was formally accepted and committed to them weekly. We worked as a team of 4-5 healers and conducted group healings in big circles. Each healer was drawn to whom he or she would work. After introductions, chakras were explained and checked and healings went on from there.

One Thursday shortly after my move, a lady and her friend came and watched with reserve. As I walked closer to the people sitting in my group, I shook hands and personally welcomed them. I was drawn to the lady and asked, "Why did you come tonight?" She explained that she wanted to learn more about types of healing since she was a hypnotherapist. I listened and thought she was truly striking. She ended, "The way my life has been going, I'm trying to discover the spiritual side of things."

"Fantastic. What is your name?"

"Petra." I looked at each person in the group and back to Petra. A strong affinity—a familiar knowing—came over me: Petra was to be an important guide in my life. She returned weekly and we did some healing together. With both of us in the field of healing we forged a great professional friendship.

Petra worked from an office overlooking a park in Bewdley about two kilometers from Kidderminster. She had a good following and loved her work relieving stress through hypnosis. Hypnotherapy fascinated me. I did regression therapy with Petra to find out my past lives. I never have had the ability to regress and Petra helped me learn much about my past as a healer.

I was thrilled making friends and professional contacts. Financially, I was not better, for the church work paid nothing save donations from the good attendees. I felt strongly that I was gaining as a healer in Kidderminster and carried on networking with as many people as I possibly could each day. My old friend David Northey telephoned. "How are you, David?"

"David Northey, you *are* psychic. I've lost my living wage with Marty Kyle. The man is in prison as we speak." He was shocked and asked once again if I would work at his hotel over Christmas. "If I did have heat in my house I might not consider you offer. The prospect of Christmas in your comfortable, heated country inn delights me already." We laughed. I called the church and told them I'd see them in January, immediately closed my house and off I went by train to be gainfully employed in nice, warm Yorkshire. We worked feverishly and spent Christmas and New Year's week enjoying time off. Margaret, Jim and the children drove down and brought me back to Northeast England for Christmas with relatives. I had a little money then and high hopes for the upcoming year.

January 2, 1994. I returned to the little closed-up rental house. It was Dr. Zhivago's Siberian summer cottage in winter ! Icicles hung from moist window glazing, frost, or was it snow, covered every surface in a blanket of crystal white. I stayed in my coat and cranked the portable gas heater, carrying it from room to room. I kept all of my clothes on for three or four days hoping to capture any heat energy I possibly could. I was miserable. Where were my warm ocean breeze spots on the seashore? I tried meditating about them daily. I layered sweaters and socks. Never warmed me fully. In despair I called a friend in London and asked if I might visit to discuss moving in with him. I didn't have to pack much, I wore it all on my back. *Dear Lord, I am in need of guidance.* I prayed all the way to London hoping to sort out my life and get back into healing. After a couple of days we decided my moving in on a permanent basis would be a good plan and I returned to close my life in Bewdley. A letter waited in my cottage post box. It was another message from a stranger, a channeled letter from the Spirit:

January 2, 1994. The Blessed Mary spoke through Kathy to David Cunningham:

"Beloved One, you above all others within the group (of spiritual energy healers & guides) and need more healing than any other. Why is this so? For, Beloved Child, your body, your chakras, your aura must be so pure and so light to receive the true energy of my Son. At present, Beloved One, the chakras in connection with the Divine Light are the Crown and the Third-Eye. Here is where the Light anchors. However, Beloved, there is some interference within the lower chakras. You are resisting releasing some old pains, some karmic links and they are still corded to you. You cannot uncord (get chakra energies back into swirling clockwise) them alone and this channel-medium has been requested to assist you in this healing process…the Light has intended to embed in the lower level, your Heart Chakra, but there was resistance at your Throat Chakra. All this I tell you, Beloved, so that you may take action."

Beloved means David. David means Beloved. Thank you, Lord. I re-read the letter many times and vowed to begin healing again that very day, I was filled with such love. I knew things would be better soon after reading that letter. I meditated and prayed and went to see Petra. "I simply must leave. The house is lovely but not in winter. My life seems finished here. I must carry on healing back at Dartford where I have my reputation and clientele."

"Oh, what a shame, David. We're just getting to know one another."

That was true, I'd only just begun to get close to my Thursday groups and Petra. I went back to the cottage to think. The house was damp and cold. I prayed. *Dear God, I do not believe in suicide. Please take me back home, back into the Spirit.* I was spent, not even a tear left. I had a loving letter, a place with heat in London and hope seemed as up and down as a roller coaster.

Then Petra called.

She volunteered to help in any way.

We discussed her options. She lived in Kinver and worked out of the Bewdley flat. We finally agreed that I would stay in the office flat as a live-in apartment and we would work together out of an office in Kidderminster, two kilometers from the Bewdley flat. Petra stated that whatever housing subsidy I currently had would satisfy the rent. What a whirlwind of emotions ! I was out of the refrigerator and into the lovely park apartment Petra had shown me. *Thank you God for the contrasts of life. May I appreciate the positive whenever I am living the reverse.*

Petra had been struggling for years in her marriage to Chris. In spite of 24 years of abuse, she had made a personal vow not to leave until her son, James, was older. My situation and her means to move into another office in Kidderminster afforded us an opportunity to join professional forces. We shared an advert in the local papers and formed a small practice in the joint office over a year. It was a very good modest life. Our practices were small but rewarding.

Petra was a long standing member of the Association of Stress Management and introduced me to the group of highly professional healers and healthcare givers. Through my work with Petra and our local reputations in the Thursday groups, I was asked to demonstrate a healing session at the Association of Stress Management Annual General Conference nearby. I was nervous thinking of being in front of over 100 professionals with a video camera up my nose taping the whole while. Petra worked on my stress management and reminded me that it was all just what I loved doing: sharing my healing gift with others. *This is what you love doing, David. This is what you love doing...this is...*I repeated Petra's comforting words over and over.

Shortly before the conference I received another letter of guidance. The timing was perfect, as always.

> June 7, 1994 Trisha channeled a message for David Cunningham by Sananda(Jesus):
>
> David is a being of golden light, from out the Central Sun.
> Soon to be recognized within the Earth Plane...
> Enclose those who search within that (Golden) mantle.
> Heal them, protect them, lead them to the Light
> Sing the song of Ascension, link hands of Light
> around the Earth so that she, with you, will ascend into the Light.
> Work together, reconnect lost memories (in meditation),lifetimes with family,
> working for the Light, with the Light, and through the Light.
> Loving and supporting Me and each other.
> Remember - Reawaken - Re-create that which is and will be...

I breathed in deeply as the letter's message calmed and strengthened me for those hundred professionals, some of whom were surely skeptics. *Stay with your true purpose, David. Heal those who are ready.* The conference began by Petra introducing me to many serious professional healers who generously shared their healing philosophies and work. My session time arrived and I worked without a hitch. I focused on the volunteer patient and not the video camera, nor the 200 eyes focused upon me. After the session I found that the Association of Stress Management's attentive audience was filled with individuals who had been highly affected from within. They had participated with us on stage ! One woman came directly after my conclusion and said, "I saw an angel standing behind you !"

"I saw a red light coming out of your healing hands," shouted another.

I thanked Petra for her help and for including me in the conference. Several stress management professionals requested private sessions and I booked the rest of the day doing some half a dozen healings that evening.

The last powerful session of the conference was with a hypnotherapist, George. At the end of our healing I called his name gently, arousing him from the depths of meditation. "George…George…" It usually took one or two calls and clients open their eyes. This gentleman did not awaken after ten minutes. I raised my voice for fear he was more than just in a trance. "GEORGE !" *My God, has he left the body never to return?* At last, some twelve minutes after my first call, George came back from wherever he'd been. Opening his eyes he said, "Dear God, what did you do to me?"

"Just my normal healing session, Sir."

"I have just had an experience with God !" His face was blanched in a form of shock, wobbling as he sat up. "I have a plane to catch home to Scotland," he said, slowly regaining a bit of composure. I made sure he got into a taxi, grateful he was flying rather than driving. He was in no way compus mentius. Hopefully, by the time his plane landed he would be functioning properly.

At the end of the conference I was approached by a couple of therapist attendees who had local practices. "Are you available? We think many patients will be interested in your healing technique." We shook on it and my private healing practice was set to fly.

Thank you, Lord, for Petra.

What an exhilarating, energizing conference day. I laid down for sleep, but couldn't. I had more of God's energy than I'd ever had and was brimming wide awake with excitement. Then George, the hypnotherapist, called, "David, your healing was deeply profound. As I replayed it in my mind on the plane I realized I healed others during my healing session with you ! Your healing hands have changed my life. Thank you upon thank you." I slept very well indeed after George's good news.

Through the colleagues in the Association of Stress Management, I had the pleasure of building clinics in various therapists' practices all over England: the West Country, the Midlands, Yorkshire, across to the East Linlconshire and even Frankfurt, Germany. I was asked to do work with a German woman outside Frankfurt, whom I visited by flying to her house on numerous weekends. My weeks were filled to the brim at last. Additionally, I received more letters from strangers who sent the messages they received during their prayerful, still time.

July 5, 1994 Through Kathy, Joshua spoke:

Words of wisdom for David Cunningham: He has much talent but needs to initiate himself in the world of spiritual planes. Time has gone before and after his pledges to give the world a new teacher. He has many times attempted to emulate the wishes of the Spirit but constantly turns away from his responsibilities. For it is our wish you now join forces of Light in order that the Universal Plan is put into action (plan for all to join in the Light).

For you both are of the same pathway homeward. You come from the world of the stars and so does the being David Cunningham. Jointly, it is ordained that you must go forth and sing praises of the Lord and show poor beings whose Light doth not shine so brightly, the way homewards.

…Yes, yes we mean him to preach to the masses but in a way that is transcribed in modern language. Surely you know this to be true, David of Light.

Re-reading this passage always takes my breath away.

Mike and his wife Lynn, from Dartford, also remained a large part of my new life in Bewdley. We communicated on the phone frequently, especially about clients I had seen or if someone in his family needed healing. Mike and I developed strong absent healing techniques over the phone together. Before I left Dartford, Mike's wife, Lynn, had been plagued for years with migraine headaches— twenty-one years of pain. I'd worked with her once, but afterward Lynn said, "I feel as if you've drilled a hole in my head and relieved all of the pressure." Following this session, Mike had reported she never had another migraine again, a few headaches but not of migraine caliber.

One day, Mike called sounding disturbed. "David? Lynn was taking out the Sunday roast and badly burned her hand. Can we do an absent healing together?"

"Mike, of course. I will use your hands. Place them on the burn and pray with me." He did this as I spoke aloud, "Light of Lights please mend Lynn's skin and relieve her pain." I closed my eyes and concentrated.

Then Mike spoke," David, healing is an amazing thing ! We've witnessed the big red blister melt away. Lynn's hand is fully healed !" I smiled. "Thank you, David."

I wished him a good Sunday supper. My body, my energy centers were feeling very bright indeed.

I spent much of my time living in Bewdley and either driving to sessions or healing. It was exhilarating, successful and I reveled in sharing it all with my partner and soul mate, Petra. Here are some of their stories.

*** One gentleman came for help oppressed from work. Only in his thirties, he had extensive allopecia with not a hair on his head. After only one session he returned the following week with hair growing in again.

*** I was called to the East of England by a woman whose husband had major surgery but awoke paralyzed. John had one of the first aorta replacements with early side effects of pain down one leg and paralyzation in his other leg. I drove to their sprawling, gorgeous home on the sea where their garage had been remodeled to accommodate his condition. John desperately wanted to get well. "Look," he told me, "I don't believe in your kind of stuff. My wife called you so I'll try anything. Get on with it."

I cautiously explained my work and found all his center chakras and his left and right sides blocked. His left side energy was stagnant making the leg appear dead. I worked on re-flowing his energy, particularly focusing on his left side with my energized hands. He opened his eyes and said, "David, I can feel my left leg. It isn't dead !" His wife stood with us, all cried with elation. This was one of the most powerful sessions of my healing life to date and the first time a paralyzed limb awoke in my hands. Tears still come when I think of John. I later traveled back to see him and focused on his painful right leg. The last word was that John walked with crutches. He's

learned to drive with a specially equipped car no less !
(An interesting aside: John remains skeptical of my work
with God and tells no one of our teamwork.)

*** Jacob, a man in his late forties, had a malignant
tumour in his chest and was sent home to die because
the tumour was too large for surgery. I did four sessions
with him. Between the third and fourth session he went
back to the medical doctors for tests. "My tumour is
completely gone, David. It was not just shrunk, it is all
gone ! They still suggest surgery in case there's any
tumour left. They don't believe the test results !" Jacob
was beside himself. I asked what he was going to do.
Jacob was covering all bases and going ahead with
surgery. He visited after the surgery to tell me the news
in person. When they cut him open not one doctor could
find a trace of the tumour. Jacob's still doing fine today.

*** The wife of a famous English ball player and star
came to me with a large tumour in her breast. She was
scheduled for a mastectomy but heard of my work and
wanted desperately to save her breast and get well again.
I suggested we do intensive work together in several
sessions during the three weeks before her scheduled
surgery. When she went for surgery the physician could
not find the lump on her films. They decided to go in
anyway when they found nothing but a little black seed
covered in skin. Her surgeon wrote 'miracle' upon her file
in red ink.

The lady's famous husband had numerous pains
from ball playing injuries, so she asked me to do several
sessions with him. He was quite the Jack the Lad and
too skeptical to discuss his troubles with me. Later that
year this woman's husband, in his early thirties, passed
away. She told me of the day when she came home and
found him slumped in his chair. He was rushed to the

hospital but by 6 p.m. he passed away. It was discovered that he had a significant brain tumour. She cried and I suggested talking another time when she was less upset. She continued, needing to tell me more, "I've something special to share with you, David. I went to a Spiritualist Church in South London the week after my husband's funeral. During the evening, a clairvoyant said to me, "Your husband is here with me. He says he has only been in the world of Spirit a short time but he wants to tell you what happened." The clairvoyant then passed on his message, "When I was lying in the hospital bed and you were sitting around loving me, I floated above, seeing my body and all my family. I saw the tubes and machinery attached to my body. Then…then I was shown what my life would be like if I remained on the earth plane: a life like a vegetable. I decided to detach myself from my body and go on with my journey." I assured her that he was happy and still with us in many ways, for no one dies. We only pass out of physical bodies back into Spirit. She smiled.

Later telephone calls from her confirmed an ongoing Spiritual relationship that was very fulfilling to them both. I feel absolute joy that this doubting man realized his loving Sprit has been energized in helping his wife grow in Spirit with him !

*** "Would you please come do some healing with my cat?" I heard a Mrs. McKenley say on the telephone. *Cat? I could, I supposed. Why not? Pets were important friends and such loving souls to humans.* "I'd be happy to, Madam," I replied. I drove the fifty miles to a small vintage, terraced house. Mrs. McKenley opened her home; its small rooms were reasonably furnished and quite comfortable. "I know Inkie's nearing his end. I want his last time filled with more action, more energy !" Mrs. McKenley introduced me to a beautiful, old black cat, her companion for years. I placed the cat on the coffee table and worked through his chakras. He was most cooperative, sitting complacently for the full hour session. I bid farewell and asked Mrs. McKenley to ring and let me know how things worked out. I made my way back home from the kitty session; the phone rang as I opened the door. "You'll never guess what happened after you left." Mrs. McKenley could hardly contain her voice she was speaking so rapidly, "I let Inkie out for a bit of air and watched him jump right over the roof of my garage !" She giggled through more details still laughing as she hung up.

Ah, the power of God's love for all living souls.

Early 1995, Petra and I moved together into a four story Victorian house with wonderfully big rooms, in Kidderminster about a two hour's drive south to London. We planned on dual healing practices out of our home leaving plenty of space for Petra's son James, then age fifteen. Petra was busy with local clientele. I was still traveling and would not have as many sessions in our new home as on the road. I was grateful for all the healings no matter how far away. I reveled in my new life with a soul mate and a little family all my own. James and I got along famously. He is a joy in my life.

Hours after our move I looked up the center staircase and witnessed a man hanging himself. Obviously, it was a Spirit manifestation. I did not tell Petra, as I wanted our

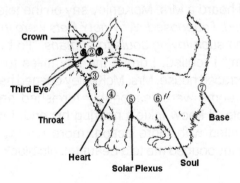

life together to begin on a positive note. I wondered about the shocking vision nonetheless, especially with me being away often.

Soon the three of us realized the troubled Spirit ways of our new home. Noises, items falling and even footsteps were heard running in every room of the house, up and down the stairs. Doors slammed when James was out, when Petra and I knew we were the only physical bodies in the house. Never a dull minute.

Christine, a talented clairvoyant and friend, was finally solicited to help us tune into the history of our grand abode. Christine meditated in various rooms and gave us the following history from her Spirit guides: A little girl was burned alive in the top right bedroom. Her guardian uncle was unable to save his niece and hung himself from the fourth story banister in his grief. Christine's reading solved the puzzle and gave us a plan to move forward in the house peacefully. Through the following months we tried connecting with and releasing the poor souls by befriending them and placing them in a more peaceful state with our love and care. Souls sometimes are not ready to go back home into the Spirit world because of their trauma. Being at peace with the karma of one's life allows one's own Spirit to move back home.

In addition I read the energy of the house and land on which it was built. The art of healing is not only for humans and animals but also for the earth. Running in a myriad of criss-cross lines, throughout the land masses of the planet are energies called 'Ley Lines'. The energy streams manifest as either negative or positive vibrations. If a building was constructed on a piece of property with a negative Ley Line activity within the structure may be affected. The building could have a strange, negative feeling, unsettling the people in it. Relationships may go awry or health problems occur. Our home's Ley Lines were neutral, but the Victorian Spirits who had lived in it remained in disharmony.

We invited other psychic friends to converse with Spirit because wild things kept us on edge. For example, all at once the four gas stove burners would alight. We'd iron and the plug would shoot out of the wall. The joys of our relationship and my efforts to befriend Petra's son were strained. Perhaps the house was a reason why I kept the intense healing travel schedule was to be away from the house. I remained fit, energized and on the road throughout the house Spirit strife.

March, 1995, Petra's 50th birthday, James and I connived a surprise gala at a favourite restaurant complete with a police-clad male stripper for a little entertainment. Some sixty friends gathered prior to my arrival with the birthday gal. They hid in the back party room titillated by the plans in store.

"Surprise !" Petra was a laughing school girl with our large surprise party guest jumping out from all corners ! Champagne corks popped, merriment abounded when, "Miss," the uniformed stripper interrupted, tapping Petra's shoulder as she drank champagne toast. "You've got to move your car this moment, it's blocking the fire lane." Petra stood-up shocked, having never received so much as a traffic citation. She grabbed her keys when the man ripped off his coat and popped open his shirt's chest buttons. The look on her face and the crowd's swell of laughter were astounding party openers. Even more embarrassing were the motions and gyrations of the man in the face of my lady. Moves I never dreamed of, all in public and in front of dozens of good friends, reddened *my* face. Suddenly, I wanted to catch a spirit and disappear.

"Don't worry, David, I'll get you back," Petra warned. She spoke quietly, but witnesses overheard, laughing evermore. Of course, James was rolling on the carpet in violent laughter. From that point on I lived in fear until my own birthday in June. My mind pondered awful celebrations that could be, instigated by Petra's calm little threat.

Based on my growing UK reputation I was invited to join the Hale Clinic near Harley Street, London. The Hale is the largest Complimentary Medicine Center in the world endorsed by His Royal Highness Prince Charles. HRH actually christened the Hale Clinic opening, some in the 1980's. It was an honour to be invited to practice there.

The Hale Clinic housed fifty-six treatment rooms offering a hundred different types of practitioners and therapists. Treatments served people ranging from Princess Diana to the postman in very professional offices. I thrilled in the opportunity to grow a London patient base and hoped this might cut down on my travel schedule. To start, I rented a Hale Clinic office for Wednesdays and drove four hours round trip to see clients weekly. Coupled with my certification by the National Federation of Spiritual Healers, I sought to build a large enough professional base in one locale to stop travel altogether. Petra and I needed more time together, as did young James and I.

The year before, to support my dedication and reputation all over the United Kingdom, I obtained British healing credentials. I interviewed with the board of the National Federation of Spiritual Healers in London and was asked to demonstrate my God gift. I was accepted that very day.

This highly respected health organization sponsored a course of study involving two years of training, culminating with two more years in practicum. The last certification step was passing the healing test. I intended to show what I was about, demonstrate a healing, then ultimately be admitted to the four year program. Since my skills are innate, with no training save the groups I worked with as I researched healing, I was willing to receive the recognized healer training. The Federation's certification would afford me the professional status to work with organizations such as the Hale and impress upon patients the serious nature of my healing work. It would afford me the opportunity to aid many more people.

Interview day at the Federation of Spiritual Healers was a marvelous and energizing experience. I focused on my energies and Spirit meditation and cannot tell you what any of the reviewers looked like, I was so intent on keeping my energies free flowing and strong.

"Come in and tell us about yourself, David." I sat down and away my life's story went, verbiage flying. The Almighty spoke through me of Baghdad, recent healings and concluded with a commitment statement about my promise to God to be a life long healer.

"Please demonstrate a session with one of us." I bowed and followed them to another room. No chakra explanation was necessary for the higher order healers in attendance. A volunteer came forward, lay down on a table and I moved my hands over his body straight away. The room was filled with wondrous, positive, surging energies. I felt strongly that I had affected every board member present as well as the man I laid hands upon. He awoke glowing and stood up.

I waited in the foyer for their decision. I felt wonderfully calm. As usual, I was rejuvenated after the healing, light and bright with the Life Force. I recall the antique crystal chandelier in the foyer sparkled in golden light.

"Will you rejoin us?" I followed the board member. "David, you have passed all of our requirements. You have earned the Federation of Spiritual Healers seal and certificate. Congratulations !"

I stood, shaking the hands of the six men and women of the board, "Thank you ! The Divine's work will be done, I assure you." I literally flew onto the streets of good old

London. I never dreamed they'd give approval certification that day. I thought I would have been accepted into their course study, only. I felt like a zillion pounds, dollars and rubles. I felt as spectacular as God's love.

Spring 1995, I hung the framed certificate on the wall of my new Hale Clinic office and carried on the schedule of healing travels. My London reputation flourished and I met Hayley Mills. (Please see the introduction.) Due to Hayley's public testimony of our healing work, my clientele at the Hale increased dramatically.

June 1995, my 49th birthday. Petra, James and I planned a sort of rehearsal for my fiftieth birthday. I knew of nothing extraordinary in store. Petra's quiet, "Wait until your birthday" comment during the stripper show still made me wonder. They had invited most of our friends from the 60's and 70's to join us in our new Victorian home, including Frank, my old chef friend, who had cancer and needed a boost.

June 11, 1995, 11 a.m., party day. James, a wonderful young man with whom I have love and respect as the son I never had, said, "Go out for a drink with Mum." This didn't make sense, we had 100 people coming and much to prepare. I must have looked puzzled, shaking my head. "No, no, I want to do the rest. Go please !" Petra and I were virtually pushed out the front door, laughing so we went for a drink at a favourite spot. All the while I wondered what was cooking.

Upon return to our lush street we noticed posters tacked on to the trees. Was that the awful photo the me in the buff? Horrified and embarrassed beyond repair, I needed no closer inspection. Each tree had a poster boasting a photo of me face down with my naked bottom in full view—a photo taken by James when I was inebriated one rare and unfortunate occasion earlier in our lives. The captions read, "Bums-up for David, it's his birthday ! TOOT AT HOUSE # 69 !" Petra was hysterical, yet apologized for her son's prank . We grabbed as many posters as possible before friends pulled me away into the party.

My reputation ! I rarely overdid drinking, yet there I was for the world to see.

Cars passed and horns honked the entire afternoon and all night long.

To add insult to injury James had mass produced the posters as going away tokens—his party favours. He stood by our lovely, Victorian front door, signing posters, giving every single attendee their proper souvenir. Ah, the perils of falling in love with a woman who came equipped with a full grown son. I had two comforts that day: James and I got along famously, plus James' eighteenth was fast approaching. I loved being loved. I was also quite sure, as I began planning my revenge, that a snide grin hung on my lips watching good old James give out parts of my bum on paper.

With my growing practice and the Hale appointment after just six months, we quit the beautiful but wild house and moved to London. We found an elegant home near the movie studios in Shepperton on a tree-lined cul-de-sac. From the large Victorian home we'd accumulated enough furniture to transform the garage into a storage facility. It was worth the move for London seemed just the place for us professionally. Petra was gracious to leave her patients and begin anew in populous London.

The best laid plans of mice and men proved a slogan for the Cunningham's in 1995-1996, as Petra's hypnotherapy work grew little. The cul-de-sac was not a mainstream locale and additionally turned into a rather unfriendly spot. If one parked a car in the street there appeared a nasty note on the window screen the very next day. With my intense traveling, Shepperton simply turned out not the right place for Petra. Though she enjoyed James's company, our London home was lonely. I wasn't home on many weekends because of the commitment with my German patient in Frankfort. I prayed for guidance and peace for my little family. The following is what I received:

July 10, 1995, David Cunningham's Channel Information after Meditation

Justice is done according to the Law of God on High. Man who persists in the negative pathway is causing the Light to fade from his Soul. Jesus walked the Earth to teach man of My Love, only a few listened, others carried on in their own selfish pathway. Man has had countless opportunities to purify but he carries on regardless of the Signs of Light that are here to show him the way.

The Light shines for all men, David, how I wish they would recognize it, but free will prevails and man stumbles in his darkness. We will show and teach him how to open his Love Chakra, to love himself and his brother. The day is dawning when man will recognize My Love and will wonder why he took so long to reach perfection. Everlasting Peace, well that is possible if man will only recognize his Love Potential. Many will come for healing so present yourself as My Servant, a Servant who carries the Spark shining brightly, others will follow - see how it unfolds. I have prepared The Pathway, no man can stop what is to come. I am The Lord Thy God, Father to all and I shall show My Love to all those who are ready. I Love All. Be at peace this day, David, all is well at this right place in time."

I kept on healing sparked by this affirmation.

One day I received a phone call from a lady in Cork County, Ireland. She and her husband read press on my spiritual healing and asked if I'd come to their son, who was ill with cancer. Daniel was seventeen and far too sick to travel. "Surely, if you can cover my fare and put me up, I'll clear my schedule as soon as possible."

I do not want to give the impression that I put off any client calls. Although a balance must be obtained when living with loved ones and implementing a busy travel schedule, I am entirely dedicated to healing. I changed my appointments only in dire emergencies, such as with the Irish family. I've treated every dis - ease as terribly important as well as tried to respect my family needs.

Busy, but thankful, I continued receiving significant guidance through my meditations:

December 31, 1995 Message to DLC from his Guides

Hereafter the Son of man shall glory in God's Light.

Speak not of doubt or fear for the Angels of the Lord are upon you. Do you not still realize how Blessed you are? Man knows of naught of things to come.

Glory in the Light, David, for you, my Son shall be a Leader of Man ! Be not afraid of signs and wonders that shall shine from afar.

The chapter of Life flows as a new and bright one appears. This coming year is more special than those gone by - just ask and you shall receive.

Abundances from the Lord God on High, for you, my son. Speechless you shall be.

Blessings this day be upon you and Mankind will soon be aware of you gifts.

January 1, 1996

To begin, the Earth responds to man's call - the Father answers all prayers. Blessed Be, Blessed Be.

The Star of David is upon you. Use all your powers and gifts well, use wise and well, my son. Be sure to remember who and what you are, a child as all God's creation. Treat all well and Love and Respect .

A stairway is ready for climbing - make sure you really know what you want and ask for it shall be given.

Be not afraid, I am with you my Son, David.
A pledge must be kept as I accept yours.
The time has come for all man to know of My
Love and Respect. This year will bring many changes.
You are Blessed this day.

January 4, 1996
Whatever language Man doth speak, he is always
heard. No man is denied access to God, for Love flows
to all and man is never far from God's mind.
Special times ahead. You will know of many
things to come as new people connect into your life
from all walks and countries of life.
Soon your travels will take off far and wide and
you will be known by thousands

I flew into Ireland. The moment I first stepped foot on
Irish soil, I felt wonderful energy and a spirituality I'd not
known in London. Seeing Dan, I also knew I was sent for
peace in his life. He was a mere skeleton obviously struck
hard by cancer. I never promise a family that life will be
restored but I do healings for peace and tranquil energy
flows, no matter what the patient's condition. Dan was in
high spirits in spite of his symptoms. His folks were
focused on my help so I immediately began explaining
the healing process. The weekend was filled with
incredible healing sessions, then breaks when we took
lovely country drives. My heart soared in Ireland. This is
difficult to explain, as I had not previously been ill or
unhappy, but this new land was energy charged for me.
The greenness of the earth, the trees, the crystal blue
sea were everywhere as we walked or toured by car. I
was enchanted. After a week back in England talking only
of Ireland I convinced Petra to join me for a visit on Easter
weekend 1996. I shared Petra with Dan and Ireland. We
stayed with new Irish friends and I delighted in having
Petra by my side. When I worked with Dan, Petra looked
about and fell in love with the land, too. "Wouldn't it be

wonderful to live here?" We pondered and discussed the dream. I knew Petra was not pleased in London as a professional healer, nor on a personal level. She helped me with my work, certainly, but her own practice needed rejuvenation. "How practical is an Ireland home with my work schedule?" We admitted I was not home much anyway. Just before going home we ran by a realtor and asked that they forward information about property or homes in Cork for rent or sale.

I had great progress with Dan to start with and my reputation was flying in Cork. When I returned with Petra the third weekend into Dan's treatments, I had eight new patient sessions besides Dan's four hours per day. *What are you saying to me, Lord?*

Petra scouted the realtor's suggestions while I worked. One house intrigued her and we met for an appointment. Driving up the tiny little pathway felt like home. When we parked alongside an old farmhouse, some 150 years old, I already fell in love. In need of hard work and care the house had tremendous repair problems with the inside a-shambles, cupboards gaping open and cobwebs matting everything. I fell in love with it anyway ! Much like the Tithe Barn restaurant with my friend Charles, I closed my eyes and saw what it could be. Petra and I walked the two acres seeing that the neighbouring farmhouses were far enough away it felt as if the place had hundreds of acres. "This is the one," I told Petra.

"You can't say that. It's only the first house and we've others to see."

"That's fine, my dear, you may look all you like. I've got to run to Dan. Please have a lovely day looking. You'll find this to be our best choice by the day's end." I said this with such great certainty it surprised even me.

We rejoined for dinner. "You're right, it is the best of the bunch," Petra said. We laughed and telephoned to see the house one more time. We took it all in slowly and knowingly. "We'd like to buy your house," we said to the owner.

He looked puzzled. "What do you mean?"

"We'd like to purchase this house." The realtor was awed. Perhaps in such quick viewings he couldn't understand that we honestly wanted the place. Later we found the house had been on the market for nine years. The house was awaiting us !

Petra owned a house from her divorce settlement, which had been rented and up for sale with no interest for two years. We arrived back from Ireland, having discussed on the plane what we could do financially if Petra's house were sold. Just as we stepped foot home the telephone rang. "Petra? I've just sold your house this weekend !" Obviously God's plan was working perfectly.

But oh what a time of separation. I concentrated my energies on healing which certainly felt scattered. Dan's health weighed heavily, I must admit. Petra was away, too, happily remodeling the farmhouse and James was knee deep in his career. Although tremendously busy, we were continually guided by Spirit that it was the right move to go to the comfort we felt in Ireland. One incident Petra and I took as a sign:

In the Spring of 1996, Petra and I waited at Gatwick Airport for one of our trips to County Cork for healings and remodeling the farmhouse. We sat in the departure lounge when an announcement came over the tanoy system, "Ladies and gentlemen ! Owing to severe weather conditions over the Irish Sea we request four of our passengers to volunteer not to fly. The plane is only a 30-seater and we must offload weight to carry more fuel which will help the plane withstand the bad weather."

Fifteen minutes passed. "Thank you, ladies and gentlemen. We have two volunteers and only need two additional. We cannot fly until the other two cancel."

Petra and I sat opposite two nuns discussing the situation. I said, "Petra, I cannot possibly delay my journey because of my sessions tomorrow."

At that moment the two nuns volunteered not to fly. Petra and I looked at each other in shock. Two nuns— had God told them not to fly?

We hesitantly boarded the plane. The flight attendants announced, "Thank you for your patience, please fasten your safety belts and ..." Silence. The sound system broke down. The attendant shouted, "We must wait for a microphone to be installed."

More delays gave us inordinate amounts of time to worry.

"Thank you, ladies and gentlemen for your continued patience. The microphone is now working, this is your Captain Paddy O'Brien. It is mandatory that seatbelts are kept fastened for the duration of the flight. The winds over the Irish Sea are 100 miles an hour plus and the journey will be rough."

The plane was awfully small. We checked our belts, looked about and were off, while squeezing hands. Within the first few minutes of reaching the Irish Sea the winds hit. I prayed to God and said, "You can deal with this, it is only the wind, after all." Petra prayed. We held hands until our knuckles whitened and shut our eyes.

Then the Captain spoke again, "Ladies and gentlemen a strange thing has just happened—the one hundred mile per hour wind gusts just stopped ! Our journey looks as if it will remain smooth." I opened and then closed my eyes and prayed. *Thank you, Creator, for stopping the wind.* A voice came into my head, *David, this incident was a test of your trust and faith: ASK AND THOU SHALT RECEIVE !* I shivered with that voice which always rang so true for me. Strange, but true, my dear readers, thus ended the lesson for that day. This incident provided us with more assurance of that the move was right.

I then received another letter from a stranger guide—as if I had an angel postman.

July 13, 1996, Sananda (Jesus) through Cath:

> "Joyous greetings, Dear One, it is I, Sananda. I sit with you this day with sunshine at our feet...David Cunningham, yet again he is in turmoil as to what he should and should not do. It is for him to reach out and call my name, for he has many helpers waiting. It is imperative that he link with us—that is to say—link with Forces of Light of the Highest (God's Energy)..."

In the midst of separations from Petra for the four months while the farmhouse was to be signed and sealed plus the distance between clients, I was comforted by this letter. The message confirmed that I must keep in good stead, stay centered, remain committed in prayer and meditation, communing with God and my clients.

Dan was not well in spite of our work. As I drove to the Hale one morning the cell phone rang. "Dan has passed on," his mother stated through her tears.

"I'll be out to see you this weekend," I promised.

Dan's parents greeted my return with intense blame for his passing. I explained that even our own subconscious is not always known to the conscious in any of us. Dan taught us love and was still learning and teaching as he moved back into Spirit. Death is sad for those who remain on earth who miss the cherished physical presence of loved ones. Spirit helped me to understand that we are not responsible for the choices other souls make. Dan had a plan which he was fulfilling both here and after he left the earth. I bid farewell and told them I was there if they decided they were in need. They've not spoken to me since. (Having lived in Cork for three years, even when we pass on the street, they have no conversation for me.)

June 1996, my 50th birthday. Petra held me captive with birthday party fear and threats after her celebration with the stripper. I'd no idea what was in store. Life was good for us as we were moving to Ireland, so I hoped she might keep it simple or even forget.

Sweet Petra gathered a dozen friends, including Hayley Mills, for dinner at The Blue Elephant in Fulham Broadway, London. Delectable food and company, but all the while my eyes darted about, looking for a James or Petra surprise. She planned it perfectly by not planning anything embarrassing at all. My fear of her revenge gave her great satisfaction. Just as we were going home Petra announced, "For your REAL birthday gift, we are going to New York." What a lovely idea, I'd not been back since Tavern on the Green days. I kissed her with delight.

I kept clear some days for a long weekend as did James who had never been to the States. Soon we piled on the plane with Petra and her surprise agenda. She had thought of everything right down to ticket reservations for Broadway's *Miss Saigon* and a gorgeous meal at Tavern on the Green. She wanted to see the places I'd described over the years. Our three spirits couldn't have been higher, or closer.

So, twenty years later, I stood in NYC and what used to be 'my place'. The Tavern had been reduced to one dining place rather than three in the '70's. Next to the Crystal Room, one of the smaller dining rooms had been transformed into a nightclub and gift shoppe. We were escorted into The Crystal Room where I said to the maitre d', "I worked here twenty years ago, I would appreciate a table overlooking Central Park." He bowed and showed us the way. The Captain came and asked, "Are you David Cunningham?"

"Why, yes," I said beginning to recognize his face, but not quite placing him.

"You hired me twenty years ago."

"Winston?" We hugged. Captain Winston dashed off to tell the manager. From that point on, abundance flowed—champagne by the bucket, samples of every food, entrees and desserts to beat the band. I felt like a king as did James and my dear Petra, queen of my existence.

In great celebration I asked Petra, "How about one more bottle of champagne?"

"Oh, goodness no, we've had too much already."

"Yes, yes, one more, please !" I insisted.

With great flare another bottle was popped. Before the birthday toast I produced from the hiding place deep in my pocket an engagement ring. In front of James and the world as witnesses I proposed, "Not too long ago James said to me, 'You're not really part of this family, are you?' Now I am making it official: Will you be my bride?" Tears danced in Petra's eyes.

James grinned, "I KNEW you were going to do this." James is rather sensitive and clairvoyant, so he probably did know ! Petra graciously accepted and the wedding day was set for June, 1997. The rest of the wonderful weekend we played tourist. It was marvelous. I'd never had time to do tourist things when I actually lived in New York. There I was with two of my favourite, favourite people. We had a ball.

Back and forth to Ireland, back and forward to Germany and to the Hale Clinic, time flew. Our wedding was to be on Monday, June 23rd, an odd day of the week, because the Glandore, Irish church we loved was booked years in advance for Saturdays and Sundays. It was a perfectly lovely and intimate spot for a wedding. Curious to this date was that James' father Chris had remarried the year before on that exact same day. Wedding ceremony and a festive celebration plans took over the upcoming months.

June 26, 1996, David Cunningham Message while in Meditation:

> England is but short-lived in your experiences. Now new green pastures await you and for you to do My Work, My Son.
> Special times ahead for you to unfold and to be who you really are and I shall make it possible for you to be known.
> You do not realize the importance of this life but soon I will tell you all that is to be known. Ireland is your safe sanctuary, a place to recoup your energies for there is much to do and little time to achieve and all before My changes to your planet Earth.
> You are special in My Eyes for you have served well over millions of Earth years I have placed you here. SO YOUR REWARDS ARE GREAT AND BOUNDLESS - JUST ASK AND YOU SHALL RECEIVE and receive in true Harmony and Love.
> Be not afraid for all is planned for you. Just wait and see how much more is to come for you. You are to be told of your mission in the near time to come and many doorways will be opened for you to move in all circles, for all mankind needs healing. Your reputation will spread far and wide as it is now in Ireland. This is your energy given out to attract all those who are ready for healing.
> So go David and just be. You do not need ever to worry, all is planned and in place for you - JUST BE. My Love to you, My Son.

As Petra remodeled the farmhouse she assembled a wonderful group of professional women and established an Irish healing team which would serve people from our new home. She'd already had some wonderful hypnosis sessions concerning the farmhouse and its past owners. It was soon my turn. Our monthly routine consisted of only one week of 'visitation' with Petra because of my healing schedule. During one of my visits, she arranged a channeling session with Alice, a gifted medium and one of Petra's healing partners, myself and Petra. I typically jot down a few specific questions before a reading. After receipt of the July letter (above) certain questions kept coming to mind which I presented to Alice. I received significant answers for my future:

July 28, 1996, Notes from Alice's reading for David L. Cunningham, County Cork

by *The GOLDEN FLAME*:

DLC: 1. Is my work on track? Do you have anything further for me to do?
2. What is the significance of moving to Ireland?
3. Connections with Jesus?
4. Reasons why Dan died?

GOLDEN FLAME: Dear One, We have come to this day from the Center of the Sun, the Sun which shines with the Gold Light. You have asked about Jesus. What is the Son of God but that which shines unconditionally on all living things. You know this and that the Sun that shines in your spirit is your home. This unconditional Light is what you absorb and then give others. Your home in the Sun is where you take others to their home. And what, Dear One, is healing if not this? The home of the unconditional sun you have experienced, and you know this place. You also know what is not home and you recognize those that are not at home in that sun, the sun of the Creator. Your healing work is your own inner experience of the Son of God. First it is yours in that experience. It then radiates as the rays of the Sun and the more you commit yourself to your home, the more the rays will emanate from you. And this, Dear One, this symbol of the golden sun is the same as your union with the Son of God and as you know that you are the sun you can help others know the same. And as you have asked, Dear One, about your healing, it is this: It is the radiation of the Light, of the Love, of the Sun, the very dream, the very—shall we say—destiny of incarnation. This is the Planet of Healing. Those spirits, those souls that choose to heal incarnate as human on this Earth to receive and to remember their Sun Origin. The power of Light through your fingers are the rays from that Sun. The palm of your hand is the home of the Sun. Your heart radiates this and the whole purpose behind your healing, Dear One, is to remind the world of their Sun home, to take people home. In this healing of taking people home you walk home yourself. We say walk. You *radiate* home yourself. You remind the body, as the sun radiates through your heart and your hands, of home of the pure dream of the Creator and this was manifested in the life of Jesus. For us to recognize where home is, what else do you need to do?

Know, Dear One, that you are growing and the radiation of the rays from your own Sun Heart are gaining strength in Light and in power through the love that you know. And just like a tree grows branches and from them others, and even the thinnest and tiniest twigs go on invisibly, so this is your symbol of balance. The roots, the branches, the Earth, the Spirit, the meeting place of the body and of the Spirit. Balance, Dear One. This is your lesson, is your gift, is your destiny, the word balance, and in that balance, the Centre Point: the Still Sun is received.

You have asked, Dear One, about your move to Ireland. This is very much to do with balance. Where there is Great Light there is also darkness. Where there is chaos the seed of need is born. As we have said before, Ireland is the cradle of the new, yet the seed was planted long, long ago. As a bird sits patiently on its eggs, so that which was seeded like an egg long, long ago, which you were a part of, is now preparing to hatch. It is quickening. You are both the egg and also the bird that sits upon it. And you can recognize and remember just the original plan for this land. It is indeed a healing and more. It is a remembering. There are certain places on the planet Earth where seeds or eggs are laid. The quickening is now. And we say to you, Dear One, that there are many that are beginning to remember the original planting and you are meeting these kindred spirits and you need to help each other remember, giving each other strength, support, healing, loving, so that the seed or the egg can bear the new. Just as Jesus planted a seed in mankind, it is quickening. You are responding and helping others respond. Do you understand this?

DLC: Yes.

GOLDEN FLAME: You have asked about Danny. His so-called death and his life is a continuous gift to all those that have had contact with him, especially his family. His life in the body was a bringing together of a great healing that will now take off within his family. You could say that he died so that others could live as they have never lived before. As Christ died on the cross so that mankind could live, so this is also the case with this boy. And his presence brings you closer now to the Christ Light. He is a helper to you and acknowledges your gift to him to help him know his purpose. His purpose is now stronger through the presence he has without a body. It will take time but his family will never be the same. They will seem to go through negativity, but this is old dregs coming finally to the surface and then they will know. The pool will be clear. They will see. He brings you the symbol of the clear, clear pool. Look into this, Dear One, and see your own reflection in His Spirit Water Pureness, and then you will know he gives you yourself. He gives others themselves. We see him as the Pure Clear Pool and His work on Earth was done impeccably. Do you understand this?

DLC: Yes.

GOLDEN FLAME: Are there any questions?

DLC: Questions, no. Comments...Obviously when I was told originally that he would live...and then he departed...I recognize this choice and free will. I hope that the healing worked on levels to help him.

GOLDEN FLAME: The twelve sessions have helped; he lives on. It has cleaned His Pool, His Spirit, His Soul. This is what you are working with. It is deeper than your mind. We see him now as a great companion in Faith and taking you deeper in Faith. Is there anything so far from what we have shared that you would like to ask or comment on?

DLC: No. It is OK. It is very awesome and very beautiful but I understand.

GOLDEN FLAME: You still have, Dear One, remembering to do. It is like puzzle pieces and each person you meet you will help them fit another piece in their lives as they will help you. The puzzle, and it is of Ireland, is still not fully seen for what it really is. The pieces are beginning to be put together and this is the same for all human beings. There has been a separation and when a puzzle is separated it is incomplete and makes no sense and each human being is a piece in the puzzle of the whole picture. And to acknowledge your piece and then help another acknowledge theirs is THE GREAT HEALING. The healing of separation: first forgiving yourself for the illusion of separation (from God) and then helping others to do the same. Forgiveness is the heart of the Law of Love and this Law of Love is the great hand that puts the pieces back together and celebrates the original picture of Love manifest (Love in the physical reality given by the Spirit). Are there any questions about anything at this time?

DLC: Have you ever been on the Earth plane or are you Pure Spirit...to help incarnate souls?

GOLDEN FLAME: We have been on the Earth plane to understand and experience Life in the body. We work on all planes with great Love and Service. Especially, Dear One, we connected with Alice in Egypt in the beginning. She knows this and this is part of her purpose and before. Is there anything else you would like to know at this time?

DLC: I've been told by various people of my lifetime with Jesus. Am I meant to know this? Please help me on this one.

GOLDEN FLAME: Dear One. This is hard for us to put into words, but you were with Him a lot as a disciple. You know this don't you?

DLC: Yes.

GOLDEN FLAME: And you have been told this before.

DLC: Yes I have.

GOLDEN FLAME: What do you feel?

DLC: Strange that thy whole thing has come together...no ego attached...I needed final confirmation. I thank you.

GOLDEN FLAME: It was strange at the time, too. There are also those that you will meet and have met in this life that know this and have worked as disciples at other levels. What is a disciple of Christ?

DLC: A follower of the Truth, Light, Love. A student, a teacher.

GOLDEN FLAME: Much is sacrificed for this and much is known. You are here to remind people of their home in the Sun. Is there anything on any level, Dear One?

DLC: No, unless you have anything on the teaching and guidance level.

GOLDEN FLAME: Dear One. You are always welcome to come to us and we are so grateful of the time this day. We remind you of the tree of balance. The power of balance. Your home is the SUN and the SON - the S - U - N and the S - O - N. Remember your rays. All blessings on you, Dear One, on this day.

DLC: Thank you.

GOLDEN FLAME: And to Dear Joanie. So let it be.

DLC: Thank you

Awesome ! Petra and I could not wait to begin our lives in Ireland. On October 26, 1996, moving day arrived and I was off to Ireland from the London flat James and I inhabited. James was a computer expert head hunter and needed to live in a business oriented city such as London for his work. I enjoyed his company and shared a place with him whenever I was in London. I flew to Cork and landed just prior to the furniture shipment over water. I led the shipping caravan to what was now an incredibly beautiful country estate. The farmhouse was transformed into a light, bright home that looked like a million to me. Petra was so proud as was I. Since the move, we extended into the barn and built a guest suite above.

Petra's team of healing professionals developed a work schedule that helped clients for a full week at a time. They came for healing of all types: aromatherapy, hypnotherapy, massage, reflexology, and clairvoyant readings. We now lived in a dream place for healing where we thrill in helping others make enormous shifts in their lives.

Historically, the house is built on beautiful earth energy and has a wonderful feeling about it—pure tranquility. This was one of the reasons healing work was always so comfortable on the land. During a weekend, Anne, another clairvoyant friend agreed to do regression therapy about the land's history in conjunction with Petra. Anne chose a stone from our earth to keep in her hand and went back to the healing room. First, I did a healing session with Anne, assuring all the chakras were in alignment. Petra then took over regressing as she does in hypnotherapy, taking Anne back in time through the house's ancestry to understand its joy.

The name of the house was Tig Na Gile which means 'House of Light'. During the first part of the 1900's, the clairvoyant witnessed a British army invasion of the land when the people living on our property, in part of the house in which we lived, were killed by the soldiers. Later the Irish Republican Army took over and the house was used for gun running. Further back into the 15th century there was a shack built on the land where the house stood presently. Anne and Petra both saw a married couple with a child wrapped in sack cloth. The woman was a healer who, apart from her spiritual healings, stitched wounds with salmon bone needles.

Further regression went back to 1201 where a hermit lived in a cave on the site. (The cave forms part of the current utility room.) He was seen also traveling extensively doing healings. Anne and Petra realized that the hermit and the 15th century mother were two of my previous reincarnations. Suddenly, I understood that I had been drawn back to Ireland for some sort of continuation, growth and sense of full circle completion.

This is why the land felt so comforting from the moment I set foot on it.

Our home in the present was for healing and loving care of people. We've come to know that the house and its land have always been used for healing for centuries. Except the brief interval with the IRA there has been little negativity there. The low point in its history has been cleansed and the healing energies have been most profound in us and our guests. Tig Na Gile is my lovely Irish home in the land called Kilbeg surrounded by the village of Leap and further to the south to Glandore, the coastal towne. It is the most picturesque of places in the world with little pubs and delicious food. Our favourite is Hays Pub. Guinness Stout's home is in the vicinity which sprouts summers overwhelmed with tourists. We love it all and have settled into work routines. I dedicated everything to absolute and full time healing and my soon-to-be bride.

February 15, 1997, a wonderful letter arrived and assured me that I, as busy as my healing schedule was, was on the correct path:

Dear Mr. Cunningham,   15 February 97

    I would be grateful if you could take Gordon Thorpe's name off your healing list as he has passed into the world of the Spirit on the 13th of February.
    I know that the healing helped him mentally prepare for his transition which was peacefully in his sleep and you have our thanks.
    God Bless you in your work.

Yours, Wendy

    June 15 - 23,1997, County Cork, Ireland. A week before the wedding and even before I'd arrived, friends and family came for the wedding festivities and settled into Tig Na Gile and local hotels. Each new day brought more loved ones in celebration. We all pitched in to clean the wedding chapel since there were no cleaning crews for the church and pigeons also called it their home and had for centuries, I supposed, judging from their build up ! We held a Sunday barbecue at our home enjoying the entire weekend together. By Monday everyone knew one another rather well.
    On June 23rd at Glandore Church the sun shone on us. We shared a precious ceremony and blessing of marriage at the little chapel. The wedding was candle lit even in the sunny weather as there was no electricity. A Catie Band played in the church then outside during photos and followed along playing for the jubilant reception. Joining us were our local partners in healing, new Irish friends and bordering farmers, who partied at the wedding reception in the church's rectory, a beautiful old building overlooking the Bay of Glandore. It was perfectly romantic and a gorgeous setting for our celebration of love. We were establishing ourselves as locales, wanting to make everyone pleased we were living with them bordering their homelands. We did not want to

be looked upon as 'foreigners', as some often think of the new people on the block. Our wedding bonded many together for what we prayed was to be a lifetime of loving co-existence. We felt safe and entirely secure.

December, 1996, James lost his job and decided to move back to Kidderminster. I was left not wanting to rent another flat on my own. This is the timeframe Hayley Mills, dear friend, was set for her road trip with *The King and I* in the States. We usually spoke on the phone often and when she heard of James' move she asked, "Would you house sit for me?" This is why and how I, a newly married man, came to live in Hayley's home for sixteen months until May, 1998. I continued commuting to sessions and conducted many beautiful healings in her home with her permission.

October 1998. Jacqui, an American with schleroderma came to the Hale. A woman of means, she had paid dearly for a countless arrays of treatment over the years and still lived in pain. Recently her home had been adapted to allow her to eat, sleep and bathe all on one level because she no longer could handle climbing stairs. Within three sessions she was healed. Understandably she was excited and wanted to tell the world of her relief. Jacqui flew back to share her news with California loved ones. She kept in touch with Petra and me almost daily. What a joy in being a team player in her life change ."Why don't you come to California for a holiday and help people here?" she suggested. Petra and I considered visiting California but were interrupted by another exhilarating invitation.

A friend and neighbour in Ireland, 90-year-old Ambrose, asked that I accompany him on a spiritual journey to India. He studied about and wanted to meet the great spiritual leader SaiBaba. "We're leaving December 26th. Please consider coming with me as I have one more vacant seat." Petra wanted to come, too, but agreed it was a chance of a lifetime for at least one of us. I'd read SaiBaba's teachings and was intrigued for years. The swami (Hindu for religious leader) had devotees throughout the world in a hundred countries and has manifested himself to these places. He is a very special soul who performs miracles. Our California trip was re-scheduled for March, and I rang Ambrose accepting his invite. My energies flew high in preparation for India.

Petra and I spent a delightful Christmas of 1998 as a married couple then drove to one of Ambrose's estates in Waterford, Ireland. We spent the night together in his centuries old Irish manor house before my departure with the India contingent. A private plane took Ambrose, his friend Harold and me to London, where we were Bentley chauffeured to Ambrose's other home, an estate next to the Queen Mother's and St. James' Palace. The trip was already an experience just landing in London and staying at his wondrous estate overlooking royal and sacred lands. I spent a most regal night dreaming of SaiBaba, feeling his Spirit.

We whisked off in an executive jet with room for only three passengers and the rest of the crew. Two pilots, two stewardesses and one steward served us with vintage champagnes, salmon, caviar. We flew into Dubai to spend the night before continuing on to India. I took the opportunity, as I had lived and worked there for a year, to rise very early and take a taxi around. I was amazed at the changes ten years had made and barely knew my way.

I was at peace regarding my past: Dubai, Suzie, Baghdad, and now my Petra and life of healing. I was set for a fresh spiritual adventure. It took six hours before landing in Putaparte, Southern India near the Temple. We offloaded to a tiny Indian hotel across from the entrance to the ashram of SaiBaba. Within thirty minutes of arriving we'd unpacked and met at the bush hotel cafe. An Indian messenger asked, "Are you David Cunningham?" I nodded, and the messenger said, "I have been sent by The Holy Man SaiBaba to invite you to come inside The Ashram and be his personal guests."

"Us?" Ambrose replied. He was utterly amazed at our great fortune.

"Please, will you get your things? I have transport. The Ashram closes very soon."

We were quickly moved to an apartment within The Ashram complex which was minimalist compared to the bush hotel we'd just left. The beds were hard, pillows made of straw and no hot water, but we were honoured guests and complaints were nowhere on our lips ! We were then given two Indian boys who tended to our needs. The 'messenger' introduced himself as The Ashram's head of security and told us that at 6 a.m. the next day a car would escort us to the Temple.

6 a.m., December 28th,1998, we rolled to see SaiBaba and were presented at the entrance to the inner sanctum of the swami. It was a special, small area within the gigantic, open-sided, ornately painted and tiled palace. The scene was striking with a domed roof of vibrant handiwork and cool, pristine marble floors. Sitting on the top tier to the right below us in perfectly neat long rows were 15,000 devotees in total silence. I had never experienced anything as awesome. I witnessed this devotion with the sudden realization of how it felt thousands of years ago when Jesus taught on earth. I shook all over with energy and exuberance. We were blessed in being chosen to enter the inner temple with SaiBaba the Swami. My heart and soul were flying.

As we waited in absolute silence I thought of what I knew about SaiBaba. He does not lecture people but guides them. According to his own guides he is a reincarnation of Jesus working on a Christ energy vibration. Hundreds of thousands flock from all over the world to be in his presence. His temple opens to everyone during darsham: the prayer times at 6 a.m. and 4 p.m. daily. People wait as early as 3 a.m. and 1-2 p.m. for a chance to sit with His Holiness. Twice daily between ten and fifteen thousand people arrive to sit in total silence. It is an inspiring and thrilling spiritual experience in which to be a part.

SaiBaba walked into The Ashram with two young men blessing and taking letters of prayer requests. The swami, a slight man, 5' 4" tall, wore orange robes and had fuzzy black hair. His hands emitted vaboti, an ash which manifests itself. He touched as many as possible with the ash. He went inside the inner sanctum where they escorted us along with six others, making nine in all. There was just room enough for us to sit on the marble. SaiBaba was on a simple throne. He spoke with deep passion for half an hour. Next swami spoke in answer to questions. He then said, "I want to speak with you three privately tomorrow."

We bowed and whispered, "Thank you."

We were led to sit outside the massive wooden Temple door until the darsham ceremony was complete. Then our two boys took us by car to lunch at the canteen. The canteens were split into male and female. One queues for food then sits at a table. We, however, were escorted to a table already set for us with servants, which caused a bit of a stir because of the special treatment. A VIP tour of the hospital and other Ashram establishments followed the lunch. We went to the afternoon darsham, then back for dinner in the canteen and candles out by 9 p.m. to ready ourselves for morning darsham, up by 4 a.m. I never slept the entire three days, but meditated, prayed and rested in a very high state of energy.

The next morning we were escorted to the feet of the holy man to wait for the appointed time of the special audience with SaiBaba. Out of the three of us the two friends of mine were much older than I and were seated to the right and left of Swami. I sat on the cool marble less than a meter from his feet.

SaiBaba knew everything about me. He looked above my head and moved his right hand as if reading the pages of my diary (He read the akashic records of my lives). He knew of my healing, of Petra and James. There was nothing I could hide, not that I wanted to hide. The atmosphere was genuinely caring and filled with Spirit.

Swami stated calmly, "This healing you do..."

"Yes, Swami," I said quietly, eager to only listen.

"Some days it's good and some days it's bad."

"Yes, how do you know?"

"David, I know these things. Do you know why you have good and bad days?"

"No, I do not."

"It is confidence. You need more confidence in your healings." He leaned forward, covering my head with his hands. "I am now going to place blessings upon you and increase your healing powers." I did not feel anything, however, spiritually it was an earth shaking experience. After that my two friends were spoken with and we left with his words, "I want to see you before you leave please." We nodded and bowed.

Our routine continued as before being the swami's honoured guests through dinner. I retired to my room early and took off my socks and shoes. As I touched my left foot with my right hand, my big toenail slid off right into my hand—no blood, no pain. It simply fell into my hand. I was shocked not knowing what it meant. I actually kept the nail for a healing colleague's advice when I returned home. The next morning we had the car packed and ready, waiting for our escort to the swami. SaiBaba is not only a holy man, he is entertainingly humourous as we found out during the last visit. While sitting in his presence he said, "Show me your watch." I took off an inexpensive watch I'd worn for years. "Place it in your pocket." I did. Realize, during all of this time, each person and everything is very still and utterly silent. We watched intently. He sat with his right hand closed. He opened it, nothing. He closed it and opened it again and there was a gold watch. See what a good fit it is, David." As I placed it on my narrow wrists, which nothing ever seemed to fit properly, *it fit perfectly*. He gave a gift of gold rings to each of my friends which fit to perfection. I had read that SaiBaba did this with certain people as a form of loving affection. One in our party of three was a brilliant skeptic and said, "He's a fantastic magician." I knew this was untrue. I sat just at his feet and I know his hands never moved from his knee, save to hand over gold gifts. He blessed us as we were dismissed, his touch vibrant and alive. We walked through the palace for the last time, brimming in awe.

As we said good-bye to our young helpers I showed them my watch. They fell to their knees and kissed my feet ! "You have been blessed by the holy man !" I found this as touching as it was embarrassing, and the most humbling experience since Baghdad. Our car headed for the runway and our mid-stop in Dubai. I was sad to see the palace become farther away. Then I noticed and certainly to our surprise, people followed us to the runway. Ambrose invited them to look inside the plane. I don't think any of them had seen such opulence. Farewell hugs and photographs went around the group of two dozen or so.

The plane leveled altitude. Ambrose and I sat staring at one another, stunned with SaiBaba. After a long silence, we slowly reviewed and shared many things about our thoughts, about our lives. I talked of my work with AIDS patients, the boys school, the university research I wanted to do. On the plane I rang Petra. It was wonderful to hear her voice yet I was so overwhelmed with emotion I could not speak.

New Year's Eve, 1998, Dubai hotel suites were reserved for us. I dressed for our New Year's Eve feast and even had my hair trimmed. My foot did not pain me at all with no large nail. Ambrose arranged a private party in another five-star hotel in Dubai. The pilots and stewardess joined the SaiBaba three dining with us, which I thought very kind and sensitive of Ambrose, dear man. It was an exhilarating welcome to 1999.

New Year's early morning the one other gentleman and I hopped a taxi to look around for a couple of hours before our departure back to London. We searched not finding the actual complex I'd previously managed, all had changed so. We spent a great time looking about and then back to the plane. It hit me as we ascended—my SaiBaba experience was ending. I resolved to take him with me in my soul.

"Imagine, Ambrose, we'd only just gone to be a part of the throngs and there we were in private discussion with SaiBaba, SAIBABA !" We all agreed it was more than we could even grasp right then.

We whisked off from our London airport landing and to Ambrose's London estate where I slept regally next door to the Queen Mother. Simply glancing back at this event always takes my breath away. Air Lingus delivered me to Petra. I spent a few sweet days with her, finally verbalizing and sharing every moment and detail. My one regret was that she was not with me in India.

I went to see our reflexologist after arriving back to Ireland. Rita is very spiritual and worked on Petra's healing team. She placed my foot in her hands and said immediately, "Ah, he was cleansing your psychic eye. The Third Eye Chakra is directly related to the left large toe. When the nail is fully grown your psychic powers will also grow and increase." Thank you, SaiBaba !

January 1999, during the second week back from India, I thought I was back in the swing of healings but my life was not at all the same. The effects of SaiBaba's energies were enormous. For the first time in my life I almost fainted with lightheaded-ness right atop patients. I was forced to apologize stating, "It appears I am not well. May we book again?" I had to lie down for hours on my own healing table and meditate, soaking in my feelings and trying to bring myself back to earth. Indeed, SaiBaba introduced a new phase of healing in me. For weeks, I felt as if I were as light as a feather floating through the days. I worried that maybe I was not grounded on earth. SaiBaba predicted there would be a great increase in my energies and much more rapid healings. It came to pass. I could not contain my delight for I was surrounded by the highest energies I'd ever felt. It was completely Spiritual, as if I were meditating round the clock.

Jacqui, the healed woman from California rang again, reiterating her idea to have me do healings for a time in California. Negotiations re-ignited and I tried going with the flow of this powerfully energized period. Petra was graciously following all of it. Petra and I decided we would go together and investigate the California potential and do a bit of vacationing. If the Almighty wanted us there we would know it together.

March 21, 1999. We arrived in La Jolla, California and were greeted by an abundance of people who craved healings. Not three weeks into our stay, a local hospital wanted us to join in a research program to document the use of spiritual healings and hypnotherapy pre- and post-operatively with heart patients. This was a dream—to document our work and help bridge science and medicine for the wellness of all people.

I was introduced to a family with a young son critically ill with a large cancerous tumour. He was one of Jacqui's friends and they returned again and again for treatments to help the sweet boy. Unfortunately, the poor young man did not respond and passed away. He passed in a peaceful state, even though our sessions were not life saving. I'd learned this lesson at Dartford, again in Ireland and now in the US. It was not easy for the families, ever.

Petra and I decided I would take the offer to work in California for a few months, hopefully conduct healthcare research and meet my clients' needs. I would rent a place in California, Petra would work in Ireland. I moved into a gorgeous apartment near the ocean, large enough to accommodate Petra and me together with visits from James. Plans were set for me to legally stay in the United States. Work in Florida, through healed clients, also materialized. At the time of this writing, I anticipate a bridge building between the spiritual healing world and modern medicine because of research between the two fields. For this, I gladly dedicate my time with those who will ultimately form an acceptance of energy healing. The accepting bridge will facilitate the healing of myriad more people, countless more than I could do alone. To this end, I share my story with you.

I place my faith and life firmly in The Divine and His wings of change. This is a moving time for me personally. I do not like being separated from my wife but spiritually it feels right and true.

Chapter Seven
Reincarnation & Incarnation

"...as to you, Life, I reckon you are the leavings of many deaths.
(No doubt I have died myself ten thousand times before.)"
Walt Whitman, *Song of Myself*

Webster's definitions are such:
incarnation: the embodiment of a spirit or deity
Incarnation: the union of divinity with humanity such as in Buddha, Christ
reincarnation: a fresh embodiment; rebirth in new bodies of life; especially a rebirth of a soul in a new human body

Part of my work is describing and sharing the Almighty's gifted information in a way that touches peoples' lives. This connecting, of the mind, soul and sometimes by hands-on experience, heals. I hope in reading this story you see that I am unique but also like you. I eat, drink, think, and talk to the Creator in my own way. I pray that your mind is flexible and open to pondering new ideas, differing thought patterns and even unusual notions which you have previously decided were not for you. Be open, life happens.

Reincarnation has been controversial for thousands of years. By its commonly understood nature one cannot research reincarnation. In the context of our physical life on earth we cannot simply die today, move about, then come right back as a communicating adult and tell everyone how all of it felt. I believe, however, at the moment of physical death all we do is discard the body and carry on living in a different way—a changing vibration in heaven or the world of Spirit—whatever you perceive this place of life after death may be. Your truth is reality for you.

With that said, one can have the ability to tap into past lives without regression therapy (looking back at one's life through deep hypnosis). For instance, one of my clients in London recalled two of his past life experiences: one was in a concentration camp in Germany. He remembers vividly being in a gas chamber with his mother. A second life he drowned at sea. He tastes salt water whenever he relives that life in his memory.

Through the aid of regression hypnotherapy, one can access past lives, but often we have hints of remembering naturally. A remembered past may be linked to a present day phobia such as the man from London. Therapeutically, a phobia can be healed by retracing the experience that caused the innate present life fear. Leftover phobias from a past life trauma are rather common, too.

I regressed and witnessed several of my own incarnations. My angel guides have told me when we are born of this life we possess memories that, as we gradually grow, we forget. This creates a life that is fresh and new in our approaches to learning and experiencing love. We can try by meditation or regression therapy to remember. Most of us do not automatically remember how our Spirits have lived. I have always needed help in remembering mine.

An example of natural remembering is in children. Their veil of forgetfulness is not fully learned, nor drawn over the soul until after the first 2-3 years. Little one can remember a great deal of their past lives. My niece Lynsey, at age two, toddled into the bathroom where her father was shaving. Standing by his side looking up at him Lynsey tugged on his trouser leg and said," "Daddy, Daddy !"

"What is it, Lynsey?"

To which Lynsey replied, "When I was a man before I shaved just like you." Margaret telephoned me and said, "David, Lynsey is weird just like you !" For several weeks before the veil was fully drawn over her memory, Lynsey recalled various incidents. My sister was told of a large house Lynsey lived in where she was served tea by servants. This was unsettling to my sister Margaret for she is not inclined to study this phenomena. It seemed natural to me !

How can we understand reincarnation, then, if we have not or cannot regress?

Faith is the best solution here, not of any one religion, but faith in a larger dimension, that of faith in one's soul. Most of us believe there is more to being human than what we see, smell, hear, touch, and taste. "Our essence or soul lives on" is a common center for the majority of earth's religions. Could we come out of nothingness to this life then back to nothingness? The mainstream of most societies say there is more.

Spirit through meditation conveyed to me, "We have something to impart with you: GOD IS INFINITE, CREATED MAN OUT OF INFINITE, MADE MAN INFINITE, BUT AT ANY STAGE CAN REMOVE MAN FROM INFINITE." I replied back, rather confounded, "How am I supposed to get my head around that one?" My understanding is that this communication was meant to show us the creative loving and far reaching inventiveness of the Divine. Spirit has nothing to do with punishment or judgements. Those negatives only belong to mankind, not to God.

There are books, television shows and Internet discussions centered around people who have scientifically and technically died, what they saw, experienced and are now sharing. This excites and intrigues us to question, wanting more. We are here on this earth and we know little, or so it seems. It then becomes a question of faith. Even understanding that life is a mystery can calm the curious. Having faith in the mystery, now that's the key and the comfort.

Knowing.

Feeling things.

Believing in a higher entity we cannot fully understand, that's key as well.

Before I go on, you should know about my daily prayer and meditation routines. Understanding what this means to me will help you follow how I think and feel and who I am. I refer to my meditations quite a lot in this book. How I have learned what I have and how I help others with these sacred knowings is through my quiet Spirit time.

Adelaide Gardner has a wonderfully practical book entitled, *Meditation, a Practical Study* (with exercises) in which she tells readers that meditation is specifically for removing the mind from the world's worries. Ms. Gardner's belief is that this quiet training to leave the mind behind is the pathway to the Spiritual realm. She practiced meditation all of her life and was successful in bringing awe-inspired meditation techniques to the world by ultimately publishing them in her book.

Meditation is a form of entering the inner world where we connect with Spirit, our guides, angels and helpers. Through internal communication (mostly us listening) we can be aided in problems of daily life without interference to our earthly free will. I love talking with the Divine. I even do it in my dreams.

I am not a psychologist, but I understand the teamwork of the mind, body and soul. I come to the art of healing by way of the spiritual side rather than scientific level. Meditation is a personal moving of my mind. It is simple. It might take on any name if 'meditation' is not a comfortable term to you. Semantics do turn some of us off for reasons of personal history. Allow me to offer alternative names for looking within:

praying	talking to God	thinking
imagining	talking to self	exercise-induced peace
runner's high	feeling	moving out of self
knowing	journal writing	communication with soul
connecting	artistic endeavours	heaven's connections, ,
knowings	painting	sculpting
experiencing	allowing spirit to work with us and through us	
	personal conversations	

(relationship with Jesus, Yahweh, Buddha, angel, guides)

Keep all things simple for Truth is simplicity.

Adele Gerard Tinning's *God's Way of Life* quotes Jesus through her own meditation thus:

Let me express myself through you, to the group (the world's audience), who are sincerely trying to bring forth my **new** teachings. Again I say, my teaching is *simple*. Keep it simple in your living it. You must first understand all experiences are for learning, for the soul's growth. Do not call it 'bad luck' or say, "God is punishing me for something I've done" when the reverse takes place. These are not reverses (negatives), but lessons. They may be reverse of what *you* would like but you would not learn this one phase of learning unless you experienced it first. Everything has its purpose and everyone has his purpose for being on your plane of existence. The experiences one goes through does not mean another has to go through them during this lifetime. He may have gone through them in a former life or former experience. Each soul growth is in different degrees of development. I say development because all will reach true perfection eventually. Your purpose is to help others understand why they are going through these so-called problems.

If all could understand the growth they are gaining with each experience their problem would become easier and joy would radiate from their countenance...

Another Jesus Message:

When I said, "No man cometh unto the Father but *by* me," I meant LIKE me. I was on earth many times before I was Jesus the Christ. I had to perfect each stage of my perfection, the same as all of you are doing. My distinction was that I was the FIRST to reach the perfection of God. I had perfected the Christ or God in me.

Many have reached their perfection since that time and they also are one with God and are capable of doing what I am able to do—even greater things than I did they are doing. These are all Master Teachers. They are helping other souls who are reaching their perfection with God. All are part of God. It is only when you reach perfection do you consciously recognize your oneness with God. I was but an example of the perfection each one of you will attain after your many incarnations. Knowing your ultimate goal is reaching this perfection is the secret to a happy life.

Look within to receive messages as Adele has, as I have, so can you.

There are variations on the quiet time approach one might use. I use the classic, sitting in peace every morning and night. A ritual of routine comforts me when I repeat the same things each day as I enter into my private space. I pray a healing intention for people with whom I am focused on absent healings and finally I ask questions of my guides. I then listen and wait. In addition, whenever or wherever I need help I tune into the Creator for anything I need. Any time, any place I ask the Deity for help. It honestly matters not where I am. The Bible says, "Ask and Thou shalt receive." How many of us feel worthy of asking the Infinite for everything we need?

The Lord can hear all of us simultaneously.

God can hear us any time and one at a time.

Whatever you choose to do, or presently practice, the path to the Creator is the same: turning inward. The more reflection I do the more love energy I have. I call this centering myself, concentrating on my eight chakras and making sure my energies are flowing well. My work is ever more effective with people because of my peaceful, yet energized state. Certainly I have challenges keeping my energy centers swirling properly, as any one does. However, after a long day of healing sessions I can feel quite elated and filled with Light. When someone is healed, I am healed. This happens best when I've begun my day and closed my day in meditative centeredness.

During personal time I receive information which I share with you over the course of this book. It is comforting to have Spirit communicate to me regarding other souls I have known, such as my father and mother, who have both passed through the veil into the Spirit World. I do not hesitate to believe these are real messages. They herald loving, accurate and often instructive intentions.

One such message stemmed from a series of healings I did with Mrs. Button, a sixty year old lady with terminal cancer. After several sessions Mrs. Button passed away. Death of clients distressed me at that stage because I did not fully understand what my healing work was all about. However, to assist and encourage me with my work, six months after the passing of Mrs. Button, I was receiving information from the Creator through a clairvoyant. Suddenly, the clairvoyant Josie exclaimed, "David, I have a Spirit identifying herself as Mrs. Button. She has come to tell you that the healing work you did with her while she was in body helped make her transition into the world of Spirit in total peace and harmony." My heart sang with that news.

On another occasion my Guide in meditation told me a major part of my work is helping souls transition to the world of Spirit and bring them home to God. Yet another reminder came in the form of a telephone call from my friend Vick: "Hello, David? I have been receiving messages saying: 'Call David, call David,' so I am calling. I am to remind you that a big part of your work is to bring people home to our Creator." I must require loads of reminders when I receive the same message many times from all sorts of sources !

To further illustrate the simple joy of quiet time, I turn to a modern Master, Wayne Dyer, Ph.D. Dr. Dyer is notorious in crafting books which ask us to feel intuitively, listen to ourselves and know the power of God's healing energies. It is all a mere shift of our minds, says Dr. Dyer in Chapter Two, *Becoming a Spiritual Being* of his book *REAL MAGIC.* For just a day, forget all the negative judgements and put aside total quiet space for yourself. Dr. Dyer calls this a personal experiment to see what happens ! I revel in his terminology for Dr. Dyer knows full well that most of us have modern, scientific culture in the backs of our minds when we approach something "undocumented or new" these days. Nonetheless, Dr. Dyer describes this little experiment you might try today: close your eyes and go within, leaving your thinking mind behind. This IS your higher self right there inside you. Stop and listen. This is the you that never dies.

If one studies the classic religious idea of life after death, couple it with the ever growing stories describing life-after-death as for sure and experienced reality, then philosopher Arthur W. Osborn's discussions of numerous souls' lives take us into the next logical step. We have and will continue to enjoy many lives to evolve into higher and higher loving souls. Please consider this: "It is this inward sense of a wider self which we must trust for it is in this direction that we can discover a (deeper) meaning for our surface (earth) selves."

Arthur W. Osborn in his classic book *The Expansion of Awareness* (1967), further affirms a common feeling we've all thought of when considering our human-ness: the unfairness of physical conditions in which people subsist. From congenital disabilities to ravaging illnesses, Osborn tells us this is the "unequal" evidence that we are having more than a couple of lives in a "cyclic series of expressions of our deeper self (ves)" until we realize our evolutionary highest Spiritual Self. The present life is not all.

Mr. Osborn continues his logical discussion of spiritual growth by highlighting two elements of his evolutionary law: *The Logic of Multi-Existence* and *The Mechanism of Karma*. It is fascinating that in any given decade and century the world's philosophers have concluded this over and over and we still resist the idea of reincarnation (please see my bibliography for a full listing of the references just in this book alone) ! In Osborn's *The Logic of Multi-Existence,* it is stated quite simply that all of earth's religions teach that this life is to prepare us for a higher eternal life. No matter what the religious persuasion we have this common goal. Osborn poses a question I pose to you: "...Is it logical to make our eternal life dependent on one embodied existence?" From our 20th and 21st century scientific cultures it makes sense to accept reincarnation. It is a logical foundation for the existence of our souls in a differing time-frame from our mortal physical bodies. It does not make sense for us, as a globe of variant religions so firmly believing in life after physical death, to reject the notion of more than one physical life !

Further, Osborn sanely states that we are where we are for the good of personal higher development within the bigger picture of cosmic drama. *The Mechanism of Karma* is the physicality of our bodies which are the locomotives of Karma. Our earthly form gives us the physical sympathetic means to come to the planet. Then we form relationships with groups of people while excluding others by a complete absence of vibrational response. This is our destiny plan, not to be born in perfect tune with everyone, but with the ones who will help us on our sacred path. The re - membering or carry-over from one life to the next comes to us in the familiar atmospheres, deja vu's and haunting phenomena people who are sensitive feel in what they view as new places (new places in the current life). Osborn states it so: " (our current)...bodies would be seed-pods from which stem forth the successive incarnations." Nature has cyclical rhythm. Osborn says that it would be odd if souls did not participate in this universal process ! By virtue of our birthplace within certain families and communities, we live out our plan without even 'knowing' it.

Finally in this small highlighting of Arthur Osborn's *The Expansion of Awareness,* I'd like to share one other link to these chapters of *Holy Hostage*: Osborn states that through our religions and cultures we all have a sense of living for the future: one in which we do not anticipate being in (physically) to even complete some of our current projects ! What, then, are we planning for?

You know the answer.

So do I.

We have hopes, dreams and knowings that...**we will live on**. This is paramount when we look at and think about reincarnation: "The present is growing into the future, which we ourselves inherit...We also participate in the fate or Karma of our group or country," Osborn continues. That is the explanation behind huge quantities of people sharing in disasters and benefits if the energies of the separate souls require that special group experience. Nothing, as I have stated often, is accidental. We are right this very moment moving and generating energies for manifestation in creation of our futures. Doesn't this give you a tremendous surge of Divine hopefulness?

It literally brightens my life.

Love lived well within this life reaps tremendous futures for us all.

Let us be.

Do you see how intricately woven are the three concepts of going within, reincarnation and the so-called sixth sense? I will endeavour to separate and concentrate on each in the next chapters. Focus on the individual concepts will give them due justice. Each is a subject worth studying for years. Remember the whole purpose of the recycling of reincarnation is: TO ATTAIN, GIVE AND BE UNCONDITIONAL LOVE TO SELF FIRST (WITHOUT EGO, WITHOUT VANITY) THEN TO FELLOW MAN. This is our highest goal.

Death is not death to me. It is going home. The soul moves back and forth to its original and infinite state of being countless times. The gifted author Neale Donald Walsch has also a perfectly simple page of explanation in the third volume of his trilogy, which you might read. I will attempt to summarize this bit of his communication with the Divine: We are life itself and do not die !

We infinitely go on living.

This physical life is but an illusion and is why people who have technologically died have this major sense of not believing their 'death' because they are flying all around. The stories of near death are rather similar: the incredible feeling of lightness and freedom to roam about is awesome and joyous.

What more 'evidence' do we need to begin paying attention to our REAL SELVES?

Intend to pay attention.

That small shift will light the way.

Let me summarize. When we look at another person, yes, we see the physical body. What mankind has learned to do is judge what is seen rather that what is felt. The physical body is not reality. It is transient, so therefore, not real and entirely temporary. The only thing that is real is the soul that is infinite everlasting.

All of us have had hundreds, if not thousands, of different bodies in the process of soul evolution by reincarnation. What I understand through my beautiful Spirit guidance is that we are not meant to judge, period. If all mankind would allow itself to feel love and intend to only love, then harmony would blossom and flourish. Remember that non-hearing and non-seeing people fall in love. How do you think this is?

They want to love.

They receive and give love *without* those senses. How is that?

For years now after my prayers and settling in, stilling myself to communicate with the Creator and the angelic realms I say, "I am here to receive any words of guidance and wisdom for my soul and fellow man." I have had the most wonderful kindications from the Most High teaching me about unconditional love. Mankind can heal its negative judgemental ways by <u>choosing to give</u> unconditional love and <u>embody the same</u>. Be unconditionally loving to any and all souls and this will transform us into high beings who are closer to the Divine.

My understanding of creation is that God created us perfect in His/Her image but as created souls we have little knowledge of how we attained perfection. God created the earth plane as a different, slower density of energy matter where souls could manifest into an outer shell (human body) to interact with others. The soul then lives and knows who s/he is in <u>relationship</u> to fellow man, learning the balance of living together. To love, to not-love, every moment that the soul allows to happen will

HEAVEN
SPIRIT WORLD

Earth Plane
of

HEAVEN
SPIRIT WORLD

Existence

HEAVEN
SPIRIT WORLD

Experience of 'Self'

HEAVEN
SPIRIT WORLD

** After each earth journey
the Soul returns to Spirit to
re-group and "blueprint"
the next incarnation **

>> At completion of
TOTAL, UNCONDITIONAL LOVE ACCEPTANCE,
the soul returns (to Heaven & the Spirit World)
to carry on with Spiritual Life, or chooses
to Incarnate to be a Teacher of Love

'teach' the loving soul about loving feelings and obtaining non-judgemental attitudes. For example: If someone slaps me across the face I know immediately who I am. I will either hate and seek revenge with that person or I will lift my vibration and love that person anyway, unconditionally. Again, this type of 'choosing moment' shows me exactly who I am and at what stage I am living along my pathway of attaining a higher, more developed self. If I give and am being always loving, I understand the balance or life, the pros and cons and still choose LOVE.

If the evolution of the soul, the eternalness of the self and the credo that love **is** our purpose were taught to our children at a very early age, we would as a whole human race evolve higher sooner. If children were shown this love in our word and deed then they, in turn, would act no other way. Love and respect must be taught in our churches, temples and the like. Rather, now in place of love, there are a great number of fear based teachings.

The Divine is not to be feared.

Our Creator is love.

We are born on this earth to experience, in the physical world, as many dimensions of love as we possibly can before we move back to Spirit. Fearing the Almighty and feeling guilty about our lives is not teaching love. If leaders of all sorts would go to their podiums saying, "We need to change. We've made a mistake. We may have needed these societal rules and regulations long ago. But now as we embark on the dawning of a new era of energy we must teach loving all without judgements. Love and respect one another." If this became a daily teaching from every single being we met, mankind would see community upon community improve their lot in life. The truth of the great Masters such as Jesus is: their ways are LOVE, pure and simple.

"Love Thy Neighbour as Thy Self."

Be at peace with God's gift: your physical body, mind and soul. Love your Self and partake of your gift of Self. Notice that when we are at peace and harmony with those around us we are well and healthy. When we have discord—fears, guilt and uncommunicated notions of hurts kept inside—all can form dis - ease. When we are still, allowing hurts to fly free into Spirit's hands, we allow the Divine's energies to flow well, light and bright as they are meant to be. We are often not taught how to deal with our emotions, explaining, expressing, and sharing with others. Pent-up feelings block our loving energy from God.

Be still.

Give your past hurts and pains to the Almighty for freedom to live in health. To help you release buried emotional pain, please allow me to suggest this form of therapy: With pen and paper write down names of people and the situations that you feel have harmed/affected your life. Then write a personal letter to the person or situation, in total honesty, stating how you have been affected. Without guilt use any language (four-letter words are acceptable). When you have finished the letter (in total honesty), sign it to affirm and confirm that it is you on paper, tear it into three pieces and in a safe place set fire to it. As it burns state: Please Lord remove this from my soul and deliver this letter. A letter writing exercise can be done several times until you feel free of the burden that is buried pain.

LET GO.
LET GOD.
JUST BE.

Now go about keeping peace, sharing love with others.

Know that your Spirit is forever living and vital. We *can* gain back our memories of previous life experiences if we quiet down and look within for guidance. The higher our energies develop through the intention of always loving the Almighty, self and fellow man, the closer we remain to Creator. Life after life, we will always be one with Spirit.

For we are God manifest.

Madeleine L'Engle, noted award-winning children's book author, wrote *Trailing Clouds of Glory, Spiritual Values in Children's Books*, an anthology of her works.

Her preface includes a wonderful story which highlights how ego-centered we can be. She asks why look for religion in children's books, anyway? Her reply is in the form of a parable:

"Once there was a very wise rabbi. A young student came to see him and said, "Rabbi, in the old days, there were those who saw God. Why doesn't anybody see God nowadays?" And the rabbi replied, "Oh, my child, nowadays nobody can stoop so low."

Egomania is alive and well on earth.

Ms. L'Engle's *Trailing Clouds of Glory* conclusion includes Wordsworth's eloquent confirmation of incarnation and reincarnation:

"Only as I keep in touch with the child within my very grown-up body, can I keep open enough to recognize the God who is Love itself, as that Love is revealed in story… and if they (my stories) do no more than remind us that we can't help loving God, for God is Love itself, then that will be enough.

There was a time when meadow, grove and stream,
The Earth, and every common sight,
To me did seem
Apparell'd in Celestial Light.

For Wordsworth, as for most of us, The things which I have seen I now can see no more.

…stories…my stories…are reminders of that Celestial Light, and that "trailing clouds of glory do we come from God, who is our home."

Madeleine L'Engle, *Trailing Clouds of Glory, Spiritual Values in Children's Books*

"Not in entire forgetfulness,
And not in utter nakedness,

But trailing clouds of glory do we come
From God, who is our home:
Heaven lies about us in our infancy !"
William Wordsworth
"Intimations of Immortality"

"We live in succession, in division, in parts, in particles. Meantime, within man is the soul of the whole; the wise silence; the universal beauty to which every part and particle is equally related; the Eternal One."   ~ Ralph Waldo Emerson
The Over-Soul

Heal yourself of negativity and the Divine will show you health. If you look, the message is there from the classic poets to 20th century children's writers. Seek and ye shall find.

Chapter Eight
That Sixth Sense: Intuition, ESP, Clairvoyance, Perception

**In early 1999, my angel guides gave me a message: "In English Time on the 11th day of August 1999, in the 11th hour and 11th minute, there will be a total eclipse of the sun; from that moment on things—life on Earth—will never be the same. That moment will spark the final stage of the Spiritual Awakening for Mankind. After this message the guide stated: then there will be a crack in the earth."

\>\>\> On August 16th, 1999, a special day in astrology, a horrific earthquake in Turkey took thousands of lives. Another earthquake took hundreds more Turkish lives the following week

\>\>\> September 1999, Hurricane season is the worst it has ever been, demolishing many Bahamian villages; half of some islands are still under water

\>\>\> September 1999, Eastern US seaboard, N.C. & S.C., thousands of animals die when tens of thousands of acres stay underwater for several weeks; dozen of people perish, thousands left homeless

\>\>\> September 1999, Taiwan, earthquake hit the island devastating over 10,000 homes, killing close to 4,000 people

>>> October 1999, Mexico, earthquake and subsequent mudslide, covered entire villages, hundreds die, accurate count of people difficult

>>> October 1999, California, 7.0 earthquake in the Mohavi Desert, trains derailed, no major population areas affected, no life lost

>>> November, 1999, Turkey on the same fault line, several hundred more die

>>> December, 1999, Venezuela, some 60,000 people drown in floods and mudslides

I have always been extremely sensitive when perceiving things outside the realm of the standard five senses. My sensitivity is to Spirit Souls on all planes. Often I receive messages ahead of earth events, which have proven time and again as truthful as the ones you've just read. My sister Margaret is sensitive along with me. We often communicate across the Atlantic without a telephone.

I struggle with my feelings of compassion. When one of the premonitions, which I prefer to call messages from God, come true and numerous people perish, I hurt. In my prayers and meditations I've asked, *Dear Lord, why have so many people died?* My guides have spoken specifically to why numerous people passed away into the Spirit: "They chose it. As part of their soul growth and progression, they choose to leave the earth together as a collective group. They may have wanted to be in the Spirit during the next stronger energy age. Perhaps they will be guides or they had so much fear of what they were feeling as the millennium energies raise, they could not live on this plane facing their fears." Choosing to not be on earth feels foreign to us, yet not so strange if one looks at the whole of the Spirit world. Remember, think of death as a passing not an ending. I do not claim to know all, nor every person's thoughts by any means. I merely pass on information I receive to help others. I have much in common with countless people in the past. Historians have documented stories for thousands of years about people who see what is to be. We are called sensitives, previsionists and preceptors.

Arthur Osborn, in *The Expansion of Awareness,* One Man's Search for Meaning, postulates the spiritual and past lives connection after his own personal experience when first meeting his mate. Before I tell his story, I realize that we all know that some foreshadowing and assumptions are easy to make if we are close to someone or pay attention to an individual's character traits, habits and style. One could predict, for example, what types of jobs, homes, even food a person will most likely choose if he or she is closely studied.

Mr. Osborn lived beyond this normal human assumption power when he received future information from a stranger. This stranger stated that he was to travel to a region of the world not planned on his agenda. When he followed this clairvoyant advice, he met a woman who was told, in similar clairvoyant vein but from a voice within years previous, to wait in this country for an important person in her life. Osborn tells, "... when I met the person in question there was an almost visual flash of recognition with a certainty which seemed born of prior knowledge."

Is this predestination?

Is this remembering from a past life?

What is this sense of prior knowing—a sixth sense, intuition or a reincarnation reconnection?

Edgar Cayce, one of modern time's pre-eminent psychics and a gifted medium, had some twenty-five years of continual, channeled information from the Spirit world. Over and over again, Mr. Cayce heard and shared secrets of lasting inner peace. Through his writings and readings chronicled at The Edgar Cayce Foundation in Virginia Beach, he has shed light and love on the real reason one is born with psychic ability—to teach others that their Spirit home is with our Creator.

Mr. Cayce's son Hugh sites a cadre of readings in the *Story of Attitudes & Emotions* (published in 1972 & 1982, from over 14,000 readings spanning some forty-three years). It is a fascinating subset of his life's work in which Edgar passed on the same message time and again that it does not matter *what* we call the Almighty (they are all Him/Her). We must—each of us as individual Soul Selves—claim our heritage as part of the 'FIRST CAUSE' (God).

Hugh Cayce is editor of *Story of Attitudes & Emotions* and writes of his father that he was a practitioner of "the whole man(woman) with an inter-involvement of all ramifications of man's past/present/future body/mind/spirit."

In Mr. Cayce's reading #4021-1, the message tells how to heal ourselves by looking within. If all healing ultimately and completely comes from the Creator, we should be looking at our attitudes of self. ".. how well do ye wish to be?"

"As ye give others, not hating them (but aiding them), to know more of the Universal Forces—so may ye have the more, for God is Love." Please refer further into Edgar Cayce's gifted medium work in *Story of Attitudes & Emotions*, most especially in the Chapters IX and X of *Health and Healing* and *Love and Forgiveness*. My Cayce's son does a splendid job compiling readings pertaining to these important subjects.

How well have our cultures evolved to welcome dis - ease ! Inordinate quantities of thought-free traditions teach small boys, "Don't cry. Men do not cry. Don't talk of feelings. Be Tough." Do we have to be unwell to receive hugs or people's love? Client after client, in my healing work, craves the love and respect I give. You deserve love. We do not have to be sick or feeling awful or in grief to ask for and receive the attentions of those who care. My guides in meditation are shouting in the quietest, persistent ways: **"Take heed parents of children: teach love. Talk and communicate with one another. Allow feelings to flow, be experienced and shared lovingly. Healing and wellness are your rewards."**

Gifted Master teacher and author of *Heal Your Body* and *You Can Heal Your Life,* Louise L. Hay, phrases and rephrases the same messages beautifully. Now is the time, here is the power. No matter how long (perhaps even from past life patterns) we've behaved in negative and unhealthy ways, we can change. If you are in a health crisis, you have the inner power to heal. In place of the old and ugly mental tapes we keep mindlessly replaying, Ms. Hay advises us by offering countless affirmations as alternative thought patterns. I believe in Ms. Hay's work. I have seen it (mind shifting into positive new attitudes) miraculously cure people in the gravest of conditions.

Listen to your heart. Listen to what the Higher Self, the Soul—your Soul—is trying to teach you. Love and respect the Self. This is without vanity or ego. Love and respect our fellow man no matter what. Get rid of hate, judging and comparing. Intend in every present moment to love. See how quickly our planet will heal. Everything is in our hands. The saving of the earth is in our midst.

Bernie Siegel, MD, comes to the healing of people through traditional modern medicine. His spiritual journey is the editorial stream of his books. He ventured forth in healing others and found his scientific training needed some filling-in, some colouring-in, if you will. Dr. Siegel 's experiences are, in majority, with cancer patients but his works surpass that particular disease to a wonderful blend of Spirit and modern medicine.

I praise Dr. Siegel for sharing a story which points to the immensity of his own (and his wife's) spirituality. It will help you see the ease in which Spirit can come into your life; perhaps it already is there. How about taking a look?

Dr. Siegel is an exquisite example of personal and professional balance when he teaches wellness workshops with his wife. This is a marvelous example of what most of us have a difficult doing in this world— balancing. During a workshop in Atlanta in which they taught jointly, Dr. Siegel told a story, which I paraphrase here:

Bobbie and I try very hard to meet during the days I am in town. We actually make dates. One fine day, we'd made a date to have lunch at a favourite spot in New Haven (Connecticut). Now you must understand that Bobbie and I are quite close. Any couple who has five children can't help it. (laughing) Bobbie has been instrumental in my life journey in educating physicians and patients about the obvious connection between the mind and the body in treatment regimes. No kidding, you might say now. Believe it or not, not too long ago this was *big* news that the head was connected by the neck to the rest of the old body ! (Big news for people who spent their formative adult lives studying the anatomy of the human body but never studied the mind.) Believe it or not.

I had a jump start being a pediatrician because I had to connect more than just the dis - ease but with the parents. There was always a relationship in which to pay attention. Let's face it, a baby can't talk very much, although I have been known to listen to babies.

To get back to our story...true to Bernie Siegel form, a patient was needing my time in such magnitude that I was running late. I did not have to call Bobbie. As I was rushing (running?) to the restaurant, I met her on the crossroads to lunch. Pretty good without a telephone call, right?

What's my point. People communicate. People who love each other and spend loads of time together communicate without speaking. It **IS** telepathic. Life is. Has anyone done this in their lives with someone? (numerous people raised their hands without hesitation…) Ah ha, see?

There you have it. We are connected. We simply have to listen. I try desperately to listen to my patients and tune in to them. Then I tell them what I know for sure. Their heads/minds ARE attached to their bodies and God gives us the free will to heal ourselves with positive thoughts, visual pictures of wellness and hope for the future. With me as their partner in healing, I try to get my patients to see that they can improve by switching their inner tape recordings to Peace, Love and then Healing.

(RE: Atlanta Workshop, St. Joseph's Hospital, 1994)
respectfully retold from LLR's personal notes

Communication has numerous forms.
Stop.
Pay attention.
You'll see.
I mean hear.

Dr. Siegel, a humourous and delightful orator, is a prime example of the new willingness of physicians to understand the individual dynamics of healing. In his present life he is committed to humanizing classic American medical education—a wonderful bridge to integrating spiritual healing with the wonders of modern scientific medicine.

As far back as the early 1880's, The Society of Psychical Research (London) was formed by Sir Arthur Doyle (author of Sherlock Holmes) and a small group of colleagues including author William A. Hovey. They published documentation of human-mind-to-human-mind communication in a book entitled *Mind-Reading and*

Beyond. The parameters of this ground-breaking, thought provoking work are as follows.

"The Society (of Psychical Research) grew out of a conference held in London, January 6th, 1882...A programme for future work was at once sketched out by the Council of the Society, in pursuance of which the following subjects were entrusted to special committees:

I.   An examination of the nature and extent of any influence which may be exerted by one mind upon another, apart from any recognized mode of perception.

II.   The study of hypnotism and the forms of so-called mesmeric trance with its alleged insensibility to pain; clairvoyance, and other allied phenomena.

III. A critical revision of Reichenbach's researches with certain organizations called "sensitive" and an inquiry whether such organizations possess any power of perception beyond a highly exalted sensibility of the recognized sensory organs.

IV.   A careful investigation of any reports, resting on strong testimony, regarding apparitions at the moment of death or otherwise regarding disturbances in houses reputed to be haunted.

V.   An inquiry into the various physical phenomena commonly called Spiritual with an attempt to discover their causes and general laws.

VI.   The collection and collation of existing materials bearing on the history of these subjects.

The Society declared that its aim to approach these various problems "without prejudice or prepossession of any kind, and in the same spirit of

exact and unimpassioned inquiry which has enabled
science to solve so many problems, once not less
obscure, not less hotly debated."
    William A. Hovey
    Mind-Reading and Beyond, 1885, page one
    Lee & Shepard: Boston

This is one of the first scientifically formal studies
done with thought, an intangible thing and it was
conducted at my alma mater, the College of Psychic
Studies. As life's synchronicity would have it, Sir Arthur
Doyle's original Society of Psychical Research evolved
into the College of Psychic Studies, which thrives today
in London. Back in the 1960s when I took courses at The
College, I had no clue that my future friend David Northey
is an ancestor of Sir Arthur Doyle. It seems that my angel
guides made sure if I did not choose to connect with The
College back in my late teens and early twenties, I would
have surely found out about The College through my good
friend David Northey later on in my life. If you, out of your
own free will, do not choose to take one of the God's
'Busses", if the event is important enough for your Spirit
development the 'bus' will come around for you. Our
Karmic, previously blueprinted messages will be
communicated. The question is: will we listen?

    Currently myriad studies are being performed all over
the world on the power of prayer, mind focusing and
healing. Larry Dossey's *Reinventing Medicine* (1999)
chronicles this ground-breaking shift in modern scientific
medicine. Dr. Dossey's work is well worth reading if you
are as interested as I am in changing our way of healing
for the better.

    In addition, *The Seth Material* written and channeled
by Mrs. Jane Roberts (1970s), covers and magnifies to
readers the nature and almost unfathomable power of
our inner potential of self healing. Try reading Mrs. Roberts'
chapters: *Health* and *Dreams*. There is much to learn

about our dream state as well. (There is enough for another book on this subject alone.)

Andrew Weil, in his chapter *The Tao of Healing* of the monumental book *Spontaneous Healing*, places the essence of a human being's capabilities to heal in a scientifically soulful, respect-for-the-body's-talents manner. He asks: "What is the relationship between treatment and healing? If I want to pursue healing, should I forego (outside) treatment?" Dr. Weil's own belief is in the Divine's gift of our immune system. Throughout his medical study and practice, Dr. Weil has seen and shares in his book that antibiotics, as an example, reduce invading organisms. His conviction is that the reduction of overwhelming numbers of germs paves the way for the natural immune system to do what it does best— cure the body !

I, the soul that is David Cunningham, *know* the intangible microscopic immune system's pilot is our Creator who tips the scales in the above scenario. His gifts of Spirit and our gift of will to survive and survive well are foundations of which Dr. Weil agrees. My trust lies in the belief in YOU—the Divine's sons and daughters and our inherited Golden Light.

Be ye awake and aware to your own Soulfullness. My guides and my senses tell me, even though I cannot see: **Know, dear ones that if one looks, one will see what cannot be seen easily, yet has been there all along.** The immune system is yet another micro-miniature example of God's greatness in the physical plane. I can't see it but I know it's there…As Dr. Dyer suggests: you've always known it was there—that you of you's. Dr. Dyer, another exceptional speaker with lighthearted wit, has written a book entitled, *You'll See It When You Believe It.*

It's all in the vantagepoint we take, surely.

Nurture what you have. Healing, wellness and peace are your rewards.

Chapter Nine
The New Millennium and The Higher Collective Consciousness

Deepak Chopra, MD, is a modern master teacher of health, healing and wellness living. In *Ageless Body, Timeless Mind,* Dr. Chopra addresses the electrifying field of quantum physics. He states that all is energy. Our bodies are energetically and physically attached to our soul energy. If we touch a flower, it truly is only one set of energy molecules (the finger) touching another set of energy molecules (the flower). These energies are grains of sand in the Universe. To us, our thoughts, our individual energies are our universe.

Look further.

Is this so difficult to change when all it takes is a little movement of molecules? Dr. Chopra reminds us that these concepts are not mysteries, but the very stuff of which our days consist. We move sets of energies all the time, why not change them all for the good? He tells us that we can choose to move our thoughts, our actions which are only energies moving around, to experience peace, harmony and unity with all people, every single day. "...in unity consciousness, the world can be explained as a flow of Spirit (Energy), which is awareness to establish an intimate relationship with Self as Spirit (Energy)."

This beautiful information illustrates the timelessness and interconnectedness of ourselves with the Divine. From the sages of India to the Bible, Koran and Bhagadva

Gita, to Hovey's 1800s research in mental telepathy to Carl Jung's 1950s and 60s philosophical thoughts on collectives and scientific subatomic research, we are one. Free will and our creative souls are one with the Divine.

As energy entities, we are separate only until we realize that we are not. So too, our minds are not separate from our bodies. What we think is connected to our bodies, therefore our thoughts most certainly affect our health state. Scientists have realized the chemistry of feelings and thoughts in on-going experimentation for years, if you seek physical evidence of the mind-body connection. If our souls do not die, we can realize the joy in *always being*. If our Spirit never dies then we have many chances to become closer to the Almighty, to live again the joys of love and to learn the lessons of the universe. Treating and loving our neighbours as ourselves makes perfectly vital sense if we awaken to the flowing oneness with all. Become a member of the remembering that the Creator is us. We are part of the whole, we are one with the Infinite.

Dr. Chopra's prose segues reincarnation and the sixth sense naturally as he explains the energy flow of the earth plane consciousness in *Ageless Body, Timeless Mind.* If we have commonalities with the small set of energies in a rose for instance—then how can we *not* see the unity of all living souls with the Almighty One forever?

In this present new millennium, we have already chosen to be here together. This is why you are reading this book—you are questioning, thinking, wondering, and awakening to the realities we cannot see but know in our souls are there.

The truth is that we can choose to gather together, those of like and positive minds, and change our present collective negativity. This switch of intentions will change and uplift our futures. Mankind does not have to be sick.

We can choose to see that we are of the Divine. See the context of your present life and choose to love. The positive and healing consequences are higher than our highest imaginings.

We are moving into a new age beginning in this new millennium. The energy is different. It is a time of renewal with intensified, more powerful energy available to us. It is a mere thought away. Now is an opportunity for mankind to grow in love not fear:

- a time of cleansing past hurts
- a time to love and forgive
- a time to respect self and fellow man
- a time to intend peace and so shall it be
- a time to 'remember' that we are one with the Deity

It is a matter of simple thought. Gently shift your mind into thinking LOVE ONLY. If another looks, acts or does something hurtful, move above it and show understanding for the other's viewpoint. Love that viewpoint as his, maybe not yours, but his viewpoint, then show only love and care for him. This approach never weighs you down. It lifts both of you. This is higher energy for you and the other soul.

In unity the lives on the earth plane have chosen this 'now here'. Together, our Spirits can surpass any loving conditions we have ever experienced. It is not for man to question who we are not, but who we ARE in relationship to God. Man is soul connected to the next soul, to the next and so the energies meander, rushing forward and flowing into one another. The six billion of us on this planet can be looked upon as one composite Energy Soul which is the Infinite, never dying, forever and ever, Amen !

It is mere illusion to think we are separate from anything, let alone the Divine. Isn't this a beautifully, uplifting thought? Dear reader, if you feel alone, just let me reassure you that you are never alone. As part of the

Energy Force presence, we are surrounded by Spirit. Our angelic hosts, guides, teachers, and loved ones are here to assist and guide us in our daily life without interfering with our free will. When you feel lonely, sit still and tune into the atmosphere of love energy around you. Listen and feel what comes to you. In *Conversations with God*, by Neale Donald Walsch, God says: "I talk to all my children all the time, but who listens to me?"

Consciously,
together,
a collection, let us listen.

This is 'The Collective Consciousness'. It is not so foreign to your every day existence. Examples of groups of souls loving and working together on this earth are:

- family
- church
- school
- work unit
- friends

Please stop for a moment and consider a group in which you work, live and love. Jot down their names. These are small clusters of souls with whom you have great caring, respect, common energies, and a knowing, warm connection. Recall that when you are with this special group and all are one in a project or a cause, that the height of joyous energies thrills all of you in the group. This is a mini-collective consciousness, free will choosing to live for a common purpose and reveling in that loving, productive, creative accomplishment which enriches and *is* your life.

Now you've also created a small list of some of your guides on earth with whom you are sharing love experientially. Highlighting the names of your close ones is key to touching the personal part you play in 'The Collective Consciousness'.

Another example of collective, like-kind intentions are those stories everyone has heard about: when a scientist in one country of the world discovers or invents a new find only to learn that someone across the seas has just accomplished a similar feat. This may be a frustration to the one who wants to own the patent of the idea or invention. However, this kind of level of awareness for a new concept raises the interests of the entire planet. Dr. Dossey's *Reinventing Medicine* also documents this phenomenon extensively. Quietly the world seems to be awakening !

So, can your decision to love above all else in your days and nights, in each of your weeks and multitudes of years change the world? Collections of love raise the world's level of Spirit+Thought+Awakening, as we have seen in our everyday community groups. Certainly it is easy to see that the reverse is true: when just one negative person decides to send negative energies around, things change rapidly. It all starts with one person then pulses to his or her clusters of soulmates.

My angels send me the same communication in various wordings to appeal to my moods and receptiveness of the moment. Positive, pro-loving actions and deeds matter. Love changes things. Everyone knows these messages if we stop and think. Not one religion forgets to tell their members to love one another. (They should focus on that entirely, as a matter of fact. Hands-up for those who do.) Poetry, lyrics, scriptures, and prose by the planet's time honoured masters say what modern singers do:

"All you need is love, love. All you need is love." (The Beatles)

This new age of energy, this next millennium after Christ's presence, has been referred to as The Age of Aquarius. What does this mean? The power is in the remembering. Together, our energies can choose to remember that we are the Creator's creations. We are now manifest, trying to achieve remembering and when we do recall, we flow into the Light. All the time, minute-by-minute, love personified is always in our daily life intentions, if we try. This is rising to meet the Divine's hope for us: that we live the perfection we were born to live. What a dream, one worthy for each and every soul equally !

In *The Expansion of Awareness,* Mr. Osborn tells that if we stop and look, we should see that nothing is by chance. We are moving and connecting energies for our futures. This image is where we can find never-ending hope ! Love now; forget rigid rules and regulations of one tradition that argues with another. Pure, sweet values in treating everyone with respect and love is all that matters. Our neighbour is God incarnate, as are we.

Arthur Osborn's writings excite me because he points to the oneness and universality of belief—our Spirit Souls live on ! How energizing it is to be one with you and all of my patients as well.

*** When I was working in the Midlands, a glorious lady Elsie, was a frequent client. She'd been damaged in WW II by a doodlebug in her back. She and I built a nice rapport, as I learned of her numerous gifts and talents. Many people in her village would come to her for advice. She shared this with me, making every session interesting. I am as much for healing myself through my patients as they are with me. One occasion, after Elsie had opened her eyes from our healing session, she gasped, "Wow, David, that was impressive."

"Elsie, tell what went on please !" I love hearing what has moved people.

"Whilst you were working my spirit guide took me by the hand and out of body. We flew together connected above the earth plane. When we were far above my guide said, "Now turn around, look at earth and tell me what you see."

I looked carefully. First I saw clearly the oceans and lands. "All I can see is the Earth and its colours. I can't see people. I do see a black ring hovering around the earth."

"Do you know what that is?"

"No, I have no idea." I said, wondering how would I know? My guide was the one I relied on to know these things.

"That's man's negativity, over thousands and thousands of years. That's what will happen to the earth plane, if not changed. So shall you sow, you shall reap. Whatever you give out, will come back to you. Not as a punishment, nothing from God, but what mankind has given out over the hundreds and hundreds of years of un-loving."

Elsie and I hugged, intent on changing our world with such profound advice.

We can save the world, this beautiful planet we call Mother Earth, by sending out beams and beams of love into the atmosphere, into the land and directly into each and every soul. This can replace anger, greed, war, destruction. This act of loving can rid us of the black cloud around the earth. It has all been going on too long, this judgemental and habitually negative way of thinking that has run its course.

It is time.

Stop it with me.

We are in charge of this.

We can save the Creator's earth.

Let us begin.

Neale Donald Walsch in *Conversations with God* (*CWG)* tells the following message in all his books, in a variety of semantics: there is one main soul that reinvents itself into individual souls to experience all of what love can and will and forever be. God and Mr. Walsch term this idea as 'A Collective', rather than just one 'Father' or one 'Creator' to illustrate the all-encompassing nature of the Infinite. Mr. Walsch, through his journaling, encourages us to think beyond our traditional or even so-called new age philosophies and thought patterns. Think past these, for the Divine is Infinite, is The All, A Collective. "By the process through which energy becomes matter, spirit is embodied in physicality. This is done by the energy literally slowing itself down—changing its oscillation, or what you call vibration." It is all God only in variant forms !

Additionally, in CWG, Mr. Walsch tells readers to think past physical death. Think further and beyond the living we consider evil, for we know not love without its opposite. The understanding is in the balance. Mr. Walsch claims that Spiritual people do not have to live negatively to understand negativity anymore. We know what is higher and best. Right now we can change the world for the higher good.

In its clarity, I trust you will find understanding to this higher calling.

Mr. Walsch's writing reiterates the essential component of my healing gift: God Energy. I am not gifted myself, but have been given the gift of receptiveness of the Divine's Energy to boost people into wellness. Along with the counseling and understanding of the chakra energy centers, the clients are moved by the Almighty through me to a new wellness. Mr. Walsch's reference to energy is the same energy in which I refer throughout my healing work and in this text. It is all the very same energy because we are all one.

I have guides—writers, mediums, friends, patients too numerous to count, which message to me. I seek, I listen and in turn give you their words for your consideration. It is through the partnership of others, the teaming of groups of like-intended souls, that we flourish and grow. Let us fill to the brim with loving energies, building our strength and resolve to live on our highest dream level.

We cannot do it alone...WE ARE NEVER ALONE.

Be still.

Listen.

Quiet within self and reap the benefits of our fellow man and masters' lessons.

WE CANNOT KNOW WHO WE ARE UNTIL WE INTERACT WITH OUR FELLOW MAN.

If someone hurts you, that is the moment to immediately know who you are—you will either lift your vibration and love or hate that person and seek revenge. Before seeking revenge, remember the ancient Chinese proverb:

Before seeking revenge
First dig two graves
The first for yourself
Because part of you will die by revenge
And the second for your victim.

Please read the following world masters' words. I find new, fresh energy each time I read their messages. Live in the golden Light of wisdom.

Carl Jung explains the dangers and challenges of collective consciousness and collective unconsciousness. Man must decide individually to break out of the mold, out of collective UNconsciousness and move forth in love. Then he must bring along his collective group.

It is not difficult, if we take heed and resolve that this day is truly the first day of the rest of our lives. I trust you shall find visions, dancing before your eyes, of people in each of the realms in which Jung so fastidiously investigated, documented, researched, and here I fill you in.

Jung says the antithesis or opposite of 'Individual' is 'Collective'. By the very word it means any like kind grouping of church, community, town, club, or membership. Jung's term, 'modern man' is one who is awake spiritually and conscious of his inner soul and spirit. The problem is, Jung says in Modern Man in Search of a Soul, 1933, that the modern man is rather alone in a sea of unconscious people. Even in his own micro-collectives he is often the only one who is bored with what goes on and on. Mankind does repeat itself. Modern, conscious man (woman) can barely speak of his consciousness for fear of others ousting him from his various groupings. Ultimately, however, Jung posits that the conscious person seems destined to choose isolation and estrangement. Granted this is written in 1933, but can we think of situations such as Jung's Modern Man in today's time?

Don't we all feel alone at times?

Listen my beloved sisters and brothers. We do not have to be unconscious, or alone. The true reality is the precise opposite. If you are reading this book you are awakening and changing your commonly known traditional way of thought. Now test the truth of these new thought patterns and love by being a living example. This is not in conflict with your old traditional thought. Try the change.

Dr. Gerald Jampolsky writes in his wildly successful book *Teach Only Love,* the essence of just this: do not talk of love—*be* love.

The Example of Love: "To me, Mary epitomizes attitudinal healing. She did her utmost to not just think *about* God but to allow God's light to pour through her for all to behold and partake. She chose not to identify with her body, not to identify with her ego personality. She demonstrated that as long as we are breathing we are here on earth to be a channel of God's blessing, to be centered in love, and in that way be of service to others.

Mary made alive two simple statements from *A Course in Miracles* that have become of central importance to me:

1. Awaken and forget all thoughts about death, and you will find that you have the peace of God.
2. Today I will let the Christ vision look upon all things for me and judge them not, but I will give each one the miracle of love instead.

Gerald Jampolsky, MD,
Teach Only Love, Epilogue

Whether it is a Christ with whom you identify, or Buddha, Ghandi, Mother Theresa or some other soul-close-to-perfection, live well in positiveness. Know that God wants us to have free will and joy and goodness that is all the positive aspects of love. Choose to love and see your mind, heart, soul and body change into the Light of peaceful, energized wellness.

FOR THOSE WHO BELIEVE, NO EXPLANATION IS NEEDED; FOR THOSE WHO DO NOT, THERE IS NEVER ENOUGH.

In the end, we must all walk in faith of what we cannot see but know.

Epilogue
More Stories of Healings

Though I am a healer, I know well that I guide others to heal themselves. I lend my energies and my counsel to assist in a person ultimately healing self and, if desired, continuing to stay in wellness pathology. Here are a few stories I'd like to share, not out of ego. I share them because over time my own personal surges of healing energy, which primarily throb right through my body and out of my hands, have increased and grown in intensity. At this point in my life, I see that all through my healing experiences I have increasingly helped heal people far quicker. So here we are, writing and reading about hands-on healing in the 21st Century ! Enjoy considering that, like Jesus, you too can heal self and assist others in healing. This is becoming a mainstream way of thinking and knowing for many people on this planet how here. Consider that if Buddha has healing energies as a physical human, so can you, so *do* you. What type of healing talents do you possess ? This book is my attempt to open your mind, feelings, souls and deep knowings and allowing this notion to walk beside you. Let us see what develops as you read some of the stories common in my everyday life.

TERRY
Over a period of at least 14 years I have suffered from severe joint and muscular pain and stiffness. The condition isn't life threatening but is debilitating. I have seen many specialists over that time who, between them,

have given me a different diagnosis on each occasion. The bottom line was in my case the condition wasn't curable. The only option available to me was to try to dull the pain with painkillers. Over the years I have tried many different drugs prescribed to me by my own general physician. Eventually I decided, along with my G.P.'s agreement, that I wouldn't take any more of them because they weren't working, I was harming other organs in my body without any benefit of pain relief. The long-term prognosis was ill health for the rest of my life. Then I read an interesting article in the local paper about a man who had the power to help people overcome their health problems. My wife also read the same article and the next thing I knew an appointment had been made for me to meet David L Cunningham.

I was very skeptical but also extremely curious as I traveled to that first appointment. On meeting David my mind was put at rest; I really don't know what I expected but who I met was a person who was able to put me at ease immediately. I was happy for him to try to help me and after the first session I noticed an improvement in my condition. In total I had seven sessions with David and now feel my health has improved beyond my greatest expectations. I now know I needn't spend the rest of my life in pain. Taking the first step to make that appointment has literally changed my life and outlook for ever.

ROB, 2006
I met David for the first time in 1993. Shortly afterwards, I put my back out for the third time in as many months and decided to risk a healing session. David began by clearing my chakras and then worked around the area of my injury.

When he had finished with my back, he asked if I had any other problems and I explained that my left knee had been giving me some grief, particularly when climbing stairs. As I lay there on my back, David's hand hovered a few inches above my knee and I felt the inside of my knee moving around as if something was beneath the flesh. It was very surreal and very memorable. Suffice to say, in the years since my back has been much stronger and I have never had another problem with my knee !

When we met, our son was three years old and had Down's syndrome. He had a congenital heart defect at birth which required surgery and in those early years was prone to chest infections and congestion. Soon after my first healing session with David I took my son along. Because of the congestion, he was unsettled and David was finding it difficult to work. David turned to me and told me that he was going to ask Spirit to help my son sleep so that he could work. Within thirty seconds, he fell asleep in my arms—once again I was amazed. I have no doubt that the healing session that followed helped my son build up his strength and fight off the constant chest infections.

David moved away from the area where I live and while we exchanged Christmas cards, we only met a couple of times over the intervening years and spoke on the telephone once in a blue moon. Then in 2005, my son had to go into hospital for heart surgery to repair a complication which had arisen as a result of the surgery when he was a baby. The surgery went well but there was great difficulty in weaning him off the ventilator and after the second unsuccessful attempt, he nearly died. Within twenty-four hours of that event, I received a phone call from David. I don't know why he called at that particular time, while our son was still fighting for life, but I believe God sent a message. David told me that my wife and I should sit with a hand over our son's heart, think of David and pray. This would enable him to channel the healing power which came from God through us to our son. I'm not sure what the ITU nurses thought of this but he grew stronger and stronger and a week later was strong enough for further surgery where a tracheotomy was fitted. This enabled them to get him off the ventilator and a few weeks later he was able to leave the hospital. On the day he was discharged, I took him to say goodbye to the ITU staff. The nurse who had been on duty when our son had nearly died told me that they hadn't expected him to survive. I believe that David's call was fate and our dear son's recovery was not only down to the skill and care of the doctors and nurses but also down to a little divine intervention via David Cunningham. Distant healing works, too.

MARGARET LESLIE
I have been suffering from migraines ever since my mid-forties—about 9 years ago. At first I would get one or two a month, but over the years the frequency and severity has gradually increased. By last year, I could often find myself having two or three a week, and it had gotten to the point where I was having to take more and more time off work. It was difficult to try and find a pattern or cause, and eventually I gave up trying to find one.

I did know that I was much more prone to getting migraines after a period of stress, although sometimes this did not happen. I visited the doctor quite a lot at first, and asked for help. I was prescribed various painkillers, plus tablets to both take to try and prevent an attack coming on in the first place and then tablets to try and ease an attack. These did work at first, but over the years they had a lessening effect.

In fact, it had gotten to the point that in May last year I was quite desperate to know what to do. I had planned a family holiday to Florida in August, which was something I had always wanted to do, but now I worried that the headaches might ruin things. Then I happened to read a local magazine that had been put through the door, and there was an article by David Cunningham in it, where he had cured someone's chronic pain. I read that David lived in the North East, and could be contacted on his website. It shows how desperate I was to have decided I had nothing to lose, and give it a try. Normally I would not have had much faith in "alternative" therapies. Anyway, I decided to contact David, and sent him an e-mail. He rang me back the same evening and arranged to see me later that week. As usual with me at that time, I was worried I would not be able to go if I got a migraine.

When I made that first visit to David, any trepidation I felt quickly disappeared; he was so kind and down to earth. We talked for a while about my problems, and David explained that he could probably help, and that he would do some healing straightaway. He explained that everyone has energy flowing within them, but if this gets disrupted or blocked in any way due to unhappiness, stress, fear etc. then it can cause symptoms of illness and pain. He believed this was why I was getting migraines. Only when these chakras are unblocked and we have energy freely flowing through us can we again start to feel grounded and refreshed.

I lay on a couch, fully clothed and first of all David tested my chakras and they were, as David suspected, all blocked. A crystal pendulum held over these centres did not move at all. However, after some unblocking healing work, the pendulum swung freely showing that energy was flowing again.

Then David placed his hands on my head. I closed my eyes and relaxed, and the healing was performed. I felt energy pulsing from David's hands, but otherwise felt nothing. After about 30 or 40 minutes the session ended, I was told to take it easy and that I might experience a healing reaction which could well be a headache. I did in fact have a headache the next day, although it was not a migraine. Then the amazing thing happened—much to my delight and astonishment I had no migraines at all that week ! I could hardly believe it; I couldn't wait to go back for another healing session the next week and tell David what an improvement there was ! I had changed from literally suffering almost every single day to being able to function normally.

This healing has continued and although I do sometimes get an occasional mild migraine, when I talk to David about it we can usually pinpoint why it happened. The healing that follows then gets rid of any remaining pain. I have also had healing for some IBS symptoms I was having, and this is now completely gone. I feel better now, but it's much more than that. I feel as though I have got my spark back, and can enjoy life in a way I had not done for years. I have also developed, in conversations with David, a better insight of why I was ill, and how to avoid it happening again.

David is a kind, caring, helpful and friendly person whom I feel privileged to know. I would recommend anyone to seek his healing if they need it.

ANDREW

I have suffered from asthma since I was 18 months old. I am now 33, and I have been on numerous inhalers and nebulizers over the years, and I was on two inhalers twice a day.

My dad discovered he had lung cancer just before Christmas 2003, and my mum decided to seek out alternative medicines and found David through the Internet. My dad started his treatment in January and is still going to this very day. He said it was the best thing he could have ever done and feeling the effects pretty much straight after his 15th treatment, so I decided to give it a go, and booked two sessions, one in the afternoon and the second the day later in the morning.

My first visit was strange and enlightening at the same time; it felt very much like a big jig-saw puzzle and I had all the pieces but not in the correct order, and after speaking to David for about 25 minutes gradually everything seemed to fall into place, at which point my mind was racing with all kinds of thoughts, such as the soul is very much like a video cassette and that it is constantly on record and as you die the soul continues to record, continuing into the next body; it was all fascinating stuff.

David then started to do some "hands on" to which my whole body seemed to go from a state of anticipation to a state of complete relaxation in a matter of minutes. After what seemed like a couple of hours (it was about 45 - 55 minutes) there seemed like a great burden had been lifted from my chest and to say I could breathe slightly better was the biggest understatement.

My second visit, the day after, was to be the biggest surprise ever ! I still had my conversation with David before moving for the "hands on" and had explained that I had not even used my inhalers since seeing him and that the night had passed of restlessness. I was slightly confused by this but he had said that the treatment works in either two ways; it will either make you very relaxed or very restless. Anyway, after completing the second "hands on" I sat up and David asked me how I felt and to my astonishment my lungs felt even more full of air than when I went in; in fact, I said that it had felt like someone had removed my old lungs and replaced them with a new set. Astonished, full of energy, excited, all of these feeling and more came over me, and for the next month I can honestly say I have never, in all my life, felt better.

My next appointment with David was made for about 3 - 4 weeks later and I had used my inhalers only once or twice since that second visit (out of habit more than anything) which was over five years ago now.

SHEILA

I first heard of David Cunningham during a conversation at work. A colleague was telling us about her husband having treatment for his knee. I had been suffering from painful knees for some time and had put it down to two things: being overweight and using a Dictaphone pedal for the past 17 years.

I contacted David Cunningham and arranged my first appointment, thinking I had nothing to lose by trying just one session.

From the moment David opened the door and invited me in, there was a feeling of calmness that I cannot explain. We talked for a while about how I felt about myself and although I did wonder what that had to do with painful knees, nail biting and being overweight, the conversation progressed to my first healing session.

The session began with me lying on a couch and after having been asked to close my eyes and relax David placed his hands on my shoulders. From that first contact there was a complete feeling of being safe and a knowing that everything was going to be all right. I felt surrounded by something I cannot explain but did feel safe and secure.

One week later, as my car drew up outside David's home, I just felt in my heart that David was about to here about me, the real me. No-one other than my husband had any idea about my past, and even my husband did not know everything.

My second session began with us discussing the events over the past week and then completely out of the blue in the middle of the conversation I began to tell David about my past. For almost 35 years I had kept to myself the fact that I had been physically, mentally and sexually abused my uncle. David heard it all. It felt like an explosion of guilt and hatred for myself had been released. My second healing session began, and again from the moment David's hands touched my shoulders I was surrounded from head to toe in an experience that I cannot explain. I can only describe it as calmness and gentleness enveloping me.

Since about my third healing session I have had no problems with my knees at all, and because I now feel better about myself I am tackling the weight problem and very slowly overcoming my nail biting habit. My healing sessions are still ongoing and I have not experienced anything other than calmness and serenity. I have to say that I do feel much better about all aspects of my life, including actually thinking and caring about myself which I had never done before.

I would sincerely urge anyone who may be suffering from any form of inner turmoil or unforgiveness to consider even one session of healing with David Cunningham. You really have nothing to lose, but everything to gain.

RITA DAVIS, May 2008

For many years I have suffered from IBS and all the inconvenience it caused. I was frightened to travel away from my home, no holidays, no meals out with family and friends. Normal medication did not seem to help in any shape or form; therefore, I was unhappy, frustrated and miserable all the time.

My daughter showed me an article in a magazine about David Cunningham's healing ability. Though apprehensive, I contacted him and my first appointment quickly followed. We discussed my problems and my life experiences and how healing could be helpful with my condition. Mr. Cunningham explained about the Chakra system (energy centres) in my body/soul and after dowsing the eight chakras explained how these centres can get blocked by emotional experiences in life.

All mine where blocked.

Mr. Cunningham began the healing process by sending the healing energies through each one to unblock them. He then began the healing process on my IBS problem. There was no discomfort at all and the whole experience was relaxing and rewarding. I visited him several times for ongoing healing sessions and I now have a totally new lease on life and am doing the normal things in life, which I had not been able to do for years. I am now healed of my disease. I cannot thank Mr. Cunningham enough.

SPIRIT HELP, Always !

A woman came to see me with her problems; in addition, she was grieving from the loss of her beloved husband. We talked about survival of the soul to which the lady replied 'I wish it were true and I could have evidence'.

As we were talking a voice spoke in my right ear telling me he was the deceased husband of the lady in front of me. He them told me to thank her for the beautiful card and then in my third eye showed me a white background card with a heart of red roses and in the centre one single red rose.

I described this vision to my client; she went white and said, "Oh my God, that is the card I put in his coffin." Her heart and soul healing began in that moment of evidence of survival

911

The mother of a victim of 911 was sitting with me one day, grieving about the sad demise of her beloved son. As usual, I was explaining survival and the eternity of the soul and how her son would be at peace now on the other side of life.

The grieving mother was looking for evidence of this and as she explained it would help her to know her son was okay and not in any distress of what happened that day.

As we were speaking, the young man identified himself to me in my right ear and told me to tell her that he watched her move his photograph to a new position on a corner table on top of a lace cloth.

She looked at me in total amazement and said, "Yes, that is right, I did move his picture yesterday."

...Just a bit more evidence that our loved ones are okay—actually perfectly well—after leaving the body.

July 2010

Back on June 11, 1990, just prior to my departure for Kuwaiti Hotel job and my ultimate hostage imprisonment, Suzie telephoned me with a surprising announcement (see page 161). I was diagnosed with diabetes and now upon more reflection, I can whole-heartedly thank her for the information she gave me, as well as initially encouraging me to have testing done. Having read the story, you can also be amazed to see that my knowing I had this disease saved my life in Bagdad. I was treated far better because I required medical care — even being released in an early group to go back to the United Kingdom, because I had diabetes. *Thank God!*

And in this new millenium, this new decade, I continually live in awe as I realize time and again how very precious are the family, friends and people in my life. Today, through the miracles of Facebook, Suzie and I have now found each other again after 22 years of divorce and silence.

We've realized anew that it had been a difficult period for us both back in 1990, our tempers were high. But now, after the passing of 22 years and mellowing of age, we are friends. I enjoy hearing and knowing that Suzie's life improved dramatically during the 22 years of our silence. Suzie founded a chain of stores throughout the UAE and is a very successful entrepreneur. I am overjoyed for her and her self-empowerment as a successful business woman. We talk regularly and we are even better friends than we were as a married couple.

So my advice to those readers how may have or had emotional problems with a loved one, pick up the phone or try and find that person via the amazing Internet social networks and make peace now, if at all possible.

I am deeply please that Suzie and I are now friends and can communicate like loving human beings. So, a healer can heal himself, too.

APPENDIX

WISDOM OF MY GUARDIAN ANGELS

Master Teacher Messages from the Spirit Guides to YOU !

Eight Stages of Perfection
(Each Soul Must Achieve)

1. TOLERANCE
2. TRUTH
3. PRAISE
4. PATIENCE
5. LOVE
6. KINDNESS
7. UNDERSTANDING
8. FORGIVENESS

In 1994, this was given to me by Spirit:

I was told to write the word LOVE then follow the instructions:

L O V E

reverse it:

E V O L

add: # V E

bring it
down to:

E V O L V E

L O V E

is

to

E V O L V E

is

to

L O V E

Spirit said, "This is the SECRET OF ALL LIFE. Nothing else is reality."

Prayer

Dear God-
I am a Light Being
I radiate the light throughout my being
I radiate the light to everyone
I radiate the light to everything
I am in a bubble of light
And only light can come to me
And only light can be here
I thank you God for everything
May I help people to protect themselves
by Being in the Light.

by David L. Cunningham

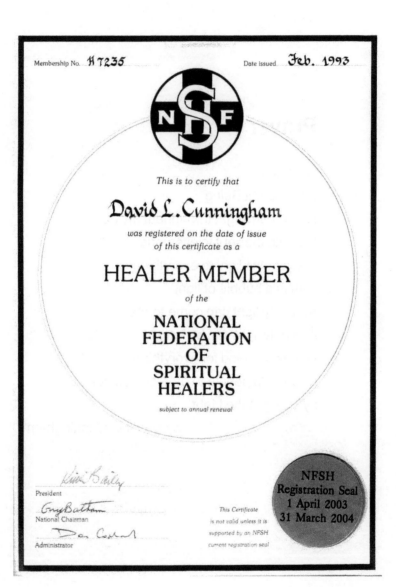

0915 841238

105,Ninelands,
Houghton-le-Spring,
Tyne & Wear.
DH4 5QD.

2nd November,1990.

Richard Branson,Esq.,
Virgin Records Ltd.,
120, Kempton Hill Road,
London W8 7AR.

Dear Mr. Branson,

My name is David Cunningham and I was
fortunate to be on your flight from Baghdad.
I would like to express my gratitude to you for your bravery
in allowing your aircraft to be used in such a delicate
situation.

After all. no one could predict the mood in Baghdad and both
you and your brave crew could have found yourselves in the
same position as ourselves.

The flight from Baghdad is one I am sure no one involved will
ever forget, as I should think it was a "first" of its kind.

An experience of a lifetime.

Your crew who I believe volunteered for the flight were
exceptional for their courage and bravery apart from their
service,I trust will be rewarded for their valour.

Mr. Branson there is no real words to express my thanks and
gratitude to you for delivering me/us home safely to our
families and friends.

I am overjoyed to be home and sad in the fact of leaving all
my companions behind and trust that they will soon be safely
home to join their families.

I am concerned that news of the remaining hostages will become
back page news as it did before. You can imagine how we felt
contribute in keeping it alive. Not to sure how I can
when for weeks no one mentioned our exitance. Our only link
with the outside world was "Gulf Link". So if you have any
suggestions on this matter I would be grateful for your
comments.

Once again Mr.Branson my deepest gratitude for bringing us
home safely to family and friends.

Yours faithfully,

David T. Cunningham.

15 January 71
Houghton-le-Spring
Co. Durham

Dear David

I hope you are keeping
well. I received the
Christmas cards and I was
pleased. Marilyn is as
daft as ever. What
would you like for
Christmas. I am going
Xmas shopping on Saturday
with my best friend
Wendy.

I am good at school
and a teacher called
me into Miss thinks
I am best scholar.
Give my regard
Lots of love
Margaret

X X X
X X X
X X X
X X X

𝔖𝔲𝔫𝔡𝔞𝔶 𝔐𝔢𝔯𝔠𝔲𝔯𝔶 𝔑𝔢𝔴𝔰 1976

Gadabout

Esther Walker

Good sport at the Tavern

NEW YORK — Liza Minnelli was such a good sport the Tavern On The Green had to keep the band on overtime the night of the party celebrating her Broadway opening in "The Act."

"There were 500 guests. It started at 11 p. m. and ended at 5 a. m.," David Cunningham, maitre d' at what has become New York's "in" restaurant, reported. "At 4 o'clock she sat down at the piano with the band and sang for all of us for a whole hour. We had to keep the band on over-time."

Before report-

LIZA MINNELLI
. . . 'The Act'

ing the above intelligence, Mr. Cunningham had seated me at a table in the restaurant's Crystal Room, a three-sided glass pavillon with a view of Central Park and the Manhattan skyline across the way. On the terrace were some over-sized pumpkins I assumed were Halloween remnants that no one had gotten around to replacing with Christmas trees which was refreshing what with the way everyone in commerce rushes Christmas these days.

The table was covered with white linen and set with crystal and hand painted china which I later learned were imitation, the real McCoy being too expensive on account of the breakage.

Tithe Barne - Sussex Express & County Herald, Nov 19, 1976

It is small — but extremely stylish

By LEE PATEMAN

TAKE one former antique shop owner. Add one former schoolteacher. Blend both into a well matured tithe barn and you have the recipe for a first-class restaurant.

The Tithe Barn at Sedlescombe is run by 66-year-old Mr Charles Harris, previously owner of an antique shop, and 30-year-old ex-housemaster, Mr David Cunningham.

The restaurant opened in March and both readily admit they had virtually no experience in this type of business before they brought the 400-year-old Tithe Barn back to life after a two-year vacancy.

But, inquire into the change of professions and you find a common denominator. In the words of Mr Harris: "A love of good food and wine."

Novices the partners might admit to being, but there is nothing amateurish about their restaurant. It is small but extremely stylish and, most important of all, the food is good.

Mr Harris says: "We set out to provide a very high quality as economically as one can afford to do it."

Our meal started with Bisque d'Homard — cream of lobster soup with brandy — at 75p, and prawn cocktail Mary Rose at 80p.

The main courses were Steak au Poivre Flambe (an entrecote steak cooked in butter with onions, mushrooms, flambed in a brandy and cream sauce), and escalope de Veau Normanie Flambe. They cost £2 and £2.50 respectively.

ABOVE: The small but stylish restaurant. BELOW: The attractive timbered exterior of the 400-year-old building.

THE GULF CRISIS   YORKSHIRE POST, OCT 25, 1980

TOAST TO FREEDOM: Freed hostages on board the Virgin Atlantic flight to Gatwick cheer Mr Edward Heath, who ended their captivity in Iraq.

0915 841238

105,Ninelands,
Houghton-le-Spring,
Tyne & Wear.
DH4 5QD.

2nd November,1990.

Richard Branson,Esq.,
Virgin Records Ltd.,
120, Kempton Hill Road,
London W8 7AR.

Dear Mr. Branson,
My name is David Cunningham and I was fortunate to be on your flight from Baghdad.
I would like to express my gratitude to you for your bravery in allowing your aircraft to be used in such a delicate situation.
After all no one could predict the mood in Baghdad and both you and your brave crew could have found yourselves in the same position as ourselves.
The flight from Baghdad is one I am sure no one involved will ever forget, as I should think it was a "first" of its kind. An experience of a lifetime.
Your crew who I believe volunteered for the flight were exceptional for their courage and bravery apart from their service,I trust will be rewarded for their valour.
Mr. Branson there is no real words to express my thanks and gratitude to you for delivering me/us home safely to our families and friends.
I am overjoyed to be home and sad in the fact of leaving all my companions behind and trust that they will soon be safely home to join their families.
I am concerned that news of the remaining hostages will become back page news as it did before, not to sure how I can contribute in keeping it alive. You can imagine how we felt when for weeks no one mentioned our exitance. Our only link with the outside world was "Gulf Link". So if you have any suggestions on this matter I would be grateful for your comments.
Once again Mr.Branson my deepest gratitude for bringing us home safely to family and friends.

Yours faithfully,

David I. Cunningham.

zo.ou a sq ft, said the total space on   the route.

In Saddam's hell for three months

A YEAR after the Iraqi invasion of Kuwait, one of Saddam Hussein's human shield hostages has been appointed manager of a Fawkham hotel.

David Cunningham, 45, survived three months imprisoned by the Iraqis just six days after taking a post at the Kuwait Plaza Hotel.

Now he can relax at the Brandshatch Place Hotel, Fawkham.

Mr Cunningham first knew of the invasion when he was woken by gunfire on August 2 last year.

He said: "I woke up but thought I had dreamt the gunfire and tried to go back to sleep. But then I looked out of the window and saw tanks lining the streets and soldiers firing guns in all directions."

The next 10 days were peaceful and many of Mr Cunningham's guests managed to escape. But orders from Saddam Hussein to round up Westerners threw the city into panic.

Mr Cunningham said: "I had to hide 20 Filipino guests, along with several English families, on the top floors of the hotel. We reprogrammed the lifts to stop soldiers getting up there and had to play a game of cat and mouse with them for a month.

"There was so much to do I didn't have time to even think about being scared. I had people to take care of."

After a month, Mr Cunningham was taken on a gruelling desert bus journey to Baghdad.

Human shield

The hostages spent a night in a hotel before being transferred to a tank factory next to a gas bomb plant as part of Saddam's human shield.

Mr Cunningham said: "We were told we were in a tractor factory, which we thought was suspicious, but it wasn't until I was back in England I realised what it was. We were sitting on a time bomb.

"Conditions were quite good. The worst thing was the food.

DELIGHTED: David Cunningham

"We lived for two months on a diet of rice, tomatoes and cucumber. I lost a stone-and-a-half in weight."

His faith in Britain kept Mr Cunningham's morale strong but one night he thought he would be killed.

He said: "I was woken at 2am by very smart soldiers who were obviously part of an elite force. They told me to dress as I was going to hospital because of my diabetes.

"I thought I was going to die. It was such a strange time. I had to secretly gesture to my room mate to take my address book and let my family know if anything happened to me.

"But they were genuine and I was taken under armed guard to Baghdad, where a specialist examined me."

Mr Cunningham's nightmare ended last October when he was released thanks to extensive negotiations by MP Ted Heath.

He said: "I can never thank enough everyone who got me out. Everyone was marvellous and made me welcome."

He is now finding joy in his work. Mr Cunningham said: "The hotel is lovely. It's wonderful to be on British soil."

INVK

ZAN
AUT(
* 850/1(
spin s
* 20 pr
comb

Model N

PREVI
PRICE
£399.9

NOW

£

ZANI
* 12 plac
* 4 prog
* Residu
* 65°C w
temp:
Model N

STOF
CHA

; Clubs and Villages 17; School Report 19; What's On 20; TV 21-23

(D) Kentish Times, August 1, 1991

COVENTRY CATHEDRAL

A SPECIAL SERVICE

OF

PEACE AND REMEMBRANCE

TO MARK THE LAUNCH OF

"THE HUMAN SHIELD"

THE BOOK WHICH COMMEMORATES THE

STRUGGLE OF THOSE WHO WERE IN

KUWAIT

FROM

AUGUST 1990 TO DECEMBER 1991

SATURDAY 30TH MAY 1992 AT 1.00PM

In honour of David Cunningham
and other human shield victims

Dartford & Gravesham Health Authority

ACUTE SERVICES UNIT

30th April 1992

Mr D L Cunningham
79 Watermill Way
Sutton at Hone
DARTFORD
Kent
DA4 8BE

Dear Mr D Cunningham

Following your informal and formal interview with Dr P Key, Mrs
W Liddiard and myself, I am pleased to inform you that your
application for the post of HIV Counsellor to be based within the
GUM Clinic at West Hill Hospital has been approved.

Notification of your pending appointment was put to the AIDS
District Co-ordinator Group meeting on Tuesday 28th April where
your pay scale and verbal job description were accepted.

Your hours will be 37 per week and you will be notified of your
pay scale by the Administration and Clerical Staffing department
and your first day of employment will be on Tuesday 5th May 1992.

May I take this opportunity in welcoming you to Dartford and
Gravesham Health Authority and hope that your stay with us will
be an enjoyable one.

Yours sincerely

H J Smith
HIV Prevention Co-ordinator

AFTER years of scepticism, the NHS is embracing complementary medicine. Having seen the benefits that healing offered her mother and son, who both fought cancer, Angie Buxton-King decided to train as one herself, and has become the first paid healer on the NHS at University College Hospital in London.

Daily Mail
June 29, 2004   **GOOD HEALTH**

How Angie took her dying son's treatment into her own hands ... and became the first NHS healer

CHILD was screaming as I arrived on the ward. The young boy had cancer and was terrified of needles. The doctor was trying to insert an intravenous needle and the boy was distressed. He looked at me with tears in his eyes and I felt a flood of understanding, as if he knew I was there to help.

I took a deep breath, explained what I was going to do and laid my hands on his head. I glanced down to see the child's vein plump up and the needle go in without him noticing. The doctor said: 'Nice trick.' I smiled, thinking of Sam.

The boy was the same age as my darling, brave son Sam was when he died. It is because of him I am here today, a healer at one of London's busiest hospitals.

Having seen what healing achieved for Sam — fewer side effects from treatments, less pain, and feeling more positive — I wanted to offer those qualities to other patients. I am the only paid NHS healer.

Sam's nightmare began when he was seven. During a half-term break, he began to complain of headaches and breathlessness, so I took him to see our GP, who carried out blood tests.

Doctors said Sam had AML — Acute Myeloid Leukaemia — a cancer of the blood and bone marrow. The consultant said there was very little hope treatment would work because Sam was suffering from a quickly progressing form of the disease.

We were told Sam might have just a few months to live. I vowed to try every therapy — conventional and complementary — to give Sam more time.

My mum had died of ovarian cancer a few years earlier and it was during her illness we began to look at healing. She enjoyed the feeling of warmth, and it seemed to ease her pain.

Sam had a private room at Great Ormond Street children's hospital where he had chemotherapy. At night, I would watch over him and place my hands gently on his body — just like the healer who treated my mother.

The doctors and nurses no doubt thought I was completely bonkers, but they had no objection. The more healing I did, the more I became convinced.

The chemo made Sam lose his hair, which he hated and cried about. But he surprised the medical staff in other ways.

We were told the drugs would make him feel nauseous but Sam was often as bright as a button. Doctors were baffled that the treatments weren't producing the usual horrific side-effects and that Sam remained so well.

Energetic: Sam with his beloved Jack Russell, Zack

His blood recovered enough for the doctors to agree to a bone marrow transplant. His brother Nick, then 13, was the only one of the family who matched as a bone marrow donor and after eight months in hospital, Sam underwent the transplant.

All we could do afterwards was wait. Six weeks later our consultant said we could go home.

The future wasn't guaranteed. The cancer was in remission but we would need to visit the hospital for blood tests.

There were some happy times in that year — when we went to collect the puppy we'd promised him. He and the Jack Russell he named Zack became inseparable.

I continued to learn more about healing and to heal Sam daily at home. Life settled down and Sam even went back to school — sporting newly-grown hair. In October 1996 we went on holiday to Cyprus and went on to have a fantastic Christmas. Then, in February 1997, a blood test showed the leukaemia had returned and doctors warned us Sam could have as little as three weeks left to live. I felt as if my heart had been ripped out.

We began visiting the University College London Hospital where Sam underwent a procedure whereby some of Nick's cells were given to him. I continued to heal Sam. He had more energy than the rest of us put together.

In September 1997, Sam went back to school, but the leukaemia returned.

DOCTORS continued to treat Sam, but said there was no hope of a cure. We flew to Florida, where Sam was to swim with wild dolphins. A few weeks later he developed a chest infection and began antibiotics.

On August 4, he became sleepy and we spent the day cuddled up on the sofa. I realised he would die that night. It was the first time I let myself think we might lose him. At 2am, when his breathing became more laboured, David and I held him and spoke softly to him as he died peacefully.

We were devastated — but it was a comfort to know Sam had lived three years longer than the doctors had first expected, and had been happy.

I believe healing played a crucial part. A friend said Sam was never a child dying of leukaemia — just a child living each day.

Since Sam died, I've become a qualified healer. I had to begin at the hospital as a volunteer. My first day was almost exactly a year since Sam had died. I was run off my feet — practically everybody I spoke to wanted to try healing.

A month later, the ward manager said he was convinced of the benefits of healing for his patients. I would be paid.

Today I work on the haematology unit at UCLH, which has 40 in-patient beds. Many of the patients are in severe pain.

One girl I remember fondly was Sarah. She was miserable and angry. She would not mix with the other teenagers and would not eat. After healing, Sarah asked if I would come back. An hour later the nurses called me to say she had demanded food, then gone out to mix with the others.

Another time I was asked to see a young woman called Linda who had a cancer of her lymph glands and was in a great deal of pain.

I was aware of a lot of energy flowing between us. Afterwards, Linda looked astonished — her pain had gone. I continued to see her twice a week and today she is alive and well.

To those who are sceptical about healing, all I would say is: try it for yourself.

Sam was an inspiration. If it weren't for him, I would never have become the only paid healer in the NHS. I hope he's proud of me.

STEPHEN ROWLEY, clinical manager at UCLH, says:
ALTHOUGH, clinically, healing remains little understood, the effects are evident. We have seen patients find more relief from healing than strong pain-killing opiates. We have also seen them report significant reductions in chemotherapy-related side-effects.

Patients are often in states of desperation. We have seen them find huge comfort in healing.

■ *The NHS Healer by Angie Buxton-King is published by Virgin on July 8, £16.99.*

SUNDERLAND ECHO   The Big Feature
Tuesday, April 11, 2006

Good
Faith healer David Cunningham says he has the power to heal in the palms of his hands. People with all kinds of diseases visit his Washington home in the hope of a cure from the man, who claims his God-given healing touch has cured cancer and helped lame people walk. LINDA COLLING meets this remarkable man who, after being taken hostage in Iraq and held as a "human shield" in 1990, developed his amazing gift.

vibrations

AMAZINGLY David Cunningham has the power in his hands to perform what seem like miracles. It's a God-given gift, he says, as I lie down on the bed.

Could he help me, I wondered, this man who claims he has healed people of cancer, given life to paralysed legs, brought blurry vision to blind eyes and made migraines disappear.

David told me: "It would be very unprofessional to promise anybody anything. I can just do my best to help them."

He most certainly helped me. After scanning for problem areas, he told me all my "chakras" were blocked. These are the energy centres that run from the crown of our heads to the base of our spine. By simply placing his hands over my body he unblocked all eight and showed me the first "miracle" – the dowser that had hung limp before when he held it over me was now spinning.

With his eyes closed in intense concentration, he turned to the crucial healing session.

Within seconds of his hands being laid on my back and the base of my spine – major problem areas of mine – I could fee a warm, comforting heat and the energy radiating down my legs to my feet.

Some people feel warmth or a vibration or both. It was so comforting, calming and tranquil that when David asked me to turn over I was ready to fall asleep.

He placed his hands on my right shoulder, which I injured last year and still gives me trouble at anything repetitive, such as chopping, cleaning windows, or vacuuming.

That doesn't mean I lead a charmed life, just one where I rub on gel to numb the pain.

FLASHBACK: The Echo's picture in October 19[..] of David with his sister Margaret Hanson who lives in Houghton. He had been detained and held as a "human shield" in Iraq

That goes too for a little toe that I broke last summer and then traumatised again. Walk too far and it protests.

Now I'm hoping all that's a thing of the past because a most amazing thing happened after David had worked on me.

From feeling lighter, muscles less taught and not in any real pain – all the places where I'd had problems were in pain.

"That's the pain going out," David reassured as he told me to focus on my little toe which was aching from the base of the joint, along the side of my foot and down to the nail.

I told it to be still and the pain to go. The same with the shoulder and neck. I'd forgotten how the pain used to radiate down my arm to my fingers and into the back of my head.

I wasn't worried because I just knew the pain was going. There had been what David calls "a healing crisis."

That night I could lie on my back without pain in my left hip and I could lie on my left side for the first time in ages.

The next morning the little toe joint felt tender, so did my back and shoulder, all ached slightly. But, David said that meant the healing process was continuing. I believe it still is.

prisoner of Saddam changed my life

DAVID Cunningham hasn't always filled his days applying his healing touch to the physical and emotional pain of his fellow man.

He's a remarkable man who managed international hotels all over the world, meeting celebrities and the rich and famous.

All that changed in 1990 when he was taken a captive of Saddam Hussein for 100 days during the Gulf War.

He was one of many "human shields" strategically placed in prisons adjacent to Iraq military's armament facilities.

It was during this critical time that David made his personal peace with God and pledged to use his spiritual healing "gifts" to heal others, if and when he was allowed to live and released from captivity

"During the time I was a hostage I made a pact with God that if I got out I would start using my healing gift. It comes out of the palm of my hand and I scan and tell you where you have a problem. Over the years the gift has evolved more. My hand is like a scanner," says David.

What's his success rate, I ask. "Pretty high, especially with breast cancer and tumours disappearing. Others have been almost instantly healed of IBS, migraine, asthma, alopaecia and I'm working with a former Durham University professor with tinnitus.

"The first thing I tell people is I can't promise them anything. It's just giving it a go."

A forthright man, when he talks of his successes, it's easy for those who have never felt his power at work to write it all off.

That's why it was great meeeting Bill McKinnie, who honestly told me his story.

Of the scores of people David has helped, one young woman in her early thirties stands out.

Wheelchair-bound for two years and unable to walk, she got off the table and walked after two sessions, he says.

And a whole roomful of people witnessed it.

Only the other morning, a taxi driver David knows, brought round his wife who had broken her wrist. In one session, he says, her wrist had healed in what would normally take six weeks and the hospital can't understand how that's happened. Of course David can.

A friend of David's who was there when I called, admitted she had once had her doubts and told me: "I thought it was incredible the mobility in the driver's wife's wrist. It was incredible that could happen with something like a broken wrist. I take back all I have said."

RESOURCES

www.SpiritualHealingCentre.com

www.LindaLeeRatto.com

www.CivilServices.us

www.Renaissance2.eu

For Traditional Mail Connectivity:

Linda Lee Ratto
P.O. Box 622
Tyrone, Georgia 30290
USA

ABOUT THE AUTHORS

DAVID I. CUNNINGHAM
Certified Minister of Healing

Since I began my days as a professional healer after my return from being held as a Human Shield in Baghdad, I have worked with thousand s of people UK, USA, Hong Kong, and Quatar. The common factors in 99% of clients illnesses have manifested from unresolved emotional issues, when we are not at peace our bodies are not at peace.

I have and still working with issues, cancers and M.E. (Epstein Bar Virus), as well as everything you can imagine would happen to people. In the cases of M.E. the dis-ease seems to manifest from parental unresolved emotional issues, my clients tell of many years of verbal abuse and in some cases physical abuse.

Children who hold onto the pain well in to adult hood combined with a stressful life style in trying to prove themselves worthy to the parent in order to seek their love and approval succumb to the mind closing the body down and enduring pain and total lack of energy, in some cases having to live in darkened rooms, because daylight cause painful eyes.

I am blessed that people treat me as a confidant and confide in me with personal details they would never tell another human being, this of course is great healing to share a secret that is cancerous if not dealt with, i.e. eating away at the body from the souls unhappiness.

How long has humanity to evolve before it realises that we are all one and love and respect is the only we can be at peace and create this beautiful planet as heaven on earth? I still hear that religions are teaching our way is the only way and everyone else will go straight to hell. One would think by now, in the period of a new millennium, that we could move out of the dark ages of judgementalim and learn to live in brotherhood and harmony.

The way I survived my days as a hostage was to treat the Iraqi Solders as my brother with love and respect. So, dear reader, please search inside your soul and allow the pain to be dealt with and live a happy peaceful life.

Linda and David launch Holy Hostage in Chicago, 2008

**LINDA LEE RATTO, Ed.M.,** is an educator, counselor and international speaker with decades of experience in the education, leadership rehabilitation and self-development fields. She has served as a classroom teacher, corporate CEO, co-founder of a learning system, private school program consultant, and guest professor. Ms. Ratto has authored twelve books: this biographical, spiritually-based self-help book, counseling titles for living with disability, young peoples' books highlighting inner-spirit strength and the power of dreams, a non-fiction overview of the highly successful Youth Challenge Academy, a boarding school system for at-risk youth, and numerous educational books including a companion book for NY Times best selling author, Neale Donald Walsch's book *Happier Than God.* She has written articles and columns in several newspapers, most notably for the *Atlanta Journal/Constitution* covering such topics as the Paralympics and healthcare.

Ms. Ratto's writing technique is centered on personal relationships and interviews with children and adults. She then sculpts a story about their gifts and miracle-making. Her books are available on her website www.LindaLeeRatto.com or on-line through **www.amazon.com.**

You may contact her directly via:

Linda Lee Ratto, Ed.M.
Post Office Box 622
Tyrone, Georgia 30290 USA
email: Ratto@mindspring.com

"David and I met a decade ago at a family wedding. He told me of his 100 days as a hostage and I immediately responded, "You should write a book!" to which David stated, "I do not write well." I'd been writing all of my life and told him without another thought, "I will write the book for you..." Thus our co-writing began. David walked miles of Bahamian shoreline on a vacation following that 'coincidental meeting' and recorded the healing events in his life. I took his biography from there and in your hands, dear reader, is the fruit of our partnership. Please, relish the miracles David shares within. He and I have experienced together countless more miraculous events —such as walking for over a mile together while each streetlight turned off and then back on as we passed some 13 of them! Enjoy this true story from David's life through my fingertips into your hands. Know that you, too, may learn healing. For more specific techniques on healing, see our first book: *SHIFT Your Life !* "

~ Linda Lee Ratto, Ed.M.

Atlanta Airport, 2005
David with colleagues:
Anne-Marie Barbier, certified Chopra Instructor, "Mille Petales-Yoga Institute" owner (Toulon, France), member, Board of Trustees of the School of the New Spirituality (founded by Neale Donald Walsch) and Linda Lee Ratto, Ed.M., co-author of David's two books: *SHIFT Your Life !* and *Holy Hostage*.

ABOUT THE ILLUSTRATOR

CHRIS PHILLIPS is a talented and well established artist. Her life drawing and sculpture is based on the human form. Much of her work has an allegorical theme. She has taught painting and drawing for a number of years. The Arts Council has sponsored her to run community based art workshops. She has held classes for disabled people using art as a therapy. She has been a member of The Women Artists Slide Library and her work has been exhibited at Fulham Palace in London, The Graves Art Gallery in Sheffield and she has won the open exhibition at The Cooper Gallery in Barnsley. She has also exhibited in many other venues in Britain. Her work has been published in books internationally and reproduced for advertising posters including theatrical productions. She undertakes commissions and can be contacted at:

www.chrisphillipsart.com

Chris Phillips with David Cunningham
after a healing session in Tyne & Wear, England

Index

A

Ageless Body, Timeless Mind 269, 270
Al Fayed 160

B

Baghdad
1, 5, 7, 9, 10, 19, 22, 23, 25, 26, 27, 28, 32,
34, 35, 36, 41, 42, 46, 49, 78, 128,
163, 178, 179, 181, 190, 196, 212,
234, 238, 309
BBC 20, 24, 25, 31
Big Apple, The 99
black magic 45, 126, 127, 131
Bloomers 115, 116, 117, 134
Browne, Dr. Samuel E.
182, 183, 184, 190, 193, 194
Buddha 242, 246, 279, 280

C

Cayce, Edgar 261, 262
Chakra 59, 60, 61, 62, 63, 216, 231, 271, 313
46, 59, 60, 61, 62, 63, 64, 67, 68, 191,
194, 205, 215, 221, 224, 228, 246, 279, 313
Children 45, 256, 257, 309
3, 6, 8, 9, 10, 14, 32, 45, 46, 59, 69, 91,
111, 115, 120, 121, 198, 243, 255, 256,
257, 258, 263, 264, 272
Chopra, Deepak 269, 270

Clacton 82, 83
College of Psychic Studies
    36, 47, 48, 79, 80, 165, 177, 267
Collins, Joan 154
Conversations with God 64, 272, 275
Cosmic Dance 57, 58
Course in Miracles 66, 101, 313

D

Princess Diana 114, 117, 211
Dickinson, Emily 67
Dossey, Dr. Larry 267, 273
Doyle, Sir Arthur (Sherlock Holmes) 265, 267
Dubai 154, 155, 156, 157, 158, 162, 164,
    191, 234, 238, 239
Dyer, Dr. Wayne 249, 268

E

Energy Power 62
Expansion of Awareness 250, 251, 261, 274

G

Galloway , Don 36, 47, 79, 80, 81, 165, 177
Gardner, Adelaide 245
Geordie 76
Ghandi 279
GOLDEN FLAME 225, 227, 228, 229, 230
Guernsey 145, 151

H

Hale Clinic 163, 211, 213, 223
Hamilton, Lady and Lord 83
Happiness Is a Choice 45

Harrods 121, 151, 159
Hay, Louise L. 213, 222, 231, 233, 263
Healing Stories 55, 84
Hovey, William A. 177, 265, 267, 270
Howard, Peter 82, 83
Hussein, Saddam
   1, 5, 10, 12, 13, 14, 17, 20, 21, 42, 163, 181

I

Incarnation 242 226, 231, 236, 242, 243, 244,
   247, 250, 251, 252, 253, 257, 261, 270
India 49, 163, 234, 235, 239, 240, 269
Ireland 163, 216, 217, 218, 219, 222, 223, 224
   225, 226, 228, 230, 231, 232, 234, 239, 241
Isle of Wight 144, 145

J

Jampolsky, Dr. Gerard 278, 279
Jesus 46, 47, 59, 81, 201, 215, 221, 225, 226,
   227, 229, 235, 236, 246, 247, 255, 280
judgemental
   48, 61, 62, 65, 90, 253, 254, 275, 310
Jung, Carl 270, 277, 278

K

Karma 67, 209, 250, 251
Kaufman, Barry Neil 45
knowings 53, 245, 246, 251, 280
Kuwait 1, 2, 4, 6, 8, 9, 19, 21, 22, 26, 33, 34,
   42, 43, 44, 128, 160, 161, 162, 163

L

Londenderry Hotel 148

R

reincarnation 231, 236, 242, 244, 250, 251,
    252, 253, 257, 261, 270
Reinventing Medicine 267, 273
Roberts, Jane 267

S

SaiBaba 234, 235, 236, 237, 238, 239, 240
Seth Material,The 267
Sherlock Holmes 63, 265
Shining One 38, 39, 40, 41
Siegel, Dr. Bernie 263, 264, 265
Society of Psychical Research 177, 265, 267
Soskins, Julie 57, 58
Spontaneous Healing 268
Swami 234, 235, 236, 237, 238

T

Tavern on the Green
    101, 102, 103, 110, 111, 149, 164, 222
Tinning 246
Trailing Clouds of Glory 256, 257, 258
Travolta, John 103, 104, 105, 164

U

unconditional love 61, 252, 253

W

Walsch, Neale Donald 64, 252, 272, 275, 276
Weil, Andrew 268
Whitman 242